TALES FROM THE RED & WHITES

TALES FROM THE RED & WHITES

A collection of writing inspired
by Sunderland Association Football Club

Volume One
Edited by Lance Hardy

TALES FROM
www.talesfrom.com

First published in Great Britain in 2015
by Tales From

Printed and bound by SS Media

ISBN 978-0-993-2381-2-3

Tales From Ltd
2 Gaddesden Lane, Redbourn, St Albans, AL3 7NP
Registered company number: 9082738

www.talesfrom.com
info@talesfrom.com

TALES FROM THE RED & WHITES

CONTENTS

INTRODUCTION

BY THE EDITOR

Welcome to *Tales from the Red and Whites*, a unique collection of original writing about Sunderland AFC featuring contributions from three famous former players and several top sports journalists, who all have one thing in common – a deep affinity with our club.

Three of the chapters feature Sunderland legends. Jim Montgomery, Gary Bennett and Gary Rowell each enjoyed extraordinary careers at Roker Park and it is a privilege to feature their special stories in this first volume of *Tales from the Red and Whites*.

Jim is Sunderland through and through. He made a record 627 first team appearances for the club. None of them more famous than that special day at Wembley on May 5, 1973. Over 40 years on, he is now an ambassador for the club.

Like Monty, Benno could have recalled many moments from his long career at Sunderland. In this edition, Gary details his own record of being the only man to represent the club three times at Wembley Stadium. He still manages to mention the Clock Stand tussle with David Speedie though…

When I was a boy, one of my most treasured belongings was Gary Rowell's autograph. Today, I am proud to call him a friend. At the start of his career, Gary was also in awe of Sunderland players. He was a youth player at the time of the 1973 FA Cup run and his chapter details his own experience of that never-to-be forgotten and never-to-be-repeated fairytale.

There were a few occasions during my editing of this anthology when I found a smile appearing on my face – but Gary's recollection of giving Billy Hughes' boots an extra shine on the morning after his two great goals in the fantastic 3-1 FA Cup fifth round replay win over Manchester City probably produced the widest smile of them all.

Two special contributions come from Sunderland-supporting television presenters. David Jones, of Sky Sports, is a well-known Red and White. Here, he tells his own personal story of following the Black Cats, explaining the background to the huge affection he holds for the club. Meanwhile, Jeff Brown, of BBC North East and Cumbria, has produced a wonderful stage play about the life and times of 1985 League Cup finalist David Corner.

BBC Radio Newcastle commentator Nick Barnes has covered Sunderland AFC since 2003. He details his own special relationship with each of the nine men who have occupied the managerial hot seat at the Stadium of Light during that time.

Two newspaper journalists have written fabulous chapters about three great Sunderland strikers of the past. Graeme Anderson, who covered the fortunes of the club over many years for the *Sunderland Echo*, recalls those momentous early Premier League days of Kevin Phillips and Niall Quinn while Doug Weatherall, formerly of the *Daily Mail*, reminisces about the best manager we never had; the one and only Brian Clough.

Pete Sixsmith was a major contributor to my book *Stokoe, Sunderland and '73*. He went to eight of our nine matches on that famous FA Cup run. He still watches The Lads home and away. In this book, he remembers The Great Escape of 2013-14. Pete writes for salutsunderland.com and his views on the club also regularly appear in the *Observer*.

The other featured story of recent times is the historic Five in a Row over the Magpies. A Sunderland fan in exile, Mike

Grady has his own story to tell about that amazing winning sequence of results – just as each one of us do.

Rob Mason also went to eight of the nine FA Cup matches back in 1973. Like many others, including Pete, the only one he missed was Reading away. Rob wore the red and white scarf that features on the cover of this book to every one of those cup matches, including our magical day at Wembley. As club historian and publications editor, he was the obvious choice to tell the wonderful story of the Team of All The Talents, who won three First Division championships back in the early days of the Football League.

That leaves just my chapter. The first football match I ever saw on television was the 1973 FA Cup final. The first Sunderland match I ever saw in the flesh was three years later and it happened to be the first match in a club record run of ten league matches without a goal. Could the highs and lows of following our club be summed up any better?

However, that 1976-77 season so nearly turned into the greatest relegation escape of all time, making the remarkable events of 2013-14 seem almost mild by comparison. The fact it ended in the way that it did still hurts many fans to this day, myself included.

My thanks to Tales From for offering me the opportunity to produce this book for Sunderland fans. And, of course, my thanks to all the contributors for making it so special.

Hopefully, it will be the first of many such volumes…

Up the Red and Whites!

Lance Hardy
Bawtry, South Yorkshire
September, 2015

1

No one has played more games for Sunderland than **Jim Montgomery**.

But one moment from those 627 matches spent between the posts stands head and shoulders above anything else.

The stunning double-save to deny Leeds United in the 1973 FA Cup final at Wembley will never be forgotten. Some consider it the greatest save a goalkeeper has ever made.

This is the story of a Sunderland lad who spent the best 15 years of his career at his home town club and, although he didn't realise it at the time, created a moment that will live on for ever.

NUMBER ONE

BY JIM MONTGOMERY

I was born in Hendon on October 9, 1943 and stayed there for a few months before we moved to Southwick, where I spent all my adolescent life. After I got married in 1967 I moved to the Barnes area of Sunderland. If I hadn't been married to Joy I probably wouldn't be the person I am now.

My mam used to clean the premises at a place on Frederick Street. She cleaned there for many years and then she also cleaned at the Savoy in Southwick. It used to be a cinema and changed to a bingo hall. She used to love her bingo. My dad would never ever praise me but if he was with his mates he would praise me to the high heavens. I had one sister, Maureen, who was two years older than me. She lived in Hylton and used to work for Milburn's and Greggs' doing all the cake decorating. We always had a tightly knit family.

I always played in goal from when I was about eight or nine years old. I remember one game I played centre forward, it was up in Ryhope, I played outfield in the first half and scored to put us 2-0 up. I went in goal in the second half and we lost 3-2. I was playing for St Hilda's school against the Ryhope school.

In the schoolyard, especially when the snow was around, I would go in goal and I loved diving around. Even diving on the concrete was done in those days and I just loved it. Dixie Thompson had a farm, at the bottom of our street in Carley Road. We used to run across the farmer's field and jump over the wall, then walk down to Cleadon where they kept the nets up. I got a ball from Roker Park from one of the ground staff when I was about 16 or 17 and we used to play for hours on end on a Sunday morning. I just loved playing football – that was all life was about.

As a young lad, just making my way, I joined Burnley. Over the years they have taken many a lad from the north east. When I was there they were a top side with Harry Potts from Hetton-le-Hole and Jimmy Adamson from Ashington. Jimmy won the Footballer of the Year award not long after I was there.

The path to playing in goal for the first team looked very difficult. Ahead of me were Colin McDonald, who had played for England, Jim Furnell who would later keep goal for Arsenal, and Adam Blacklaw who would go on to play for Scotland. I came home and hadn't been back long when there was a knock at our door. It was one of my schoolteachers, Mr Alfie Lavender, with Sunderland's physio Johnny Watters. Johnny was a great character who had played for Celtic and he arranged for me to come down to Roker Park for a trial. I joined Sunderland as an apprentice on June 1, 1958. The club was reeling after its first ever relegation. At first, I didn't have to worry too much about that because I was playing for the youth team, which I enjoyed.

First team goalkeeping duties were shared by Willie Fraser, a Scottish international, and Johnny Bollands until manager Alan Brown bought Peter Wakeham from Torquay United. I particularly enjoyed watching Johnny and used to enjoy standing behind the goal watching him play for the reserves. He was a spectacular 'keeper and I wanted to emulate him. Willie's time at Sunderland came to an end after a few heavy defeats prompted Browny to sign Peter. He became the regular goalkeeper and barely missed a game for about three years, during which I was working hard to earn my first professional contract, which I signed when I turned 17 in 1960.

Five days before my 18th birthday I was given the present I wanted most of all. The League Cup was in its second season and Browny named me in the side for a second round match at home to Walsall. I didn't know I was in the team until I saw my name on the team sheet when it was pinned up the day before the game. I was gobsmacked to say the least. I later learned that our captain Stan Anderson had put a word in with Browny saying that I should be given a chance. Mind you, we agreed that had probably cost me a few games because Browny might have picked me earlier had he not had someone trying to tell him what to do!

We won 5-2 on my debut with Brian Clough scoring a hat-trick. Having had a taste of playing in the first team I wanted more but it was no surprise when Peter was back in goal for the next league game three days later at Derby's Baseball Ground. Oddly enough it would be the return fixture with Derby on February 24, 1962 when I would get my chance to make my league debut. Peter had actually kept a clean sheet in his last game, giving him two shut-outs in his previous three matches, but Browny was always willing to give youth an opportunity.

Charlie Hurley and George Herd got my league debut off to a good start by putting us 2-0 up at half-time and although Derby pulled a goal back I had done enough to keep my place and was in the side when we drew 1-1 at Orient a week later. I played in the next four fixtures and kept my first clean sheet in a goalless draw with Preston.

A big moment for me came the week after I missed my first game after getting into the side. Peter did well on his return, keeping a clean sheet in a 1-0 win at Middlesbrough but when the team sheet was pinned up for the next game at home to Southampton, it was my name at the top of it. Thankfully, I kept a clean sheet too and would only concede twice in the six games from then until the end of the season.

After seven wins in a row we went into the final match of the campaign at Swansea in with a chance of promotion but could only draw and missed out by a point. Only two went up then and we had edged into second place for the first time after winning our penultimate game at Rotherham. That capped a perfect Easter where we took maximum points from three games including a Good Friday 3-0 win over Newcastle United in my first derby match, watched by over 57,000 at Roker Park.

The season was finishing so I was very apprehensive over the close season, thinking about whether I would be able to do the same thing the next year or wondering if it was a fluke or beginner's luck. The first game of the new season was at home to Middlesbrough. I was named in the team and played every one of our 53 league and cup games that season.

It was terrific to be playing week-in, week-out – especially considering I was still a teenager when the season finished – but it was a very frustrating year. We'd missed promotion by a point when I first came into the side but it was even closer in my first full season when we missed out on goal average. We were top going into the last game of the season at home to Chelsea and all we needed to do was draw to go up. The game was an early lesson for me in how cruel football can be. It was a horrible day and a scrappy, physical game but Chelsea boss Tommy Docherty got his tactics spot on. We lost 1-0 to an ugly goal from Tommy Harmer which gave Chelsea the win they needed to overtake us.

We had a couple of decent cup runs, reaching the fifth round of the FA Cup and the two legged semi-final of the new League Cup. We were beaten 3-1 at home in the first leg by Aston Villa and, with the big freeze of 1962-63, that was one of only two games we played at home between Boxing Day and March. The second leg wasn't played until late April and while we managed a goalless draw at Villa Park it had been inevitable since the first leg that we weren't going to reach the final.

What had made that more likely was the injury to Brian Clough on Boxing Day. At the time we were second in the table and Brian had scored 28 goals in 28 games up to that point. Cloughie was the most natural of goal-scorers. In the 36 games I played alongside him he scored 39 times. Phenomenal. Undoubtedly we would have gone up that year had he not been injured. Brian would have secured many more than the one extra point we needed.

Brian would make a comeback over a year later but I was injured at the time and didn't play in the three games he managed in the autumn of 1964. A decade and a half later he would sign me for Nottingham Forest, by which time he was one of the most successful managers in the world.

A couple of weeks before his injury, Brian scored twice in a 3-0 win at Huddersfield. George Mulhall got the other goal with all three coming after half-time. It was possibly as well as I ever played. It was one of those games where I was constantly called upon, especially in the first half and I had to make a number of reflex close-range saves, more than one from the former Newcastle forward Len White.

We weren't a one-man team and even without Cloughie we went into the 1963-64 season determined not to miss out again. Of course there were no play-offs then and you had to finish in the top two out of 22 so there was little or no margin for error.

Our big rivals for promotion, Leeds United, were managed by another former Sunderland centre forward who went on to become a big-name manager, Don Revie. He was still at Roker in my first few months on the staff and by this stage he had assembled a fiercely competitive team. It was to be a glorious season as we achieved our goal of promotion but Leeds pipped us to the title by a couple of points. I am sure we were the better side though. We played them twice between Christmas and the New Year, drawing 1-1 at Elland Road and beating them 2-0 at Roker Park. By February we were top of the table but the demands of a strenuous FA Cup run possibly cost us the title.

We raced into a 3-0 half-time lead against league champions Everton in the fifth round and resisted their fight back to win 3-1. When the draw was made for the quarter-final it sent us to Old Trafford to face the cup holders Manchester United. To say the tie was dramatic would be an understatement. All the big names were in their forward line: Bobby Charlton, George Best and Denis Law but we had a canny team ourselves and we knew each other's games inside out. That season we had a very settled line-up.

I was one of four ever-presents, two others missed just one match and another three played nearly every game. On top of that Nicky Sharkey and Martin Harvey played over 30 games each without missing a match once they got into the side, in Martin's case he had been so difficult to leave out Browny had felt able to transfer Stan Anderson, of all people, to Newcastle.

We were full of confidence and with four minutes to go at Old Trafford, led 3-1. I got a knock and had to receive treatment. When I got up, Bobby Charlton pulled one back from the corner that re-started the game and a minute or two later Bestie made it three each with a shot that managed to drift through the legs of several players.

It has often been put to me that when I was injured I should have taken a lot more time to have treatment and delayed the re-start but I was okay and it is not those late goals that bother me so much as the one in the replay. I played 627 games but sometimes people don't remember 625 of them! They remember the 1973 FA Cup final and the game against Manchester United when I kicked the ground!

That replay was incredible. We probably played in front

of Roker Park's record crowd that night although the official figure was much less as the gates were pulled down and tens of thousands poured in – which ruined our crowd bonus! We were supposed to get £5 each for every thousand over 55,000. The supporters were vital to us. They always have been and they are now. Alan Brown liked us to be charged up by the crowd. At away games he would sometimes stop the team coach short of the ground and let us walk the last bit amongst the fans, led by George Curtis, who was the trainer. We had done this at Old Trafford.

For home games, we used to meet up for a pre-match meal on the sea front, usually at the Roker Hotel or sometimes the Seaburn Hotel and then walk up to Roker Park. We did this on the night of the replay and certainly by the time we made our way to the ground we were in no doubt whatsoever as to the fact that, even though we'd had crowds of over 60,000 before, this time it was going to be many more than that, and every one of the supporters was as up for the replay as we were.

Nicky Sharkey gave us the lead with a tremendous volley but then came my nightmare moment. I stubbed my toe taking a goal kick. Could I have done this in a league game where we were three up? No, I had to do it in a cup quarter final replay and send the ball to Denis Law. He couldn't believe his luck and clinically equalised. I mentioned how vital the crowd always are and they were brilliant with me. I had made a big mistake but they were right behind me, and that helped enormously in enabling me to put the mistake behind me. The match went to extra time where we re-took the lead through an own goal by Maurice Setters but Matt Busby's side came back and equalised again with seconds to go through Charlton.

We fought hard in the second replay at Huddersfield and kept it goalless to half-time but when Nicky Sharkey gave us the lead they levelled straight away, went into overdrive and, with our lads out on their feet on a heavy pitch, we were well beaten in the end. We had given it one hell of a try but once that chance had gone we had to make sure that we got the club promoted so the top sides like Manchester United and Everton were on the fixture list for the following season.

We had no intention of making any mistakes but there were still a lot of butterflies around before we took on Charlton Athletic in the last home game of the season, knowing it was in our hands to take the club back into the First Division. We had been in this situation before and missed out so we desperately didn't want a repeat but when Eddie Firmani gave Charlton an early lead it certainly didn't help, neither did the sight of my predecessor Peter Wakeham having a blinder at the other end for them. Peter looked to be in unbeatable form but we kept plugging away and got a bit of luck just before half-time as we drew level when George Herd's shot looped over him, having hit defender Brian Tocknell.

You have to work for whatever you get in football and that proved to be the case again in the second half when once again we scored right at the end of the half. This time it was the winner as our top scorer Johnny Crossan sealed promotion.

It had been a fantastic season and at the end of it I was a player about to make his bow in the top flight. On top of that I was by now an under-23 international. I had previously played four times for England at youth level but in February, with Sunderland top of the table, I had been selected to play against Scotland U23s at St James' Park, where we won 3-2. I was only 20 at the time and delighted to get the call-up.

The first day of the season after promotion wasn't how I had envisaged it. For a start I was injured and 15-year-old Derek Forster debuted in goal. Not only that but we were without a manager. It had been a big shock when Alan Brown walked out following a dispute with the directors and it was the directors who took charge until November when they appointed George Hardwick.

Derek kept goal for the opening three games but with ten goals conceded, Sandy McLaughlan was bought from Kilmarnock, which meant I had a fight on my hands if I wanted to get back into the team and play in the First Division. My chance came at the end of October. The team were struggling – we were third from bottom having won one of 13 games and had lost 5-2 at Forest the previous Saturday. Things didn't start well as we trailed at half-time to Stoke City but came back to draw 2-2.

Away form continued to be poor as we lost the next three but we were picking up at home. Burnley were still a decent side. They had never finished out of the top half since I had been there but beating them started a run of three home wins. The last of those made it back-to-back wins as a first away victory of the season had been registered at Leicester City. Despite winning four games in six though our position hadn't changed and we were still 20th.

What did change is that after that I was out of the team. After Boxing Day I didn't play again until the penultimate game of the season when I stood in for Sandy but I was straight out again after being beaten three times in the reverse fixture with Stoke.

I was playing reserve team football in the North Regional League but reserve team football was of no use to me. I had been used to being in the first team from a young age and so I asked for a transfer.

I didn't really want to go, I just wanted to play. Anyway, I didn't get the chance as the chairman Syd Collings made it clear to me that I would be going nowhere. It wasn't long after that our manager George Hardwick got the sack. I spoke to him and said I hoped my asking for a move hadn't contributed to his dismissal but he was good as gold about it and told me it hadn't been a factor.

Ian McColl was appointed as manager in the summer of 1965 and when the season started I found myself out of the side with Sandy McLaughlan preferred, so while he was in goal away to our old rivals Leeds on the opening day of the season, I was in the reserves who started with a home defeat to Carlisle on the same afternoon.

I got into the team for the sixth game and while we lost 3-1 at Aston Villa, I stayed in the side. We won the next two at home without conceding but I got injured against Forest in October. Martin Harvey took over in goal. I was out of the side for the rest of the year but when we lost heavily at home to West Brom on New Year's Day I was brought back 48 hours later and managed to keep a clean sheet as we beat Newcastle. From then on, I didn't look back really. I didn't miss a game for nearly two and a half years. The team had changed a bit since we'd won promotion in 1964 though.

We pulled Leeds out of the hat at home in the fifth round of the FA Cup. After two hard-fought draws we ended up meeting Revie's side at Hull's Boothferry Park in a second replay. When we had lost to Manchester United in a second replay three years earlier, we had ran out of steam and were beaten by a brilliant team. On this occasion we couldn't accept we had been beaten fairly and squarely. The tie was eventually settled in Leeds' favour by a massively contentious penalty that resulted in us having George Herd and George Mulhall sent off.

Leeds' right-back Paul Reaney had been my team-mate earlier in the month when I had been called up for England under-23s. As with my previous cap three years earlier it was against Scotland at St James' Park. Although we lost 3-1 I must have done okay because at the end of the season I was selected to play against Austria. It was back at Hull but it was a more enjoyable night than the cup meeting with Leeds as we won 3-0 and I was chosen to go on an England under-23 tour to Greece, Bulgaria and Turkey.

The Tottenham Hotspur manager Bill Nicholson was in charge. I played really well in the first match – I saved a penalty in a goalless draw with Greece in Athens – and did well again in the next game where we drew 1-1 with Bulgaria in Sofia. I stayed in the team for the last game of the tour as we beat Turkey 3-0 in Ankara. I would have loved to get a full cap but the nearest I came was sitting on the bench at Wembley a couple of years later in 1969. We played against France and beat them 5-0 on a horrendous night. Gordon Banks was in goal for England.

Sunderland had ended 1966-67 comfortably placed in the league and started the next one well but inevitably things fell away in what was to be a season of change. Ian McColl was sacked after winning his last game away to Alan Brown's Sheffield Wednesday in February – and within a week Browny was back at Roker Park as Sunderland manager! That was good news for me and those of us who had been at the club when we won promotion, because we knew that we had nothing to prove as he knew what we were capable of.

We lost the first four games under Browny to drop into a relegation position which we had never been in under McColl but we recovered and finished well after losing only two of our last 12 games. We even won at Old Trafford on the last day as Manchester United lost their title to rivals Manchester City.

Browny's first full season of his second spell saw us finish comfortably as he fashioned a new side. As in his first stint in charge he was keen to blood youngsters; Dennis Tueart and Ritchie Pitt being among those who came into the team while my old mates George Herd and George Mulhall's days at Roker came to an end.

We had been in the top flight for five seasons and never

really pushed on from the excellent promotion side we came up with, though on the other hand we had no serious scrapes at the wrong end of the table. That was to change for the worse in 1969-70. We got off to a bad start, didn't win until our 11th game and spent all season in the bottom three. Only two went down then, but we ended up second from bottom and were relegated after losing to Liverpool. I only missed one game that season and was playing well, so it was a crushing blow.

I played every game of the first year back in the Second Division but we never got going and finished halfway down. There was an improvement in the second year as we finished fifth but we never looked likely to go up.

Twelve years had passed since Alan Brown gave me my first team debut when 'Bomber' was sacked after a goalless draw with Fulham that left us 14th at the end of October 1972.

The previous season's promising fifth place didn't look like being built on and the club put Billy Elliott in temporary charge. Billy's big decision was to switch Dave Watson to centre half. Dave had played there at the beginning of his career and quickly transformed from a good centre forward to a great centre half.

Bob Stokoe was appointed manager at the end of November and just over five months later we had gone from being a struggling club to being the darlings of the nation after beating not one of the country's best teams but three of them as we magically won the FA Cup.

It is sad to see the way the FA Cup no longer has all of the glamour it traditionally boasted but back in 1973 it was the dream of every player to win it beneath the old twin towers at Wembley. I have heard members of England's 1966 World Cup-winning team express their regret that half a century on England have still to be world champions again. By the same token, it is over four decades now since we won the cup and

Sunderland supporters still cling to that achievement. Like the rest of the lads who lifted the trophy, as much as we deeply appreciate the esteem we are still held in by the fans, we would love to lose our claim as Sunderland's last cup winners and we would be thrilled to see the modern generation of supporters have their own day to savour.

We came close in 2014 when a great cup run led to an appearance in the League Cup final. Prior to the kick off, we were introduced to the crowd and received superbly 41 years after our greatest day. Believe me we hold the supporters as dear to our hearts as they do with us. I like to listen to what people did during the cup final, I want to know where they were that day. People say things like: 'I was six and I was too young to go,' or 'I was 12 and I went round to my mate's because he had a colour television.' I love listening to those little stories.

The cup run began modestly. Third Division Notts County were almost the giant-killers as we were a division higher and nearly lost at their place in the third round. Dave Watson scored a vital equaliser back at his first club and I remember an important late save from Les Bradd, who had opened the scoring.

We won the replay to set up a home tie with Fourth Division Reading who were managed by none other than Charlie Hurley. Their 'keeper Steve Death had an absolute blinder to earn them a draw at Roker but we quickly swept into a three-goal lead in the replay and progressed to be faced with cup favourites Manchester City at Maine Road, where we drew 2-2.

The replay was voted the greatest game in Roker Park's 99-year history when the ground closed in 1997. The Roker Roar was at its best that night and so were the team. Bob Stokoe had just added centre forward Vic Halom from Luton. The manager had already brought in two defenders who were surplus to requirements at Newcastle in Ron Guthrie and David Young. Bob had also signed Billy Hughes' brother John but 'Yogi' as he was known suffered an injury that finished his career on his debut. That was so unfortunate for John and Billy but had it not happened Vic almost certainly wouldn't have been signed and the course of history might well have been different. As it was, Vic was playing just his fourth game when he scored a truly unforgettable goal, beating giant Joe Corrigan at the Fulwell End with a pile-driver from the angle of the box.

We went on to sensationally win 3-1 and played fellow Second Division side Luton at home in the quarter-final. We had lost at Luton in the league seven days before the cup meeting and they had already beaten us at Roker Park – when Halom had scored for them. We made no mistake though, winning with two goals at the Roker End, a bullet header from Dave Watson and a great shot on the turn from Ron Guthrie.

Vic Halom had made his debut for us at Hillsborough against Sheffield Wednesday and would open the scoring on the same ground in the semi-final against Arsenal, who were bidding to reach their third successive final. Billy Hughes made it 2-0 with a header but six minutes from time Charlie George pulled one back. I got my hand to it but just couldn't stop the ball from trickling across the line. One I had stopped was a deflected shot from George Armstrong just before half-time. I had to change direction to keep it out and it was a good save. World Cup winner Alan Ball was good enough to congratulate me on it. We deserved to beat them and as it sunk in we had reached the cup final all we could hear as we celebrated in the dressing room was the sound of the fans demanding to see Bob Stokoe.

Inevitably, given all that had happened between the clubs since we had gone up together in 1964, the team we would face in the FA Cup final were Don Revie's Leeds. In the meantime, our league form had been on the rise. We had been 19th when Bob Stokoe took over but we went into the cup final in seventh place with two league games still to play. We would end up sixth but there were no play-offs then. The team who goes up from the play-offs is often the team with momentum. Had there been play-offs in 1973 might we have gone up on the back of winning the cup? It would have taken something special to stop us. As it was, by the time we went up three years later we had lost some of the cup team's best players so we will never know how successful we could have been against the top sides over a league season.

The only match I missed in the cup-winning season was at Orient on the Monday night before we played at Wembley. We spent the week leading up to the final at the Selsdon Park hotel where we had a great time. We were completely relaxed all week. No cup final team had ever gone to the Football Writers' dinner before but we were there.

Teams often freeze at Wembley and of our own side only Ritchie Pitt had played there before, in a schoolboy international. We knew we were about to play the best team in the league but we had knocked out Manchester City and Arsenal, we believed in ourselves and while Don Revie was renowned for producing dossiers on their opposition, we concentrated on ourselves. Besides, we didn't need to spend our time thinking about them, they were full of household names and if we had thought too much we might have developed a fear factor. That is not to say we were anything other than professional and prepared – we just prepared in the way that was right for us.

Tactically, many pundits thought left winger Eddie Gray could be Leeds' match-winner but Bob Stokoe detailed Bobby Kerr to double up with Dick Malone when needed and in an era of only one substitute, the fact that Gray was the man taken off tells its own story.

If Leeds had heard about Billy Hughes' laughing box on our TV interviews they realised straight after kick off we weren't at Wembley for a laugh. Ritchie Pitt's instant tackle on Allan Clarke showed them we weren't in awe of their reputation.

We thought that Clarke might not fancy it if he was hit hard enough while his partner Mick Jones would just keep going so Dave Watson was detailed to look after him. I am remembered for the save, Ian Porterfield is remembered for the goal but it was Dave who was man of the match.

We were the better team on the day. Their 'keeper David Harvey had more saves to make than I did. We worked for everything we got and not one of us was a weak link. If we had a weak link, Leeds would have capitalised on it.

The goal came when Bobby Kerr hit a looping shot that would have been an easy take for David Harvey – but we chased everything. Billy Hughes raced in at the goalkeeper who, with the ball wet, played safe and just helped it over the bar instead of trying to catch it.

Billy took the resulting corner, Dave attracted the attention of the defenders as Vic got the touch that knocked the ball to Ian. 'Porter' was a 'maker' rather than a 'taker' of goals and was all left foot but he cushioned the ball on his left thigh and then met it full on with a crashing right foot shot that flew past Harvey and made the rain splash off the netting as he indelibly wrote his name into the record books.

I have got Allan Clarke to thank for my name also being remembered from the cup final. When I made the double save everyone recalls it was from Trevor Cherry and Peter Lorimer but Dick Malone insists had Allan Clarke not fouled him he would have cleared Paul Reaney's cross, which his fellow full back headed back across me. I was already committed to going one way and had to change direction to get to the header. I couldn't hold it but managed to palm it out. I had always trained hard at making second saves; so many goals come from rebounds off the 'keeper so I was always anticipating a second save if I parried a first. I worked hard at pushing myself off the ground without using my hands to give myself a better chance of making a second stop with both hands free. I had seen the loose ball go to a white shirt. At that moment I didn't realise it was to Peter Lorimer, but instinctively I reacted with a hand out to the ball and managed to knock it up and onto the bar. As I got up I saw Dick getting the ball clear.

There were 25 minutes still to go and I didn't give the save another thought until after we had been presented with the trophy. Of course at the final whistle Bob Stokoe made a beeline for me but even then it didn't strike me that the save was anything different to saves I had been making for over a decade. It was only afterwards when I kept getting asked about it in interviews that I began to realise the importance of it. I don't think there has been a day since when I haven't been asked about it but I have never got tired of talking to people about it. I am grateful to be remembered and I am so proud to have been a part of a team that brought the FA Cup to my home town.

As we travelled home the following Tuesday, after playing another league game at Cardiff, we didn't know what was about to hit us. As we came up the A1 there were people waving on motorway bridges but it was when we got to Durham that it really sunk in. We transferred to an open-topped bus and as we travelled the 13 miles to Sunderland there were more people cheering us than I realised lived in the north east. People had climbed on to rooftops and scaled lamp-posts to get a better view. It was absolutely brilliant and when we got to Roker Park to do a lap of honour it was simply spine-tingling. Amazingly, the following night we played another league match against already promoted QPR.

Promotion was what we wanted, of course – and as soon

as possible. But we quickly found out that as the cup holders in the Second Division we were the team everybody wanted to beat. We were third after being unbeaten in the first five games but fell away, spent most of the season in mid-table and only climbed to a final position of sixth late on.

I played all but one of our 52 games that season. Ten cup games included four in Europe in the Cup Winners' Cup. We won both legs against Vasas Budapest without conceding a goal and then were 2-0 up in the first leg against Sporting Lisbon only for Hector Yazalde, who was the top scorer in Europe that season, to snatch a last-minute away goal. We went out on aggregate after losing 2-0 in the second leg. I had a testimonial at the end of the season and was grateful to the 29,625 who attended the match against Newcastle.

We had a really near miss for promotion in 1974-75 when by now three went up. From the start of November we were never out of the top three – until we lost the final match at promoted Aston Villa and ended up fourth.

We finally went up in 1975-76 when we won 19 and drew two of the 21 home games, although we lost at home on the windiest of days to Crystal Palace in the quarter-final of the FA Cup when we had ambitions of a Wembley return.

Three years and three months after winning at Wembley, just Dick Malone, Bobby Kerr, Billy Hughes and myself of the cup team were in the side that returned to the First Division. We drew our first three games. It wasn't a bad start but it became one as we took only one point from the next seven games. I missed the first two of those defeats, came back for the draw and then appeared in two more losses. I played in a drawn League Cup tie with Manchester United and made what proved to be my 627th and final appearance for Sunderland in a second replay at Old Trafford, where we lost 1-0 to a goal from Brian Greenhoff.

It was October 6, 1976, 15 years and two days since my debut, in the same competition. It was three days before my 33rd birthday but as I blew the candles out I didn't think I would never play in goal for Sunderland again. Barry Siddall – who is a great lad – had been bought from Bolton Wanderers the previous month so I knew I faced a challenge.

By the end of the month I was playing for a team wearing red and white stripes but it was Southampton, not Sunderland, and it was back in the Second Division on loan for Lawrie McMenemy. I played five games without particularly enjoying it.

Bob Stokoe had been feeling the pressure at Sunderland and resigned five days before my debut for Southampton. When I came back from my loan spell, Ian MacFarlane was in charge as caretaker but he was quickly replaced by Jimmy Adamson, who had been a star player when I had been at Burnley as a kid. Like most of the senior players, I found I didn't feature in the new gaffer's plans. I had looked forward to the 1976-77 season, having won promotion, but by March I was playing for my third club of the campaign after spending a lifetime at Sunderland.

Willie Bell signed me for Birmingham, initially on loan. I saved a penalty from Charlie George in a goalless draw on my debut at Derby. I still remember it now. We had some good players like Howard Kendall and Trevor Francis. But Willie left and went to America to join a religious cult. Alf Ramsey took over and was just so calm he never lost his temper. He was brilliant and still got his points across. Then Jim Smith came in. I had some good times with Jim.

Amazingly, before the end of the 1976-77 season, I was playing at Roker Park again – but playing against Sunderland. When I came back I did a little article for the *Sunderland Echo* and said as we were both struggling to stay up, it would be great if we could get a 0-0 draw and both of us could go on to avoid relegation. Birmingham lost 1-0 but the reception I got was unbelievable from the moment I got off the bus.

I missed only one game for Birmingham and was player of the year as we finished halfway up the First Division the following season, ending with a clean sheet at Nottingham Forest, who would win the league title under Brian Clough.

A year later, Cloughie would sign me for Forest after I had lost my place at St Andrews. I never played a first team game for Forest or after I returned to Sunderland a few years later so what proved to be the final appearance of my career came for Birmingham against Forest on April 21, 1979. It was the only game I played after February and Birmingham went down.

I moved from a relegated team to a club who had just won the European Cup! I got a European Cup medal myself after we beat Kevin Keegan's Hamburg in the final in Real Madrid's Bernabeu Stadium to retain the trophy but I never played as Peter Shilton was not only Forest's number one but England's. He was very focussed and never missed a game.

Being at Forest was a great education. Cloughie and Peter Taylor were probably the best partnership ever. We never trained much, we would do things like go for a wander down by the river. We used to sprint to one tree, walk to another. Then we got down to the pitches, which were all five-a-side. Clough and Taylor used to come round and walk the dog, maybe shout a couple of obscenities to someone off the ball, walk off and that would be it. It was a great education to see how different managers manage. Some people like Revie knew what you had for breakfast but then people like Cloughie never spoke about it.

One of our best players was Trevor Francis, who used to live in Birmingham as I did. We would take it in turns to drive to Nottingham. I used to have a Ford Orion and Trevor would turn up in a new XGS. He was a lovely lad and a smashing player. It was a nice time. I did play in the County Cup final where we beat Notts County 2-1. I loved playing in all the reserve team games though, it was brilliant.

After one year with Forest, I took the opportunity to return to Sunderland on August 8, 1980 after three and a half great years in the Midlands. My wife was absolutely gutted because she didn't want to go back as we had built a new life with a lot of new friends. It was a great chance to return to my club in a new role though. Sunderland had just been promoted back to the top flight under Ken Knighton and I accepted a position as player-coach.

I had two seasons without adding to my total of 627 appearances. After leaving Sunderland for a second time, I had seven enjoyable years working with future Sunderland Academy manager Ged McNamee at Meadowfield Sports Centre in Durham and also worked as a goalkeeping coach at various clubs including Newcastle, Sunderland, Darlington and lastly working with George Herd at Ryhope C.A.

Of course, I am a Sunderland lad and Sunderland have always been my club. In recent years, I have been heavily involved in the Sunderland Former Players' Association, being chairman for a while. I have also been honoured to take on an ambassadorial role with Sunderland AFC, attending many events in this country and abroad.

I still desperately want Sunderland to win. One of the most exciting moments for me came in January 2014 when I found myself hugging chairman Ellis Short at Old Trafford after we had beaten Manchester United on penalties to reach the League Cup final. Sunderland went on to lead in the final at Wembley against Manchester City before being beaten 3-1. One day Sunderland will win silverware again and I hope to see it.

Jim Montgomery holds the all-time record for most Sunderland AFC first team appearances with 627. His double save in the 1973 FA Cup final against Leeds United is known throughout the world. He is now an ambassador for the club.

2

The late winter and early spring of 1977 saw Sunderland put together a run of form that would have put them in the running to win the league title.

Unfortunately, they had been rock bottom at Christmas, with only nine points from 18 matches. There was also a club record run of ten games without a goal.

Relegation looked a certainty until a blistering change in fortunes that saw Sunderland almost pull off the greatest escape British football has ever seen.

As **Lance Hardy** explains, the key word there is 'almost'. In the end, relegation was confirmed in agonising and controversial circumstances…

DO YOU REMEMBER THE FIRST TIME?

BY LANCE HARDY

It was around 10.30pm on Friday, November 26, 1976 when it happened. Earlier that day, the Sex Pistols released *Anarchy in the UK* on EMI Records. But, as an eight year old boy, I wasn't aware of that at the time.

I was at a school disco in Lound, a small village in north Nottinghamshire. I don't remember too much about the party – apart from it costing me three pence for a cup of orange squash and the music being played was by Tina Charles and Leo Sayer. Hang the DJ!

But I distinctly remember the conversation I had with my father when he turned up to collect me.

'Do you know who Sunderland are playing tomorrow?'

'Derby County,' I replied in a nanosecond.

'Do you want to go?'

I didn't need to answer. My face said it all. I didn't know where Derby was. I didn't care. It could have been on the moon. It didn't matter…

Little did I know that this match would go down in history as the start of a record run of ten league matches without a goal for Sunderland AFC. Little did any of us who were there on that cold autumn day know that what was to follow could so nearly have gone down in history as the most miraculous relegation escape ever seen in British football.

My father worked on Saturdays. We also lived 125 miles south of Sunderland. So, I usually followed my team courtesy of *Grandstand*, Radio 2, a very bad Tyne Tees TV reception and Colin Diball's match reports in the *Daily Mirror*.

While I was old enough to watch the 1973 FA Cup final on television, I am sadly not old enough to remember it! Although I did run round the settee in celebration when Ian Porterfield scored, apparently. The first Sunderland side I can properly recall is the 1975-76 Second Division championship team: captain Tony Towers, Mel Holden, Pop Robson and all.

After six long years in the second flight and three years after winning the FA Cup, First Division football was back. Sunderland had romped to the Second Division title with 19 wins and two draws at home and Towers – whose face now adorned bubblegum cards and magazines alike – played for England in the Home International Championship against Wales and Northern Ireland. He won another cap in the USA Bicentennial Cup tournament against Italy later in the same month.

Shoot! magazine's popular League Ladders became my pride and joy from the early part of that successful season. The white-on-red Sunderland team tab was at the top of the Second Division almost throughout. But, after promotion to the top flight, I soon had to get used to seeing it at the bottom of the First Division. And there it stayed for what seemed like forever…

Sunderland manager Bob Stokoe said that he needed to make four new signings for the club to compete at the top level. He talked about a new goalkeeper, a new central defender and a new centre-forward. He went in search of a whole new spine to his team. But by the time our season kicked off at Stoke City's Victoria Ground in August, he had bought nobody.

He had, however, caused an element of disharmony within the club's ranks. The bearded winger Roy Greenwood, who had signed from Hull City – with beard – for £110,000 during the promotion season, was banned from appearing in the club's official team photograph for the 1976-77 season by 'The

Messiah' on account of having a beard and refusing to shave it off!

Incidentally, three other players – Dick Malone, Mel Holden and Billy Hughes – also returned home from an exhaustive summer trip to Australia, New Zealand and Tahiti sporting beards. Fortunately for Stokoe, they agreed to shave. Otherwise, the official team photograph would have featured just over half the first team!

Letters poured in to the *Sunderland Echo* from disgruntled supporters – many of whom had beards themselves – complaining about Stokoe's decision and, perhaps more pertinently, what it actually signified. There had been concerns about the manager's health for some time: he had missed a number of key matches due to migraines and his decision to part company with his loyal and well-respected assistant manager Arthur Cox and replace him with the burly and outspoken Ian MacFarlane had also been questioned, not least by his own chairman. As pre-seasons go, it wasn't the best…

Sunderland began the 1976-77 season with three draws. But the situation quickly worsened after a 4-1 thrashing at promoted Bristol City in the next match. Three of the following four league games were also lost – Joe Bolton's 30-yard screamer at West Ham United earning a solitary point.

Injuries had been mounting up too: Jim Montgomery, Bobby Kerr and Tony Towers had all missed vital matches and the situation was exacerbated when Mel Holden fell down the stairs at his home. He would be ruled out for six weeks. Tragically, within five years he would be dead; a victim of motor neurone disease. Holden died at just 27. His fall at home was the first sign that something was wrong with his health. Although there was sadly little sympathy shown towards him on the training ground at the time. Supporters of a certain age will have fond memories of a banner that was regularly displayed at the back of the Roker End with the words 'Mel Holden Rules The Sky' written on it.

Bottom of the table, Stokoe suddenly splashed the cash: Bolton Wanderers goalkeeper Barry Siddall and Leicester City forward Bob Lee signed for the club within 24 hours of each other for £90,000 and a club record £200,000 respectively. Jim Holton and Alan Foggon also joined from Manchester United.

Holton, a Scottish centre-half who had played in the 1974 World Cup finals in West Germany, came on loan with a view to a permanent £80,000 deal while Foggon became one of only a few men to play for Sunderland, Middlesbrough and Newcastle United when he signed for £25,000. However, Holton hadn't played for 18 months due to injury and Foggon had hardly featured at Old Trafford following a move from Rochester Lancers in the USA just a few weeks before.

Incidentally, Sunderland and Manchester United played out three exciting and exhausting League Cup ties that autumn. In contrast to their poor league form, Sunderland led four times in the first two matches but were denied on both occasions by 2-2 draws. By the time the sides met for a third time, a home tie with Newcastle United was on offer for the winners.

It has been argued that Stokoe was much more of a cup manager than a league manager. However, the former could impact positively on the latter. For instance, in the 1972-73 season, he famously took Sunderland from fourth-bottom of the Second Division up to sixth during the club's celebrated and fabulous FA Cup exploits.

Admittedly, cup runs could sometimes become Stokoe's priority, often to the detriment of league form. Indeed, in the season following the FA Cup run, he selected a much-weakened Sunderland side in a Second Division match at Hull City in readiness for the seemingly more important upcoming fixtures against Sporting Lisbon in the European Cup

Winners' Cup and Liverpool in the League Cup. All three matches were subsequently lost and the expected 1973-74 promotion campaign never happened.

But Stokoe knew that cup runs brought in the fans in their droves. It happened in 1973 and it happened in 1976. Almost 125,000 spectators watched those three League Cup matches between Sunderland and Manchester United.

Cup fever was back and the Sunderland manager briefly looked as though he might be in his element once again. But it didn't last. The prospect of playing Newcastle was lost when Brian Greenhoff's 75th-minute goal in the second replay gave Manchester United the lead in the tie for the first time and a passage through to the next round. The Lads had nothing to show for their toils and, ultimately, Stokoe would only ever manage Sunderland in Texaco Cup and Anglo-Scottish Cup matches against their great rivals; the club that he won the 1955 FA Cup with as a player.

Undoubtedly, this would have been a massive personal disappointment for Stokoe. But it was still a shock when after just one more league match and yet another defeat – this time at home to Aston Villa – the manager offered his resignation. He felt there was no alternative and wanted to allow somebody else to step into his place. His actual words to club chairman Keith Collings were: 'I don't think I can go any further with the club. I think I have gone as far as I can.'

With no wins from nine league matches, Ian MacFarlane took charge of the team for the visit to Queens Park Rangers, who had finished First Division runners-up behind Liverpool the previous season. He promptly became the first man to select a Sunderland side that did not feature one member of the 1973 FA Cup-winning team. Less than three-and-a-half years had passed since that day.

Sunderland lost 2-0 at Loftus Road. Although Jim Holton's

header hit the post when the score was 1-0. However, MacFarlane did manage to inspire the team and two 2-1 wins – against Coventry City and Tottenham Hotspur – were recorded in his next five matches before the Rokerites and I made our separate ways to the home of the 1974-75 Football League champions, Derby County.

And so my first memory of my first Sunderland match isn't being drawn to Roker Park by those giant floodlights or walking up those steep steps behind the Fulwell End but filing into the left-hand corner of the Baseball Ground, buying a match programme (in the rare style of a broadsheet newspaper), seeing the famous club logo of a ram high above on a gable facade on the top of the main stand across the pitch from us and being greeted by the sound of the number one record at the time – *If You Leave Me Now* by Chicago – being completely drowned out by a chant of: 'Six foot two, eyes of blue, big Jim Holton's after you!' from the Sunderland faithful. Such was 1970s football. Such moments last a lifetime…

Big Jim Holton captained Sunderland that day and only Bobby Kerr and Billy Hughes, of the 1973 FA Cup-winning side, played. Barry Siddall was in goal, Joe Bolton was at left-back, 19-year-old Gary Rowell was in for the injured Tony Towers in midfield and Roy Greenwood was on the bench, along with his beard. Somewhat disappointingly for me, we played in our away kit of yellow shirts, yellow shorts and yellow socks with blue trim.

My main memory of the match is Derby's Welsh international winger Leighton James, who scored the only goal of the game, taking the ball to the corner flag in the final few minutes and playing for time. Sunderland had pressed for the last 20 minutes or so but to no avail. We lost 1-0. We were next to bottom of the First Division. I was sick on the way home. And I had just witnessed the start of an unwanted club record that still stands to this day…

Four days later, the Sex Pistols went on the *Today* programme on national television and Steve Jones swore at Bill Grundy. Punk became a national phenomenon. Seventy six days later, Sunderland finally managed to score a league goal again!

That defeat at Derby was to be Ian MacFarlane's last match in the Sunderland dugout. The club announced that they were to appoint a new manager the following week. Nottingham Forest manager and former Sunderland striker Brian Clough was the fans' favourite. He had met Keith Collings before Bob Stokoe was appointed at Roker Park in 1972 and he was once again interviewed by him for the job. However, he was once again overlooked.

Sunderland would never have a better chance of getting Clough. Within two years, he won the First Division title with Nottingham Forest. Within three years, he won the European Cup with them.

The man who was appointed on this occasion was another North-Easterner. Jimmy Adamson had played under former Sunderland manager – and Clough's mentor in his days as a Sunderland player – Alan Brown at Burnley in the 1950s. He captained the Clarets to the league title in 1960 and an FA Cup final in 1962. He was also named Football Writers' Footballer of the Year in 1962 and went to the World Cup in Chile later that same month as a player and assistant coach in Walter Winterbottom's England squad – but he didn't feature in the team, much to his disappointment. He was later offered the England manager's job ahead of Alf Ramsey and turned it down. He had also been a candidate to replace Brown at Sunderland in 1964 but Burnley chairman Bob Lord blocked the move.

Similar to Brown, Adamson was a Sunderland fan as a boy. His favourite player had been the 1937 FA Cup-winning captain

Raich Carter. He also shared the same faith in youth as his former manager. He proclaimed that Burnley would become the 'Team of the Seventies' and subsequently led them to sixth in the top flight in 1973-74 before leaving the club disheartened after a row with Lord in early 1976. Other than a brief stint at Sparta Rotterdam, he had been out of work since.

The Sunderland squad was quite different to the one that had been photographed without Roy Greenwood just a few months before: Jim Montgomery had gone on loan to Southampton after making 627 first team appearances for the Rokerites (it was one of the last acts carried out by Bob Stokoe – who agreed the move with Saints manager Lawrie McMenemy – although Ian MacFarlane concluded the deal); the previous season's top goalscorer, Pop Robson, had returned to West Ham United; Bob Moncur, who had lost his place to Jim Holton, was now manager at Carlisle United; and Alan Foggon, Bob Lee and Barry Siddall had all signed. Meanwhile, Mel Holden and Tony Towers were both out injured. Towers had also asked to be transfer-listed, as had FA Cup-winning captain Bobby Kerr.

Adamson's first words at his first press conference at Roker Park were as follows: 'I am delighted to be taking over as manager of such a famous club.' He added that Ian MacFarlane would continue at the club as his right-hand man. Ten days later, MacFarlane was sacked. Dave Merrington came from Burnley to replace him.

The day after that press conference, three inches of snow settled on the Roker Park pitch. It meant that Adamson's first match in charge would be at Birmingham City on Saturday, December 11. By which time both Towers and Kerr had both independently withdrawn their transfer requests. Sunderland lost 2-0 at St Andrews.

The following week, Kerr made his 300th league

appearance for Sunderland at home to Norwich City. There was also a debut for 17-year-old Alan Brown, who had impressed for the youth team in the Northern Intermediate League. Sunderland lost 1-0. We were bottom of the table at Christmas.

'Plenty of heart but not enough brains,' was Adamson's summary of his team's performance. As a result, the entire squad spent the Monday before Christmas watching a re-run of the whole 90 minutes at Tyne Tees TV studios in Newcastle.

Sunderland were stuck on nine points. Christmas and New Year came and went but there was no hope of me even thinking about moving the white-on-red team tab from the bottom of my First Division League Ladder. The festive season brought a visit to a packed St James' Park to play Newcastle United, where Adamson gave another teenager – 18-year-old Tim Gilbert – his debut. We lost 2-0. Two days later, a Joe Jordan goal beat us at Leeds United. A trip to Liverpool on New Year's Day brought another 2-0 defeat.

We looked doomed: four points from safety, having played four games more than most of our rivals. Further defeats against Coventry City and Leicester City worsened the situation. The FA Cup brought a chance of some respite but delivered further embarrassment after a 1-0 defeat at the hands of Third Division Wrexham in a third round replay. Sunderland had also trailed 2-0 at home in the first match but managed to draw 2-2.

It was around this time that Adamson met the Sunderland board and delivered a six-week report. Under his charge, the club had lost every league game they had played without scoring a goal. They were also out of the FA Cup. He was given permission to sign two defenders – Mick Docherty and Colin Waldron – both of whom had played under him at Burnley. He also made attempts to bring Welsh international midfielder Brian Flynn from Turf Moor but failed.

Jim Holton, who was a popular player at Roker Park and had been seen house-hunting in the area during the previous week, was surprisingly dropped for the match against Leicester. He immediately asked for a move and his wish was granted. Six other players were also transfer-listed on the same day. Fans wrote protest letters to the manager about his decision to release the Scottish international but he put them in the bin. Holton subsequently joined Coventry, of which more later...

Holton's replacement at Filbert Street was 19-year-old Shaun Elliott. Another youth team player, Kevin Arnott, aged 18, had also made his first team debut in midfield at Wrexham. By contrast, the first match against Wrexham marked the last Sunderland appearance by another hero of '73, Billy Hughes. Adamson was making big changes and big decisions. He had now given debuts to four locally-produced teenagers while another, Gary Rowell, had featured regularly over the previous few months.

'Shaun Elliott and I came through the ranks together but Kevin Arnott seemed to be plucked out of nowhere,' Gary Rowell remembers. 'Kevin was a stylish midfielder, Shaun was a battler and I loved to get forward and score goals.'

'Charlie's Angels' were born. Named after veteran Sunderland scout Charlie Ferguson, it was also loosely based around the popular American TV detective series of the same name, which was a big hit in the UK at the time. Arnott, Elliott and Rowell were to join up in a new-look Sunderland midfield with another famous Ferguson find, Bobby Kerr. The old stalwart became a great influence on the three youngsters.

In the next match – at home to Stoke City – Adamson started with Arnott and Rowell. In the following game – away at Arsenal – he started with Arnott, Elliott and Rowell. This echoed what Adamson had done at Burnley. It also echoed what Brown had done at both Burnley and Sunderland.

'Tony Towers was our star player in the centre of midfield so I had only really started a game if he was injured or suspended,' Rowell explains. 'Number 11 wasn't my natural position but Jimmy Adamson told me that he wanted to play me in the team and that was the position that became available.'

Rowell never looked back. And neither did Arnott or Elliott. None of them were to miss a single match during the rest of the season. The reason for that was an astonishing run of results that so nearly achieved the greatest relegation escape of all time.

The games against Stoke and Arsenal were both goalless draws. So, at least one unwanted run had been stopped. After nine successive league defeats, Sunderland had finally moved into double figures in the points column and now had 11. But the other unwanted run continued. It was now 11 long weeks since Sunderland's last league goal – Billy Hughes' thrice-taken penalty in the 3-1 midweek defeat at Ipswich Town. Meanwhile, the Stoke attendance (22,901) was the lowest home crowd of the season so far. That was to drop even further (21,407) for the visit of Bristol City the following week.

However, there were encouraging signs. Stoke goalkeeper Peter Shilton was the man of the match and the point at Highbury was achieved against the fifth-placed team in the First Division. It was also shown on *Match of the Day* and I can vividly remember Sammy Nelson kissing Bobby Kerr on the cheek after one of many near-misses by the Rokerites.

Sunderland impressed at Highbury with their youngest team in years: Barry Siddall was in fine form in goal; Jack Ashurst and Mick Doherty were solid in central defence; the new-look midfield was beginning to gel nicely; and the new partnership of Mel Holden and Bob Lee up front was also starting to click. Substitute Alan Brown also hit the underside of the Arsenal bar late on.

'I know most people think we are down already,' Adamson said after the match at Highbury. 'But after a show like this, I don't think we have had it yet.'

It was a terrific performance. Although, admittedly, the overall feeling at that time – at least for a nine-year-old boy – was the resignation of relegation. Sunderland had 11 points from 25 games and were firmly rooted at the bottom of the table. If we had any realistic hopes of survival, Adamson will have known more than anyone that the next four games – all to be played at home – against Bristol City, Middlesbrough, West Bromwich Albion and West Ham United – had to deliver wins. And the last one of the those had come against Tottenham Hotspur way back in November. Spurs were now the side positioned one place above the relegation zone, six points ahead of us with two games in hand.

First Division, bottom (February 5, 1977)

Pos		Pld	Pts
19	Tottenham Hotspur	23	17
20	Bristol City	21	16
21	West Ham United	23	13
22	Sunderland	25	11

(42 matches to be played, two points for a win)

Sunderland's First Division goal famine finally ended after two-and-a-half months on a Friday night in the second week of February with Mel Holden's 58th-minute header against fellow strugglers Bristol City. Furthermore, a third successive clean sheet won the match. The result put Sunderland three points behind their opponents in the table, although they had played four games more!

Incredibly, the following week – seemingly out of nowhere

– Sunderland's biggest Wear-Tees derby victory was equalled when Middlesbrough were flattened 4-0 with goals from Bob Lee, Mel Holden, Kevin Arnott and Gary Rowell.

However, highly-rated defender Jeff Clarke suffered a serious knee injury in this match. It would keep him out of action for the rest of the season. Tony Towers also remained unavailable for a further eight matches due to a thigh injury. It was now down to the kids…

'Jimmy Adamson was asked in a press conference why he had all these youngsters in the side and why he wasn't playing the "stars" instead,' Rowell remembers. 'He told the press that we were the stars! We were young lads and that gave us a tremendous confidence boost.'

Three days later, West Brom were battered 6-1 at Roker Park. Bob Lee scored after 25 seconds and went on to hit a hat-trick. Shaun Elliott, Gary Rowell and Mel Holden got the others in Sunderland's biggest victory in the top flight since 1956.

Astonishingly, that record only lasted until the next home match! This time, West Ham were thrashed 6-0.

After 1,020 minutes of football without a single league goal, Sunderland had somehow scored 16 in three matches. After picking up two points in two-and-a-half months, Sunderland had now won eight in just 22 days. Furthermore, they were out of the bottom three for the first time since September.

First Division, bottom (March 5, 1977)

Pos		Pld	Pts
18	Sunderland	29	19
19	Tottenham Hotspur	27	19
20	West Ham United	27	19
21	Derby County	25	18
22	Bristol City	25	18

'We can do it,' Jimmy Adamson boomed afterwards. 'Let the rest of them do the worrying.'

Sunderland could have had concerns about the four extra games they had played over some of their rivals or the recent form shown by others; West Ham, with Pop Robson up front, had won three matches in a row before they had been annihilated at Roker Park. But the word 'worry' was not in the player's minds at all.

'It was an incredible time,' Rowell says. 'I was living the dream. We weren't just beating teams, we were totally outplaying them and scoring so many goals.

'But it had been coming,' he adds. 'We hit the woodwork three times against Coventry and at Arsenal. Jimmy Adamson always used to tell us that it would come. He believed in us. We had a great team with a great spirit. We thought we could go out and beat anybody, we really did.'

Next up came a trip to Maine Road to face title contenders Manchester City. It was to be an eventful match and the importance of those events would turn out to be critical. Referee Bert Newsome wrongly ruled out a Mel Holden strike after 15 minutes for offside and then awarded the home side a penalty in first half injury time after Jack Ashurst had beaten Gary Owen to the ball. Dennis Tueart scored from the spot. City won 1-0.

'It must be the joke of the season,' Adamson remarked about the disallowed goal. Former Sunderland centre-half Dave Watson, watching from the stands, said about the penalty: 'I would have been very proud of myself to have made such a tackle. He took the ball clean as a whistle and there was no suggestion of a foul.'

'They were two massive decisions and they both went against us,' Rowell says. 'The disallowed goal should have stood and it was never a penalty either! It is easy to look back now and pick out one match that made a difference, but I honestly think that one did. We should have won it, not lost it.'

A crowd of 35,376 – the biggest home attendance since early November – saw a Colin Waldron goal beat Ipswich. But the former Burnley captain was sent off as Sunderland surprisingly capitulated 4-1 at Aston Villa four days afterwards.

It was to be a rare blip. The Rokerites began a busy April – with seven matches to play – sixth from bottom in the table. They ended the month unbeaten with a further ten points gained from three wins and four draws.

Another Bob Lee goal was enough to beat QPR at home. Kevin Arnott then produced a wonderful chip from over 20 yards to help Sunderland into a 2-0 lead against Newcastle in the Good Friday derby, played in front of 46,056 fans at Roker Park. But we were pegged back to 2-2. The following day, Mel Holden put Sunderland 1-0 up at Leeds, but again the match was drawn. There was a 2-1 Easter Monday win over Manchester United with another goal from Arnott and a penalty from the fit-again Tony Towers. Two 1-1 draws against Tottenham and Derby followed before West Brom were beaten 3-2 at The Hawthorns by two more goals from Towers and one from Lee, who took his season tally up to 13 in the league.

Sunderland were out of the bottom three – on goal difference – going into May. But the relegation dogfight had now extended to ten teams.

Bristol City remained bottom and West Ham – with just one win in nine matches – were next to them. Tottenham had climbed above the Hammers after beating Aston Villa 3-1 on the last day of April – but they were running out of matches.

Above Sunderland came QPR. Stoke – with just one win in their last 11 matches – had also slumped into the danger zone. Back-to-back wins for Coventry had lifted them up to sixth-bottom, following a run of 13 matches without a win. Derby, Norwich and Birmingham were just above them.

First Division, bottom (May 1, 1977)

Pos		Pld	Pts
13	Norwich City	40	35
14	Birmingham City	38	34
15	Derby County	38	32
16	Coventry City	37	32
17	Stoke City	38	32
18	QPR	36	31
19	Sunderland	39	31
20	Tottenham Hotspur	40	31
21	West Ham United	38	30
22	Bristol City	37	28

Sunderland were the form team in the First Division. The Rokerites' league record of eight wins, five draws and two defeats from early February to late April was better than any other. Only champions-elect Liverpool – with eight wins, three draws and one defeat – came close.

After the horror show of a first half of the season where only nine points had been won from the first 23 league matches plus early exits in both cup competitions, Sunderland had played more matches than all of their rivals. The remarkable turnaround in form had begun in early February but only now – with three games remaining – was the league table beginning to properly take shape. It had been a hell of a run – but it looked as though we still needed something like three or four points to be safe.

With so many teams playing catch up, the situation was ever-changing and after Pop Robson scored both goals for West Ham in a 2-0 midweek win at home to Coventry, Sunderland found themselves back in the relegation places.

A hero came back to Roker Park for the final home match

of the season as Jim Montgomery returned with Birmingham. He received a welcome comparable to the one that had greeted Reading manager Charlie Hurley during the 1973 FA Cup run.

It was still somewhat surreal. Montgomery had only been granted a free transfer by Sunderland a few weeks before. After a loan spell at Southampton, he had briefly returned to the club before being officially released after 17 years of service. Ironically, he was now playing against the club he loved in a relegation clash.

'It was hard for us to get our heads around it,' Gary Rowell remembers. 'We were attacking towards the Fulwell End and standing in front of us and in front of all our supporters was Monty! When we scored it still felt like we had scored against our goalkeeper.'

Mel Holden's ninth goal of the season settled the match and earned Sunderland a ninth home win of the campaign. It was enough to climb out of the bottom three once again.

Elsewhere, apart from Tottenham – who were thrashed 5-0 at Manchester City and subsequently left on the verge of relegation – every other team in the bottom ten drew.

This meant that QPR (32 points) had joined Tottenham (31) and Bristol City (29) in the bottom three. Four teams – including Sunderland – were just above them on 33 points and two more had 34. QPR and Bristol City also had games in hand. It was far too close to call.

The final Saturday of the league season was a week away. But with so many fixtures still to be played, the relegation battle was going to stretch beyond that weekend. Sunderland's season was due to end at Everton on Thursday, May 19.

At the other end of the table, Liverpool were challenging for an unprecedented treble of First Division, FA Cup and European Cup honours. The league title was almost theirs, the FA Cup final against Manchester United was to be played at Wembley the week after the final Saturday of the league season and the European Cup final was to be contested against Borussia Moenchengladbach, of West Germany, in Rome four days later.

Interestingly, The Reds' final three league games were to be against Coventry, West Ham and Bristol City. Intriguingly, Coventry's last match of the season would be another re-arranged fixture against Bristol City.

Surprisingly, Coventry held Liverpool to a goalless draw in their midweek match. Bristol City beat Leeds 1-0 on the same night. Twenty four hours later, Stoke drew 3-3 against Manchester United. Five points now separated the ten teams at the bottom. Any of them could still go down. Any of them could still stay up…

First Division, bottom (May 14, 1977)

Pos		Pld	Pts
13	Birmingham City	40	36
14	Derby County	41	36
15	Norwich City	41	36
16	Coventry City	40	34
17	Stoke City	40	34
18	Sunderland	40	33
19	West Ham United	40	33
20	QPR	38	32
21	Bristol City	39	31
22	Tottenham Hotspur	41	31

The final Saturday took Sunderland to Norwich. As for the rest: Tottenham – needing something of a miracle to survive themselves – were at home to Leicester; Bristol City were away at Middlesbrough; QPR were away at Leeds; West Ham were at

Liverpool; Stoke were at West Brom; Coventry were at home to Manchester City; Derby were at home to Ipswich; and Birmingham were at home to Everton.

Sunderland lined up unchanged for the fifth game in a row: Barry Siddall, Mick Doherty, Joe Bolton, Kevin Arnott, Colin Waldron, Jack Ashurst, Tony Towers, Shaun Elliott, Mel Holden, Bob Lee and Gary Rowell. Bobby Kerr was substitute.

With seven minutes left, Sunderland trailed 2-0 at Carrow Road. With nothing to lose, Adamson threw on the old stager Kerr in place of Towers. It changed the game. Rowell pulled a goal back when he headed home a Kerr cross and two minutes later – with the game heading into injury time – 'The Little General' himself powered home a left foot drive from outside the box after goal-bound efforts from both Lee and Holden had been partially cleared. There was pandemonium on the terraces. It finished 2-2.

Elsewhere, Tottenham won 2-0 – but it was in vain. QPR beat Leeds and draws for Bristol City and West Ham – along with Sunderland's point – put Spurs down. Elsewhere, a draw for Derby and a win for Birmingham meant they were safe. Coventry and Stoke both lost. Five teams were now on the same number of points and four of them had just one to play…

First Division, bottom (evening of May 14, 1977)

Pos		Pld	Pts
16	Sunderland	41	34
17	QPR	39	34
18	Coventry City	41	34
19	West Ham United	41	34
20	Stoke City	41	34
21	Bristol City	40	32
22	Tottenham Hotspur	42	31

The following morning was the first time that I tried – with pen and paper in hand – to work out permutations. I had chosen a difficult task. The newspapers called it 'the most dramatic First Division relegation battle in over 50 years'. Nearby, my *Shoot!* League Ladders looked in the best shape they had been in all season. But, of course, the situation was far more complicated than that.

However, if Bristol City lost to Liverpool – the best team in the country on course for the treble – and West Ham lost to Manchester United – the other FA Cup finalists – or Stoke lost at League Cup winners and fifth-placed Aston Villa the following night, I quickly worked out that Sunderland would be safe. This was due to a combination of a lot of paper, our superior goal difference and the important factor that Coventry had to play Bristol City – and therefore both of them couldn't win! So, it was simple: defeats for at least two of our three relegation rivals on the Monday night and all would be fine and – on paper at least – all of those required results looked more than likely.

But life doesn't work like that. Both Liverpool and Manchester United played weakened sides at Ashton Gate and Upton Park and both Bristol City and West Ham won. For the record, QPR won as well to secure their survival. Stoke did lose at Villa and were therefore effectively relegated – but that felt almost incidental that night. I sat there watching the results caption on the *Nine O'Clock News* open-mouthed.

It was suddenly one from three teams to go down with Stoke and Tottenham: Sunderland, Bristol City and Coventry. Each had played 41 games and each had 34 points – but Sunderland had a goal difference of -6, Bristol City -10 and Coventry -11.

Therefore, a draw for Sunderland at Goodison Park three days later would be enough. It would not even be necessary if there was a winner in the match at Highfield Road on the same night. But if it was required, two defeats in our last 18 league matches suggested that it shouldn't be a problem, particularly given mid-table Everton had nothing to play for.

In terms of the other two sides: Bristol City required a draw to be safe and Coventry needed to win. The only possible combination of results that could relegate Sunderland was a defeat for us and a Coventry-Bristol City draw. However, given the Sky Blues needed a win to be safe, surely they wouldn't gamble on that?

Bobby Kerr's heroics at Norwich persuaded Jimmy Adamson to revert to the midfield that had started to shock the nation back in February. Tony Towers was relegated to the bench. It would be the last time he wore a Sunderland shirt.

Sunderland lost 2-0 at Everton. Bob Latchford scored after ten minutes. Then, late on, with ten men pouring forward in search of the equaliser that would preserve our First Division status, Bruce Rioch scored a second goal in injury time.

But that wasn't the story. Kick-off in the all-important match at Highfield Road had been controversially and – many would say – conveniently delayed by several minutes due to crowd congestion.

Coventry had led 2-0 against Bristol City but were pegged back to 2-2 in the second half. With the Sunderland match over, the possibility of an all too predictable and totally unfair scenario arose where two teams could now play out a draw in the knowledge that they would both be safe.

And so it was that Coventry chairman Jimmy Hill raced up to the Sky Blues radio booth and demanded that the Sunderland result was broadcast. His request was carried out. Sunderland's result was also displayed on the electronic scoreboard, presumably just in case somewhere in the stadium somebody had failed to hear the radio announcer.

Two former Leeds United team-mates, Norman Hunter (Bristol City) and Terry Yorath (Coventry) were on opposite sides that night. In his autobiography, Yorath recalls that, on hearing the radio announcement, he shouted out to Hunter: 'There you are, you can tell your lads to back off now.'

Both sides played for time, passing the ball to each other to ironic cheers from the crowd. Jim Holton, released by Sunderland earlier in the year, was in the Coventry side that night.

The scene at Goodison Park was almost as surreal. As Sunderland's players left the pitch, the latest scoreline from Highfield Road was incorrectly announced via the public address system as 2-1. Around five minutes of play remained at Coventry at that time.

Thousands of Sunderland fans, who had made the long midweek trip to celebrate the most miraculous relegation escape ever known, now stood still in silence and waited for confirmation of the result that would determine their club's fate.

As we now know, the outcome at Highfield Road was never in doubt from the moment that the Sunderland result was announced. The match finished 2-2. Players from both sides embraced each other afterwards. It was a cruel and ugly relegation for Sunderland to suffer.

When the sad news finally filtered through to Goodison Park, there were tears on the terraces and in the away dressing room. Back at our house, I cried as well.

'We were in the dressing room for ages not knowing if we were staying up or going down,' Gary Rowell recalls. 'It was chaotic. One minute, we were told one thing and the next, we were told the other. In the end, it was confirmed that we had been relegated. It was such a shame. It had been a great three or four months for us and it was in our hands at the end.

'We didn't know about the late kick-off at Coventry until the next day.' Rowell adds. 'That made us feel even worse. In hindsight, you are left thinking about what could have been? Tony Towers left us soon afterwards and we had to start all over again in the Second Division.'

'That's life,' Jimmy Adamson said as he gathered his thoughts in the tunnel that fateful night. 'You have to learn to take it on the chin.'

The man who had lost an FA Cup final as a player with Burnley and was also overlooked for an England cap, despite winning the Football Writers' Footballer of the Year award, added solemnly: 'I was proud of the team. We went down all guns blazing. This was the biggest disappointment of my life.'

First Division, bottom (final table)

Pos		Pld	Pts
13	Birmingham City	42	38
14	QPR	42	38
15	Derby County	42	37
16	Norwich City	42	37
17	West Ham United	42	36
18	Bristol City	42	35
19	Coventry City	42	35
20	Sunderland	42	34
21	Stoke City	42	34
22	Tottenham Hotspur	42	33

Over 30 years later, I was on the television gantry at Craven Cottage when an 80-year-old Jimmy Hill was booed by hundreds of visiting supporters during a Premier League match between Fulham and Sunderland. A commentator nearby took off his headphones and asked me what it was all about?

'1977,' I told him.

He shook his head and said: 'Your lot have got long memories.'

'Too right,' I replied.

The week after those final matches of the 1976-77 season had been played, the Sex Pistols finally released their second single *God Save the Queen* on their third record label, Virgin. It was subsequently banned by the BBC but still reached number two in the charts amid rumours that it was the best-selling record in the country and it had been fixed to prevent it from reaching number one in the UK at the time of the Queen's Silver Jubilee.

Meanwhile, Alan Hardaker, the Football League secretary, was instructed by the Football League Management Committee to seek an explanation for the controversial radio announcement at Highfield Road. The outcome was that he later reprimanded Coventry in a letter. But there was no points deduction and Sunderland's relegation stood.

As Johnny Rotten once said: 'Ever get the feeling you've been cheated?'

Lance Hardy is the author of *Stokoe, Sunderland and '73*, which was shortlisted for Best Football Book at the British Sports Book Awards and nominated for the British Society of Sports History Literary Prize. He is also the editor of *Tales from the Red and Whites.*

3

After Martin O'Neill's departure and the short-lived gamble on the Italian Paolo Di Canio, Sunderland found themselves deep in trouble again.

With the team sucked into a relegation fight it had begun to look like the surrender might be meek.

That was until Gus Poyet arrived, led the team to a cup final at Wembley and masterminded a late run of four wins – including victories at Stamford Bridge and Old Trafford – to steer the ship to safety.

Pete Sixsmith remembers the Great Escape of 2014…

THE GREAT ESCAPE

BY PETE SIXSMITH

I suppose it all began on March 30, 2013, when Martin O'Neill was in charge of his final game as Sunderland manager. Knocked out of the FA Cup by Championship Bolton Wanderers, the January transfer window had seen the distinctly underwhelming arrivals of Alfred N'Diaye and Danny Graham and it looked as if the club were sleepwalking to relegation.

I left at half-time; a Titus Bramble own goal had given Champions-elect Manchester United a 26th minute lead and I had bigger fish to fry. My home town team, Shildon, members of the Northern League, were hoping to turn around a two-goal deficit in the FA Vase semi-final. Opponents Tunbridge Wells would surely not fancy an encounter in front of a boisterous crowd and I wanted to be a part of it.

It turned out to be a miserable day. Sunderland lost in as timid a fashion as you would expect as the United juggernaut rolled on. Shildon, leading 3-0, contrived to let a no better than average side back into the game and missed out on a Wembley place. And then came the shock news of O'Neill's sacking.

For me, this was as sad a day as I have had as a Sunderland supporter. Here was the manager we had all wanted, who had got off to a flying start and who looked as comfortable in his role as any of the many Sunderland managers I had seen. But it all went wrong for him. Was it because there was no John Robertson alongside him? Was it because he had been out of the game for the best part of two years? Was he just too old to fully comprehend the mindset of players who earned thousands for doing very little?

Whatever it was, Sunderland chairman Ellis Short terminated his employment with the club heading for a relegation spot, the support muted and the multi millions of the Premier League beginning to disappear in the rear view mirror.

We awaited the appointment of a new saviour, someone who was going to grab the club and the players by the scruff of the neck and make Sunderland into an outfit that would be challenging for a top half place rather than one that seemed to be permanently struggling.

We got Paolo Di Canio.

As appointments go, it was as bizarre as the directors running the team as they did after Alan Brown had left in 1964 or as left-field as Howard Wilkinson appointing himself in 2002. It was an odd one that was for sure. The Italian had been out of work since his departure from Swindon Town, had no experience of coaching in the highest league and brought some baggage with him. Rather unpleasant baggage as well.

A fine player and revered at Parkhead and the Boleyn Ground, Di Canio had never shied away from controversy. He had been suspended for laying hands on a referee while at Sheffield Wednesday and had returned to his beloved Lazio where he had been photographed participating in a commemorative service for a recently departed Lazio ultra.

The photograph showed him making a Fascist style salute, one that was associated with a reverence for the dictator Benito Mussolini, a man who drained the Pontine Marshes, got the trains to run on time and whose body ended up swinging upside down from a lamp post in Milan in 1945.

Di Canio's politics made Sunderland front page news for a few days. The Durham Miners Association wanted their banners back. David Miliband resigned as vice chairman.

Suzanne Moore, not noted for her footballing enthusiasms, wrote a column about it for the *Guardian*.

Meanwhile, Di Canio and his coaching staff set about saving the club from the Championship. A new fitness regime was introduced and players said that they enjoyed it. His first game saw an unfortunate 2-1 defeat at Stamford Bridge. Leading at half-time thanks to an own goal, a similar aberration put Chelsea level just after the break and they went on to win it through Branislav Ivanovic. But things looked better. The players looked animated and it set them up for a visit to Newcastle United.

Whatever Di Canio did in the preparation it worked well. A Stéphane Sessègnon opener was added to in the closing stages by sensational strikes from Adam Johnson and David Vaughan and we got the full knee slide from the enthusiastic Italian. John Carver admitted he wanted to hit him and a Newcastle fan decided to punch a horse. Many Red and Whites wanted to hug him but some of us had grave reservations about Di Canio as a coach and as a man. His enthusiasm was wonderful after the torpor of the O'Neill period but…

Still, he won the next game at home to Everton and things looked distinctly better. The players worked hard, dug in and got a win that lifted the club, the support and the head coach. And then, the wheels began to wobble…

A 6-1 thrashing on a Monday night at Aston Villa brought us all crashing back to earth but a pair of dull home draws against Stoke and Southampton cemented our Premier League place as Wigan tumbled down after winning the FA Cup. We finished 17th on 39 points, three ahead of Wigan and two behind Newcastle. Relegation avoided, we awaited the summer rebuild with a mixture of optimism and trepidation.

The trepidation was justified. In came players we knew little or nothing about; Valentin Roberge, Andrej Celutska,

Modibo Diakité, Charalampos Mavrias. Those that we had heard of were perpetual reserves – Vito Mannone – or players who had already had a crack at the Premier League and had struggled – Jozy Altidore. The new Director of Football brought in one player that excited us in Emanuele Giaccherini, an Italian international with a splendid pedigree. He was to be the catalyst of the new Sunderland, a player whose guile and craft would set up Steven Fletcher, Connor Wickham and Danny Graham and enable us to sit comfortably in the middle of the table. Or at least that was the theory.

The practice was different. Reports were coming out of the Academy that all was not well. The opening game against a Fulham side that looked like strugglers was lost because we failed to defend a corner and we never looked like scoring. A trip to Southampton almost brought back a win as Giaccherini opened his account but a late equaliser thwarted us – and then it all went downhill.

Three days after the Southampton match we were 2-0 down at home to MK Dons in the League Cup before we dragged ourselves back into the game to win 4-2. The supporters were not impressed and rumblings of discontent started and were not assuaged by a battling performance against Arsenal which might have brought a point had it not been for a bizarre decision by Martin Atkinson, bringing the ball back for a free kick after Altidore had ridden a challenge by Bacary Sagna and had put the ball into the net.

Di Canio was sent to the stands for complaining about that decision and it appeared that he was giving himself enough rope to perform his own execution – although not upside down from a lamp post as his political hero had. It was reported that there was a climate of fear amongst the players and shocking news of no ketchup or mayonnaise in the canteen confirmed to some that all was not well.

That was confirmed with a truly wretched performance at The Hawthorns, where West Brom, prompted by recent signing Sessègnon, crushed a feeble Sunderland side 3-0. Di Canio urged the support to lift their heads up, but the damage had been done. He went within three days amidst stories of a huge argument with the players who told him that they no longer believed in him.

One point in the bag, four games lost and bottom of the league. You could hear the chuckles from the O'Neill and Bruce households and the chortles from Tyneside as the search began for yet another manager.

Two names were frequently mentioned; an out of work Italian (Roberto Di Matteo) and an out of work Uruguayan (Gustavo Poyet). After Di Canio, the Italian option was not a good one. And was a Champions League-winning manager really going to come to Sunderland? Hadn't he also made rather a mess of things at West Brom?

Poyet had some baggage as well but he was seen as young and ambitious. He had done well at Brighton, had taken them to the play-offs and had had a couple of decent cup runs. But there was a mystery surrounding his departure from the Seagulls, something to do with a falling out behind the scenes and a gagging order that guaranteed his pay off.

After the madness of the Di Canio regime, Poyet seemed a relatively safe pair of hands and he was appointed as head coach on October 8, 2013 with the club very firmly anchored to the bottom of the Premier League. Two games under caretaker Kevin Ball, at home to Liverpool and Manchester United , had not improved the points tally or the league position, so Poyet was starting with an almost blank canvas.

He brought with him the backroom staff that had worked with him at Brighton notably Mauricio Taricco and Charlie Oatway, a man with 11 first names as his parents blessed him with the moniker of each of the Queens Park Rangers first team of 1973. That was the team that beat us at Roker Park after the 1973 FA Cup final and included Stan 'If he could pass a bookies as well as he could pass a ball he'd be set up for life' Bowles.

The Poyet era opened 300 miles away from Wearside at the Liberty Stadium, Swansea, a ground where we had drawn on our previous two visits and where a third successive one would double our points tally for the season.

It didn't happen.

The general consensus was that we did okay for nearly an hour and then imploded. Phil Bardsley diverted a corner into his own net and before we had a chance to recover, Jonathan de Guzman put the game out of reach. A Wilfried Bony penalty and a Steven Fletcher own goal left us with one point from eight games, a worse start than the one we had under Lawrie McMenemy in 1985 and far worse than the one in the 15-point season, where we had four by this stage.

And the Mags were up next.

And we beat them. Fabio Borini, introduced in the 69th minute, struck a glorious late winner that sent the crowd wild and lifted us off the bottom of the table, depositing Crystal Palace there and giving us hope. Fletcher had opened the scoring, Mathieu Debuchy had equalised and the visitors had chances to win it – but they didn't and the Italian, on loan from Liverpool, wrote his name into the SAFC book of derby legends, alongside the likes of Marco Gabbiadini and Gary Rowell to give us our first win of the season and lift the clouds of gloom around the heads of Sunderland supporters everywhere. Was this the beginning of a run that would get us out of the bottom three by Christmas, we all asked, as it was a well-known fact that the club bottom at Christmas would be relegated in May?

It wasn't. We travelled down the A19 to Hull and a meeting with former manager Steve Bruce full of optimism and with a fair amount of bile to aim at the man who had got us to the giddy heights of tenth place a couple of years previously.

Bruce had spent much of the time since his dismissal complaining about the misconceptions that Wearsiders had of him. As a fully paid up member of the Geordie Nation, he never quite managed to win the hearts and minds of the Sunderland support but his constant whining did him no favours. And he was roundly abused by many of those who had travelled and who had filled the pockets of pub landlords with gold.

Of course, Sunderland being Sunderland, we messed it up. In three mad minutes before half-time, Lee Cattermole and Andrea Dossena were sent off for tackles that could best be described as 'agricultural' and Keiren Westwood was replaced by Vito Mannone after injuring himself in not saving Carlos Cuellar's own goal in the 26th minute.

Moans and groans in the Sunderland end and much opprobrium aimed at referee Andre Marriner but the lack of self-discipline was worrying and it meant that both players and the keeper were out of the team for the next game against title-chasing Manchester City.

So, three games in and one win and two defeats for Gus; 19th in the league and four points behind Norwich City who were sat in 17th; were things getting better or were we heading for an early relegation?

Poyet had now had time to look at his squad. Wes Brown was fit, Ki Sung-yueng came back and Phil Bardsley joined Darren Bent, Ji Dong-won and Adam Johnson as City's slayers. A relatively early goal from the United-supporting Salfordian compared with Bent's and Ji's but, like those two, it was a backs-to-the-wall job which we came through thanks to Brown and John O'Shea and some hard graft in midfield from

Seb Larsson, Jack Colback and Ki. We were still in the bottom three but were within striking distance of Fulham, Stoke City and West Ham United. There was hope but as all Sunderland supporters know it's the hope we can't stand.

It didn't get any better the week after when we visited Stoke. It's a gloomy place at the best of times and not exactly a happy hunting ground for us; a measly 1-0 win a couple of years before was the only bright spot amid a whole host of defeats. The weather was miserable, the trip was miserable and as I entered the Britannia Stadium I heard the England rugby league team had slid out of the World Cup in agonising fashion to New Zealand

Enter Kevin Friend, who did our chances of building on the previous week no good at all, by sending Wes Brown off for what the majority of spectators, pundits and television viewers saw as a perfectly good tackle. Down to ten men, we tried to get back into the game but to no avail. It left us bottom of the table, level with Crystal Palace on seven points, with Fulham and West Ham three points away and Cardiff and Norwich four up on us.

The week after, I opted to go and watch Australia crush an exhausted New Zealand in the World Cup final at Old Trafford, missing out on a tedious 0-0 draw at Villa Park – but it lifted us off the bottom of the table prompting Palace to bring in Tony Pulis and his particular brand of pragmatism. Clubs were beginning to worry. We had changed managers, Palace had. What next? We awaited the opening of the transfer window with anticipation.

In the meantime, there were fixtures to negotiate. Chelsea arrived at the beginning of December and won an enthralling game by the odd goal in seven. It was a game that sticks in the memory for two reasons. First of all, there was a wonderful individual performance from Eden Hazard, one of the best I have ever seen and one which had the crowd gasping in admiration. And then there was something which we never expected to see – a league goal from Jozy Altidore! The big American had struggled in his second spell in English football and was rapidly becoming an embarrassment. He was being likened to other big money flops up front like Andy Kerr, Tom Ritchie and Lilian Laslandes and it surprised most in the crowd when he put us into the lead. Hazard's brilliance soon put an end to any hopes of a valuable point and we were comfortably beaten – but the towel was not thrown in and there was a glimmer of hope.

That glimmer faded in the next three games which brought a mere two points. Spurs won 2-1 at the Stadium of Light, the points going their way thanks to an O'Shea own goal and there were two uninspiring 0-0 draws at West Ham and at home to Norwich.

As Santa crept down the chimney on Christmas Eve, we were struggling. The old maxim that bottom at Christmas meant relegation was trotted out numerous times. Palace were upwardly mobile, but Fulham were struggling and there was mayhem at West Ham, with Sam Allardyce seemingly on the point of dismissal.

Presents opened, turkey scoffed and strong drink taken, we set off for Everton with about as much hope of winning as the fattest turkey in the pre-Christmas yard has of seeing the next year's FA Cup final. If a win at Stoke was a rarity, one at Goodison Park was a rarity times ten.

In 50 years of following Sunderland, I had seen just one triumph there – Craig Russell and Michael Bridges with two were the scorers and Lionel Perez saved a penalty when he was still a hero, but we were still relegated at the end of that 1996-97 season. What chances this year?

Looking at the team sheet, not much. Brown and O'Shea

were out through suspension and injury so in came Modibo Diakité and Valentin Roberge, neither of whom had impressed in their short spells at the club. They had their shaky moments here, but held on as Ki's first-half penalty saw us home.

It was a game dominated by goalkeepers. Vito Mannone had a superb game for us, performing heroics against Romelu Lukaku, Phil Jagielka and Ross Barkley and instilling confidence in a back four made up of a Czech, two Frenchman and a Salford Lad.

And it was a Korean who won the game for us when he was pulled down by Everton's American keeper, Tim Howard. Ki picked himself up to put the ball past the Spanish replacement Joel Robles. It was a goal that was to play a huge part in keeping us up.

Ki was having a good spell at the turn of the year. He had scored the winner in the League Cup quarter-final against Chelsea a few days earlier and looked a very good player. Whatever had happened between Michael Laudrup and him at Swansea certainly worked to our advantage.

There we were, in a cup semi-final for the first time since 2004 and beginning to show genuine signs of life. Off we went for our second visit to South Wales a couple of days after the Everton win for what turned out to be a very, very important 90-plus minutes.

I drove to this one, breaking the journey in Tamworth and arriving in Cardiff at lunchtime, ready for a 5.30pm kick off. I like Cardiff. It has a good feel about it and is compact. The hotel was in the city centre and next to a splendid Brains pub. Even the Wetherspoons was a decent place to drink being an old theatre with the flies still intact.

The new stadium is close to Ninian Park, a ground which always had a terrible reputation for violence in the 1970s and 1980s. I remember a particularly unpleasant afternoon in 1980 where stones, bricks and iron bars were thrown at the Sunderland fans. But this is the 21st Century and all that has gone and the City fans were open and friendly, even when we nicked a point from them in the last few minutes.

Roberge and Diakité, who had done so well at Everton struggled in this one. Jordon Mutch opened the scoring for Cardiff and Mannone performed heroics in keeping it down to one. Altidore missed another easy chance and when Fraizer Campbell made it two, desperate measures were called for.

This was probably the most important game of Poyet's season. Had we lost, we were really struggling so he gambled, replaced the peripheral Borini with Fletcher, yanked Larsson and Cattermole off and sent Craig Gardner and Colback on. Fletcher got us back into it and with a full five minutes of added time played, Colback forced a shot over the line to level. A point against the odds and, most importantly, a point against a relegation rival.

Drinks were taken post-match and the journey home through the Cotswolds and Northamptonshire – stopping off to take in Coventry City v Oldham Athletic at Northampton Town's Sixfields Stadium – was lovely. An overnight stay at the wonderful Nelson and Railway in Kimberley was the icing on the cake. Great beer, great room and a great breakfast made this one of the best away trips of the year.

But just when it looked as if we were clambering out of the depths, along came Aston Villa and Gabby Agbonlahor.

Villa were strugglers, their support was losing confidence in Paul Lambert and they had taken a single point from the previous 15. What better than a visit to a Sunderland side who looked as if they might be getting their act together and attracted a crowd marginally under 40,000? As usual, we shot ourselves in the foot, with Cattermole making a catastrophic error to allow Agbonlahor a clear run at goal, which he rounded off with a highly competent finish. For the next 75 minutes, we huffed and puffed but the big, bad, Brummie wolf was secure and comfortable and took three valuable points back to the Midlands. Things certainly did not look better. But they did by the end of the month…

It started with a straightforward win over Carlisle United in the FA Cup and continued with a victory over Manchester United in the first leg of our League Cup semi-final. Ryan Giggs was used to scoring against Sunderland but this time he scored for us, not as a result of an inspired Poyet move into the January market, but due to him aiding two of his former team-mates. Wes Brown's cross was met at the far post by Phil Bardsley and Giggs helped it over the line. Cue celebrations which were wiped out by Nemanja Vidic's equaliser and then restored by Borini's penalty to take us to Old Trafford with the narrowest of margins.

By this time, Poyet had been busy in the transfer market. Full back Marcos Alonso had come in on loan from Fiorentina and looked a quality signing. He had Premier League experience with Bolton and had been at Real Madrid. He was a clear improvement on Dossena and Colback who had filled that spot. There was also a clutch of Argentinians of which more later.

The next two games saw a rejuvenated Adam Johnson scoring goals for fun. He bagged a hat-trick at Fulham to confirm to this writer that the Cottagers were heading for relegation. Then, he bailed us out against an impressive Southampton team with a pair to grab a point that gave us hope of overtaking those above us.

Some may argue that this was the most important result of the season. To come back from 2-0 down to a side who were playing well and who had looked ever so comfortable in front showed that whatever our technical deficiencies, the players were prepared to fight for the club. We were off the bottom (Cardiff replaced us), were level on points with Big Sam's Hammers, were a point behind Fulham and two points behind Palace. We had dragged ourselves from the long-held position of *Lanterne Rouge* and were back in the *peloton*. And, in four days' time, we were on our way to Wembley.

The second leg at Old Trafford summed up everything about this wonderful football club. Huge and noisy support, a determined performance despite conceding in the first half, a late equaliser in front of the travelling support which we thought took us to Wembley and then a shocking lack of concentration to allow United to take the game to penalties.

We then had to suffer the worst shoot-out I have ever seen at any level as seven out of ten penalties were not converted. Craig Gardner and Danny Welbeck put theirs into the crowd, David De Gea saved from Adam Johnson and Steven Fletcher, with Mannone doing the same from Adnan Januzaj, while Phil Jones missed his. Darren Fletcher had scored with some aplomb for United and Marcos Alonso and Ki had done likewise for us. Up stepped Rafael to take it to sudden death, but Mannone got it right and saved to spark delirious scenes in the away end which carried on into the car park, on the coach, along the M62 and A1 and into workplaces, classrooms and pubs the next day.

The improvement continued. Kidderminster Harriers were put out of the FA Cup three days later, a game that saw one of the three new Argentinians, Santiago Vergini make his debut. Four days later came another hugely important win as Stoke were seen off thanks to another Adam Johnson goal, one which sealed the player of the month award for him. But far more importantly, we were out of the bottom three – Cardiff, Fulham and West Ham were below us, Stoke and West Brom were a point above, with Palace, Hull, Swansea and Norwich no more than a win away from being caught.

The next game up was against Newcastle United at the Sports Direct Arena. Under Alan Pardew they were bumping along quite well, sitting in eighth place and looking for a Europa League place. They wanted revenge for the last two defeats and would have hoped to push us back into the mire.

The 3-0 win was probably the most satisfying result of the season. Early goals from Borini – as cool as ice from the spot – and Johnson – a bit of a shanker if truth be told – put us ahead and prompted alarm for the equine population of Tyneside. It could have been wrapped up by Altidore in the second half and would have been a fitting reward for the big American who had his best game in a Sunderland shirt but still could not convert the chance that he fashioned for himself.

It took Colback – whatever happened to him? – to finish the Magpies off and seal a third win in a row. The future looked bright; a cup final to come., a win over our rivals, up to 14th in the table and three points away from tenth place. Poyet was hailed as a hero, the players were on the up and the support was buzzing. Things had clearly got better – Sunderland AFC were back.

But this was Sunderland AFC.

Hull and Steve Bruce rolled up the next week. Bruce had antagonised Sunderland fans with his constant whining about how he had been drummed out of the club because of his Geordie roots. Wrong, Steve: You were sacked because we had won but a single game, were out of the League Cup, had lost at home to Newcastle and were playing football that was so poor that some of us wanted Terry Butcher back as manager.

Hull beat us 2-0. Brown was sent off after four minutes for a foul on Shane Long.

It got a bit better the week after as Southampton failed to beat us for the fourth time, going out of the FA Cup to a Craig Gardner thunderbolt in front of a pathetic crowd of 16,000 with many saving money for Wembley and others not attracted by the midday kick-off.

A trip to Ashburton Grove brought nothing and there was a postponement at Eastlands as well as Hurricane Ted whipped through Lancashire scattering programme booths, roofing and trees all over the place and forcing me to sit inside the Jolly Angler in Ducie Street supping Hydes bitter until the rain stopped. It took a while but my word, it was worth it.

And then it was Wembley.

I travelled by coach, leaving at some ridiculously early hour. A trip to Stanmore and a couple of pints in a Wetherspoons there and then on to the stadium and a sense of pride as I saw the red and white hordes pouring down Wembley Way. It wasn't quite as emotional as 1973 but it brought a tear to a cynical and jaundiced eye.

Okay, we didn't win but it was a vast improvement on our only previous League Cup final appearance, where a dreadful game was settled by an own goal and victory went to a team who managed to be relegated with us, Norwich City.

This time we took on probably the richest club in the world, Manchester City, a team crammed with world class players and managed by a dignified and charming Chilean. We turned up with a mixture of top-level cast-offs, loanees and one or two who have never quite made it.

We would have won it as well had it not been for a superb tackle by Vincent Kompany on Fabio Borini. The Italian had put us ahead early on, finishing off a Lee Cattermole-Adam Johnson move with a superb finish. They were rattled and were hardly in the game and had Borini got away from Kompany and scored a deserved second, we would have won. But he didn't and the City skipper's tackle gave them a lifeline which allowed them back into the game in the second half.

Goals from Yaya Toure (a wonderful strike), Samir Nasri

(a good finish) and a late one from Jesus Navas gave the cup to City and they probably deserved it for their ruthless second half performance. But here was an opportunity for the club and the team to kick on, make progress in the FA Cup and get away from the relegation zone to mid-table comfort.

Ha! A week later we went to Hull in a sixth round game, played like drains and lost 3-0. Cattermole gave away two goals and Poyet came in for criticism for making too many changes. The wheels were wobbling on the Gus bus.

The next six games were horrendous. One point was taken out of the 18 on offer and that came as a result of an abysmal 0-0 with a rejuvenated Crystal Palace. We lost five in a row – at Norwich, at Liverpool, at home to West Ham, at Tottenham and finally at home to Everton.

The Spurs one was a total collapse, losing 5-1 after Cattermole had opened the scoring but showing neither fight or gumption. It convinced the Sunderland support there that we were looking at yet another relegation and that was exacerbated five days later when Everton stole a win courtesy of a Brown own goal. Plans were made for trips to Blackpool and Bolton.

The next two fixtures saw us visit Manchester City and Chelsea, third and second in the Premier League respectively. We had slid back to the bottom, seven points from safety and with a team that looked shot. And this is when The Great Escape really started…

A dwindling band of Red and Whites took the trail of tears across the Pennines to Manchester. Relegations at Goodison Park, Maine Road and Old Trafford had given it that moniker and there appeared to be little chance of success as City began to haul back Liverpool and look good for their second title in three seasons. When we went a goal down to Fernandinho early on, the wall looked as if it was covered in writing and the pencil would write no more. But we were playing well and then Poyet pulled a masterstroke.

Off came a labouring Seb Larsson and a blown out Fabio Borini and on came two distinctly bit-part players. Emanuele Giaccherini had struggled with injuries but was clearly a good player. Nacho Scocco had struggled full stop and was looking even less effective than Jozy Altidore.

These two, along with Connor Wickham – a man-child if ever there was one – changed the game round. Scocco played in Giaccherini with the kind of ball one expects from Sergio Aguero and the Italian international fed Wickham who stormed in to slot it past Joe Hart. And then, he did it again…

This time it was just Giaccherini who set him up and he had a bit more to do. But he did it in style and there we were, bottom of the table, on our knees and 2-1 up at the home of the wealthiest club in the universe.

They came back at us and we held on with brave tackles, strong headers and safe goalkeeping – until the 89th minute when the otherwise excellent Mannone failed to hold a drive from Nasri (that man again) and the ball wriggled over the line.

Disappointment mingled with pride as we trooped back to our transport. There was a glimmer of hope. Fulham, Norwich and Cardiff were destroying themselves by sacking managers and replacing them with men who were clearly inadequate. But Chelsea away was next for us and if Jose Mourinho thought that his expensively assembled squad were little horses, then we were plodding pit ponies.

And we won. This was the most sensational result of the season and gave us hope that we could survive. The points we had taken out of City helped Chelsea and they were relaxed and confident – indeed, some would say cocky – as the game got under way at 5.30pm. By 5.42 pm Samuel Eto'o had put them ahead and the wall was covered in pencil again.

I listened to this one while watching Birtley Town play Chester-le-Street Town in a keenly fought local derby at the romantically-named Birtley Sports Complex Ground. I was involved in the Northern League's 125th anniversary celebrations and had been placed in charge of a bus load of groundhoppers for the weekend, guiding the coach to such exotic locations as Jarrow Roofing, Ryton, Crawcrook Albion and Newton Aycliffe and gaining much sympathy from the almost exclusively male congregation. Sympathy mixed with bewilderment as many could not understand why I, or anybody else for that matter, would prefer Premier League football to a windswept field somewhere in deepest, darkest Dorset or Durham.

Off went the radio as I socialised on my circuits of the ground. It looked as if we were done for but I was told that Chelsea were not pushing on. 'Still hope,' said one Manchester City fan who had been effusive in his praise for our display the previous Wednesday – although it did come through gritted teeth.

As I completed my third circumnavigation, the news reached me via text that Wickham had levelled and that we were 'doing canny' so I stopped walking and retreated to the far end of the ground and stood there as still and erect as an Anthony Gormley statue, waiting for the final whistle.

The text went again. Fearing a Chelsea winner, I looked hesitantly. 'Penalty to us,' it said. 'Jozy brought down. Borini to take.' Pause. And then: 'Goal; Don Fabio.'

The assembled ranks of Her Majesty's Regiment of Groundhoppers were then treated to the sight of an elderly, overweight man jumping up and down, yelling something along the lines of, 'I say, we have scored a second goal at Stamford Bridge. Let's hope the chaps can hold out and bring three points back to the North East.' You get my gist?

Hold on we did. Chelsea showed what a classy club they are

when their assistant manager tried to provoke a fight and the win brought us within striking distance of Norwich who were in the safe place of 17th.

There were four games left, three of which were at home and were against teams who were around the relegation zone. The away game was at Old Trafford, a ground where we traditionally got less than nowt, but who had sacked David Moyes and had put Ryan Giggs in charge for the remainder of the season. The hope was rising but we are Sunderland supporters: it's the hope we can't stand.

The Cardiff game was the one that we had to win. They were in freefall; owner Vincent Tan had fallen out with the support big time, not least by changing their traditional blue shirts, as worn by heroes like John Charles, Ivor Allchurch and, er, Michael Chopra to red because, 'it's a colour associated with good luck in the Far East'.

Tan had got rid of popular manager Malky Mackay and replaced him with the inexperienced Ole Gunnar Solksjaer. Mackay was well thought of and Tan was hammered in the press but subsequent events have proved the owner to be right. Not many made the 600-mile round journey from the once great South Wales coalfield to the once great Durham coalfield and those that did were sent home with a 4-0 cuffing, enabling us to climb off the bottom and push Cardiff closer to whence they came.

This was probably the best performance of Poyet's time on Wearside. The team looked comfortable and were full of confidence. An early Wickham header settled the nerves and then up stepped the rotund figure of Phil Dowd to finish the game off.

In an inspired piece of refereeing, he spotted a foul by the hapless Cala on Wickham inside the box, allowed play to continue and, when nothing came of it, brought the play back, awarded a penalty and sent Cala packing for the proverbial early bath. Borini slotted home the spot kick and that was the end of the game. Further goals from a rejuvenated Giaccherini and Wickham finished the Redbirds off and, by 5.00pm, Sunderland were in 17th place with Cardiff, Norwich and Fulham below them. It wasn't going to change; the miracle that Gus Poyet famously asked for after the Spurs debacle was on.

The last time we won at Old Trafford I was still at school. Colin Suggett and George Mulhall scored for us in a 2-1 win on a day when Manchester City clinched the title with a 4-3 win at the soon-to-be-renamed Sports Direct Arena. Since then there had been a handful of draws and a bucketful of defeats including some heavy ones. We even lost the night we won the League Cup tie on penalties in January!

But United were in decline and the departure of David Moyes and the temporary stewardship of Ryan Giggs meant that they were there for the taking – and that is what we did. Larsson's early goal from a sublime run and cross by Wickham won it for us and it was a jolly ride back across the M62 for the third time since mid-January. Defeats for Cardiff and Fulham and a draw for Norwich put clear water between us and the bottom three and our game in hand – at home to a struggling West Brom side – would undoubtedly seal it.

And it did. 45,181 turned up to roar The Lads home and home they came thanks to goals from Colback and Borini. Altidore missed a sitter and we reached the dizzy heights of 14th, passing the Baggies, Hull and Villa and looking supremely comfortable in this elevated position.

TV cameras picked up a banner in the crowd which had a checklist for 2013-14: Beat The Mags (check); Get to Wembley (check); Stay up (about to be checked). Meat Loaf may have been happy with two out of three but we get the full set.

The last game was an anti-climax against Swansea and they deservedly won 3-1. We also saw how good Bony was and that if Swansea could find a player like that, why did we get stuck with the Altidores and Grahams of this world?

How were we able to survive what should have been a catastrophic season? An awful start, poor player recruitment in the summer and a rookie Premier League manager all warned of total disaster. After the embarrassment at White Hart Lane, I proclaimed to the queue for the train back to Liverpool Street that, in the words of Richard Nixon: 'You won't have us to kick around any more,' to sympathetic listeners, safe in the upper echelons of the Premier League, but still grumbling about not qualifying for the Champions League.

We survived because after that debacle, Poyet and the players probably thought, 'Bugger it, let's go down fighting.' What had we to lose? We clearly could not defend, so unleash Wickham and Borini on unsuspecting defences and let's see what happens. It worked.

We survived because confidence comes from winning and sometimes even from drawing. Those results at Eastlands and Stamford Bridge gave the team a huge surge of self-belief which carried on until safety had been assured.

We survived because there were three clubs around us who imploded due to poor management on and off the field. Cardiff lost their crowd largely as a result of Tan's thoughtless and aristocratic actions which said: 'It's my club, I'll do what I want.' Fulham appointed two managers with no experience of running a club in England after sacking Martin Jol. René Meulensteen lasted 75 days before an inexperienced owner got rid of him and appointed Felix Magath. Once he came in, that was one relegation place comfortably filled. Norwich City dithered before firing Chris Hughton and then appointed from within; not a wise move with a handful of games left. But it suited us.

In my half century of following the Red and Whites at Roker Park and the Stadium of Light, this was the only time that we have retrieved a seemingly hopeless situation and stayed up. Poyet, his staff, the players and the owner deserve praise for pulling together to ensure that we did not have to grind our way through a Championship season, playing twice a week and appearing on TV long after the cat has been put out and the doors have been locked and bolted.

To alter the words of Charles Dickens, it was 'the worst of times that ended up as the best of times.'

But wouldn't it be nice to have a similar run at the top end of the table one day instead?

Pete Sixsmith has been a regular at Sunderland home matches for over 50 years. He did his teacher training in Sunderland so he would not miss any home games and subsequently spent his career teaching history in County Durham. He contributes regularly on Sunderland AFC matters at salutsunderland.com and in the *Observer*.

4

Gary Bennett played at Wembley for Sunderland three times – more than anyone else in the history of the club.

His time at Roker Park was truly a rollercoaster ride. There were three relegations and two promotion campaigns as well as those three Wembley finals.

All three matches – the 1985 Milk Cup final against Norwich City, a play-off clash with Swindon and the 1992 FA Cup final with Liverpool – ended in defeat.

But, for Gary, nothing can beat the memory of those three trips to play beneath the Twin Towers…

TWIN TOWERS

BY GARY BENNETT

Len Ashurst was the main reason why I came to Sunderland in 1984. I played under him at Cardiff City and I did quite well there. Sunderland were struggling in the First Division and he got the call to be the manager, which was an opportunity he couldn't turn down given his long association with the club over so many years as a player. Before he left Ninian Park, he gave me a little tap and told me he would come in for me in the summer, which I was very excited about.

I had played at Roker Park once before – in the FA Youth Cup with Manchester City in 1980. We won 1-0 and I remember it was snowing! We went on to the youth cup final but lost to Aston Villa. Sadly, I didn't make a first team appearance for City but my brother Dave did, playing in the 1981 FA Cup final. We signed for The Bluebirds together.

However, the first opportunity that came my way after Len left Cardiff was to join another Second Division club, Crystal Palace. Ron Noades called me and I went down there and had talks with their manager, Steve Coppell. I had a look around and I liked everything that I saw. But, at the back of my mind, I always wanted Sunderland to come in for me. It is every footballer's dream to play at the top level.

The next day, Sunderland's financial director Barry Batey called me and explained that the club wanted to sign me but if the fee was anything over £100,000 they would have to pull out of the deal. It went to a tribunal in the end and the agreed fee was £65,000 with further payments dependent on appearances. Little did I know that I would be there for the next 11 years!

Len Ashurst later revealed that he had to go to a few supporters clubs and ask how they would feel if Sunderland signed a black player. That is unimaginable nowadays but by 1984, Sunderland hadn't really had a black player before. Rory Gregoire had played a few games back in the late 1970s but nothing more. So, I suppose it was something of a gamble. Len laid out the rules: he told me that if I did well, they would hold me in high esteem and if I didn't do well, they would let me know about it. So, it was certainly a challenge – but it was something I looked forward to. The signing of another black player, Howard Gayle, helped me settle. I think I helped him settle too.

It was a very exciting move for me, especially given that my old manager had signed me. But I remember not wanting the other players to think that I was just one of his favourites coming into the club. So, it was important for me to establish myself. I wanted to make them all aware that I was a good player. I played in a few games pre-season and did well. I was really pleased to be selected – along with three other players making their club debuts (Steve Berry, Howard Gayle and Clive Walker) against Southampton on the opening day of the season.

Running out at Roker Park with that crowd behind us was very special. To score after a few minutes was even more so. It was a tremendous start for me. My goal came from a set piece. The ball came down to me, I got my foot to it and put it in the back of the net. The goalkeeper was Peter Shilton. So, it was a truly great moment to score so early into my Sunderland career, at that ground, at that level and against that sort of goalkeeper. We won the match 3-1.

We were flying and up to seventh in the table in November after successive 3-0 wins over Queens Park Rangers and Luton Town. We also beat Manchester United 3-2 with a Clive Walker hat-trick a few weeks later. It was a great start to the season for us. These were the types of games that we all wanted to be involved in and we were doing really, really well. A top six finish seemed achievable for us, which would have been the first time Sunderland had done that in 30 years.

Funnily enough, our 1984-85 League Cup run started against Crystal Palace. We beat them 2-1 at Roker Park – Rodger Wylde got both our goals. We went down to Selhurst Park a fortnight later for the second leg. It felt like just another match at that stage of the competition. No one was thinking about getting to the final. We got the result we needed – a 0-0 draw – and then looked forward to who we would get in the next round.

We got Nottingham Forest, managed, of course, by Brian Clough, who was loved by Sunderland supporters. We drew 1-1 at the City Ground – David Hodgson got our goal – and then we had a replay the following week at Roker Park. It was on this night that our Milk Cup run really came alive.

Goalless after 90 minutes, Howard Gayle hit a tremendous strike in extra-time to win us the match. It was a fantastic night. The atmosphere was something else and scoring the winning goal in extra-time made it even more special. It gave us all a little taste of what it could be like if we could go on a cup run.

That was what the Sunderland supporters wanted. Nothing has changed in that respect. They hadn't had a cup run throughout the late 1970s or the early part of the 1980s. So, although we were only through to the last 16, you could definitely feel the excitement building that night.

Tottenham Hotspur came next. We played them at Roker Park in front of 27,421 fans – the biggest home crowd of the season so far – and it finished goalless. We got a replay but no one expected us to beat them when we went down to White Hart Lane.

Len Ashurst changed the team around a bit and credit to

him for getting it right. We had a game plan and I ended up playing in the middle of the park. But we all had a job to do. The man of the match for me was our goalkeeper. Chris Turner made a great penalty save from Graham Roberts as we held on to win 2-1 with goals from Clive Walker and Gordon Chisholm.

It was clear to us all that we had a great team spirit. That really drove us on in that match in particular and it got us the result – as well as a place in the quarter-finals of the League Cup. We also had the nucleus of a very good team: Chris Turner, Barry Venison, Nick Pickering, Shaun Elliott, Mark Proctor, Colin West for example plus all the new signings we had made.

Our next match in the competition would be away at Watford in late January. That was seven weeks away. But by the time it came around, our league form had started to crumble. Five defeats in December and a bad day at Newcastle United on New Year's Day, when both Howard Gayle and I were sent off amidst racist abuse, left us 18th in the table. Southampton also knocked us out of the FA Cup a few days later, 4-0.

A bad winter meant some postponements and we pulled together to win at Watford in our first match in three weeks. It was another great performance – Clive Walker scored the only goal of the game – and a great result on a freezing cold night.

I didn't play in the match. But I was standing on the Vicarage Road terraces cheering the team on with the Sunderland fans that night. That is another example of how the game has changed. I travelled down with some friends in a mini bus. The mood was fantastic and so we didn't feel the cold. I remember it very fondly. It is an example of the connection I have always felt with the Sunderland supporters.

Sunderland hadn't reached a semi-final in either of the two big cup competitions since 1973 so excitement was now at fever pitch ahead of our two-legged semi-final against Chelsea. The first match, at Roker Park, was won by two goals from

Colin West, one from the penalty spot. David Speedie didn't play for Chelsea that night. But after the game I went up to the players' lounge for a few 'refreshers' and was confronted by his dad, who told me his son would sort us out at Stamford Bridge!

After a few minutes at Stamford Bridge Speedie did score but it was to be our night. We played very well. Clive Walker got a couple of goals – which didn't go down too well with Chelsea supporters, because he used to play for them – and Colin West got the other as we won 3-2 (5-2 on aggregate).

It was a cup semi-final and neither team wanted to lose. For an ex-player to go back to Stamford Bridge and do the damage obviously didn't make them too happy! It was an awful atmosphere that night. It wasn't a nice time to be playing football. As a black player, I could feel it from the terraces and it could become very hostile – not just for the players but also the fans. Added to that, things were being thrown down on to the pitch that night. When Colin West scored our third goal, a police horse was on the field. Some of our supporters' buses were also smashed on the way home.

At the end of the match, we were just glad to have got it over and done with. It was as much about relief as celebration. We couldn't really celebrate our victory or reaching Wembley. We had to go to our dressing room, get changed as quickly as possible and get out of there. We only really celebrated when we got back to Sunderland in the early hours of the following morning. It was an enjoyable coach ride home though. When you spend so much time together on journeys like that, you get to know each other inside and out. It was normal for us to travel down to London or somewhere like Southampton and spend up to six or seven hours on a coach together.

Back in Sunderland, the build-up of cup fever was unbelievable. All the shops were decorated in red and white and everybody wanted a piece of us; everybody wanted to talk to us, everybody wanted to wish us well. It was a big event. The League Cup final was going to be televised live on the BBC, which was still something of a rarity in those days, and Wembley Stadium held 100,000 at the time. Also, Sunderland fans hadn't been to the Twin Towers since 1973. You could feel the excitement everywhere.

When you go into professional football, a Wembley cup final is where you want to be. Not only is it every player's dream, it is every supporter's dream to see their team there as well. I had been to Wembley to watch my brother play for Manchester City against Tottenham in the 1981 FA Cup final. The first match ended in a draw and I was there again for the first-ever FA Cup final replay at Wembley the following Thursday night for one of the great finals. Unfortunately, City lost 3-2. But it was a tremendous match and still well remembered for Steve MacKenzie's great volley from outside the box and Ricky Villa's wonder goal at the end.

The week before the Milk Cup final against Norwich City, we played them at Carrow Road in the First Division. It was seen by some as a dress rehearsal. We won 3-1. This gave us a timely confidence boost going into the final.

But our line-up was going to be markedly different in eight days' time. Shaun Elliott was suspended for Wembley. That was heart-breaking for him because he had been with Sunderland for over ten years and it was a major, major blow for us. We had lost our leader. Shaun was a great player and his unavailability meant the whole look of the team was going to change.

There was also a lot of stuff going on behind the scenes. Personally, I don't think the club was prepared for us getting to Wembley and everything that went with it. The ticket allocation for the players was poor. We were hoping for maybe half-a-dozen tickets each for the final for us to give to family members. When it came down to it, we were told we were entitled to two each! We seemed to be the last ones on the list. Eventually, we were given the opportunity to get more tickets – but we had to buy them! Naturally, that caused a certain amount of grievance. Rightly or wrongly, things like this do play on players' minds. It was a massive occasion for us all but suddenly we didn't feel particularly well looked after.

There were no bonus payments in place for us either and there were also various issues with sponsorship. Leading up to the final, all the talk was about what we were going to get and what we weren't going to get, which, looking back, was not a good situation at all.

Cowie's were the club's first shirt sponsors and the company name was emblazoned across our shirts. The kit was made by Nike and they now wanted to provide all the boots for the final. But three or four of the players – myself included – had boot deals elsewhere. Some of us were wearing Puma boots, others were wearing Adidas boots. We refused to wear Nike boots. In the end, we had to blacken out the logo on our boots so that we could wear what we wanted to wear on the day. This caused more animosity between the club and the players. It was unsettling for us. We had worked so hard to get to Wembley as well.

None of us knew who was going to play or even what formation we were going to play right up until the morning of the match. In the end, Len Ashurst decided to go with three central defenders and brought in young David Corner to play alongside Gordon Chisholm and myself at the back. He also made Barry Venison the youngest captain in a major cup final at Wembley at the age of 20 in Shaun Elliott's absence. Colin West – who had scored three goals against Chelsea in the semi-finals – was left out, which was a shock to everybody.

Did it work? In hindsight, no! We did have a couple of opportunities to take the lead before David Corner made a mistake and Norwich scored with a deflected goal early in the second half. We were awarded a penalty shortly afterwards, which Clive Walker missed. If that had gone in, maybe things might have been different. In the end, we lost 1-0.

As the match wore on, I made a few attacking runs to get us forward. I tried everything I could. I think some Sunderland fans would sometimes be asking: 'Where's he going?' But that was my style. I loved to play, I had lots of energy and I wanted to do my very best in a cup final at Wembley, as we all did.

We went to Wembley to win and we lost. Wembley is no place for losers. But we did get there. If we had lost in the semi-finals, that would have been the worst feeling. At least we got there. At least the supporters got there. But we all knew that we hadn't performed well on the day.

Wembley was a sea of red and white. I swear there must have been over 60,000 Sunderland supporters there. At the time, it is hard to take it all in. The day went by so quickly: the cameras, the dressing room, the match, the supporters, everything. There was just so much going on. Credit to both sets of fans: there was no trouble and the match went down in history as 'the Friendly Final'. The Norwich players were applauded by our supporters as they collected the cup.

We travelled on an open-top bus from Durham into Sunderland and supporters lined the streets to welcome us home. There were around 200,000 there in all. We had a reception that is something that will live with me for the rest of my life. I think the fans just wanted to say thank you.

But it was to be the biggest hangover ever. The season suddenly went flat. A few players had issues with contracts. Some of them seemed to throw the towel in. The biggest issue of all surrounded Colin West, who had been controversially left out at Wembley. He never played for Sunderland again.

Suddenly, we were in a relegation battle. The excitement the Milk Cup had given us covered up our problems in the league.

I think we felt we would be okay and focused on the cup run, which was a mistake. We slipped into the bottom three the week after Wembley and we didn't have enough to get out of it. One win in our last 12 games sent us down.

One minute we had been on a high and the next we were on a downward spiral. It was devastating. Len Ashurst lost his job just a few weeks after leading us out at Wembley. That was obviously a personal blow for me too. But when managers lose their jobs, players have to learn to be professional.

We were now a Second Division club and we all waited for news on our next manager. Rumours started to grow about Lawrie McMenemy coming to the club. He had done a fantastic job with Southampton, winning the FA Cup and taking them to second place in the First Division. He had also been linked with the England job. Sunderland got their man and when he arrived, it was like Wembley fever took over once again. The fans were out in force. He was a massive appointment for the club. Everybody was excited. Everybody expected him to turn us around. He made me captain of Sunderland.

Unfortunately, it just didn't take off under him. The money he was getting paid became national news. It was even debated in parliament. Here was a highly-paid manager coming to an area that had been very badly hit by pit closures. It was a bleak time. Within two years, we were in the Third Division.

Lawrie McMenemy was sacked towards the end of his second season in charge. The club quickly appointed Bob Stokoe as caretaker manager in a bid to avoid relegation. We desperately needed someone to come in and lift the club and I think he was the right man for the job. But he only had seven games to do it. He tried his hardest but sadly it didn't work. It was a privilege to play under Bob. He will always be linked with Sunderland and 1973.

I remember we played Barnsley at home in our last league

fixture of the season, needing a win to avoid the drop. We were 2-0 up in the first half but the wheels came off after Mark Proctor missed a penalty for us and we ended up losing 3-2. Afterwards, we waited to hear about the other results up and down the country and every one of them went against us.

We went down fighting. Bob Stokoe was a passionate man. In the relegation/promotion play-off second leg against Gillingham at Roker Park, he switched Dave Swindlehurst and me around. I went up front and brought the house down when I scored at the Fulwell End with a looping header in the very last minute of normal time to force extra-time. We had been moments away from relegation. Sadly, we just delayed that desperately sad scenario by 30 minutes. We won 4-3 on the day but lost the tie on away goals after drawing 6-6 on aggregate. We hadn't played well down at Gillingham and were beaten by Tony Cascarino.

The day before our relegation I had watched on television as my brother scored in the FA Cup final for Coventry City as they beat Tottenham 3-2 at Wembley. The greatest moment of his career and the worst moment of mine were separated by just 24 hours.

Denis Smith came in and soon afterwards he signed Marco Gabbiadini from York City. Eric Gates was going through a sticky patch with us at the time and the signing reignited him. He was maybe a step ahead at that level and he formed a terrific partnership with Marco.

Everyone wants to see a winning team and it was a really enjoyable season. Admittedly, it was the Third Division, but it is still fondly remembered by a lot of supporters. We took big support away from home and recorded big wins on our way to the title. The Gates-Gabbiadini combination worked very well and we played some really good football. John MacPhail played alongside me at the back. He was an out-and-out centre-back, who kept it simple. He also took our penalties and scored 16 goals that season.

As a team, we scored 92 goals in the league, winning 93 points. We certainly had goals in that team: Gatesy was a very good footballer, Marco was an exciting player with pace and strength – he could score a goal out of nothing – and we also had some quality young lads coming through like Gary Owers and Gordon Armstrong.

We had another good run in the League Cup two years later, getting to the quarter-finals, and had a tasty encounter against Coventry City. I had a number of famous moments in a Sunderland shirt. This tie would provide my most infamous one…

This was the first cup run we had been on since 1985. We beat Fulham, Bournemouth and Exeter City to set up a last eight meeting at Roker Park with the Sky Blues, who featured one certain David Speedie in their line-up. Every time I came up against him, it was always a battle. He was a good player but he was a pest and he always let you know that you were in a game. There was always likely to be a clash of some sorts with him.

I had passed a fitness test to play in the match. And, as I got the ball in front of the Clock Stand, I could see him coming towards me from the corner of my eye. He caught me on the top of my knee. All hell broke loose. I got hold of him by the throat and my momentum took the two of us into the Clock Stand paddock. It was a televised game and it happened right in front of the cameras so it was there for all to see. I actually thought the supporters were going to finish him off that night. But they didn't, they pushed him back out!

Twenty five years later, so many people still tell me that they were in the Clock Stand that night that I find it hard to believe it only held something like 8,000 people!

The replay at Highfield Road was a disappointment. Gary

Owers was sent off and we lost 5-0. I also needed 12 stitches in my lip after colliding with the goalkeeper so it wasn't the best of nights.

But our season wasn't over. Kieron Brady came into the side. Here was a young kid with unbelievable ability. He was magnificent in a 4-3 win over West Ham United at home. He got us going again. We started to get a little bit of confidence and we went on a good run, winning no fewer than five matches away from home.

We had belief. We aimed for the play-off positions and we got there by finishing sixth. Newcastle finished third and so that meant a Tyne-Wear derby in the play-off semi-finals with the winners going to Wembley.

The first leg was a Sunday lunchtime kick-off at Roker Park. It finished 0-0 after Paul Hardyman had a last-minute penalty saved by John Burridge and was sent off after following through. It all kicked off again. But coming off the pitch, we still felt we had a chance. We were in good form away from home and Denis Smith told us to keep our chins up.

We went to St James' Park the following Wednesday night and produced a great, professional performance. We knew that if we could keep it tight, we had goals in us with Gatesy and Marco and so it proved. They got a goal each and we achieved a very sweet 2-0 win over our biggest rivals.

Before the end, Newcastle fans invaded the pitch. I remember being kicked up the backside by one of them and I thought to myself: 'Right, I am going to have you.' I turned around to see about 3,000 of them and so I changed my mind! It had to be another dressing room celebration. After that, it later continued in the nightclubs of Sunderland.

We played Swindon Town in the play-off final. I led the team out that day. That was another great experience for me. I had played in the First Division with Sunderland and I had played at Wembley with Sunderland, I was now captaining the team at Wembley. It was rare at that time for a black player to lead out any English league team, never mind one at Wembley. So it was another huge personal achievement. I look back at it now with a lot of pride.

The Sunderland supporters were fantastic again. The coach ride down Wembley Way was amazing. There seemed to be about four or five times as many Sunderland fans as Swindon fans. To witness that was a tremendous sight.

But it was a very long 90 minutes. Swindon played 3-5-2 and they absolutely battered us. They beat us 1-0. It was an own goal again and this time I was the unlucky man. But, to be fair, it could easily have been 3-0 or 4-0. We were no match for them. Our goalkeeper Tony Norman was our man of the match. We thought we could beat them but we didn't have an answer for them.

About ten days later, I got a call from Sunderland AFC to inform me that the Football League had demoted Swindon and their decision was to promote us in their place to the top flight. There had been a lot of rumours flying about. Firstly, concerning Swindon's fate – the illegal payments case had been in the news for a long time – and secondly, regarding who may or may not replace them should a demotion happen. It was bubbly time for us. Five years after being relegated under Len Ashurst, we were back in the First Division with Denis Smith.

Newcastle weren't happy. They had finished six points and three places ahead of us and they felt that by coming third, they should have been promoted. Sheffield Wednesday also contested that they should remain in the First Division after finishing third-bottom the previous season. But rules are rules. The play-offs are a competition in their own right. We had finished runners-up and so we were duly and rightly promoted in Swindon's place.

In hindsight, promotion back into the First Division may have happened too soon for us. Money was a big issue again. Questions will always be asked about whether we could have spent more in strengthening a side that finished sixth in the Second Division. As it was, just Kevin Ball and Peter Davenport came into the club. We thought we had enough to stay up.

The second home game of the season brought another special moment for me with a last-minute winner against Manchester United. Gary Pallister had been signed by them for £2.3 million, which was a lot of money for a centre-back. I was up in attack again and when my chance came, I flicked the ball past Pallister, ran into the box and fired home. To see the ball nestle in the far corner of the Roker End net was a sweet sight. This wasn't just any goal – it was the winning goal in the last minute against Manchester United back in the First Division! I was proud of the finish too. It is every player's dream to do something like that. It was *Roy of the Rovers* stuff.

The last game of the season – against Manchester City at Maine Road – could have been even more special. I was back where I started my career. We needed to win to really stand any chance of staying up as Luton – who were level on points with us – were playing relegated Derby County at home. After going a goal behind, we scored twice just before half-time to lead 2-1 at the interval – and I got the second one. We took something like 15,000 fans down there and – at that moment – I think every one of us thought that we were going to do it. Sadly, it wasn't to be. We lost 3-2 and were relegated after just one season back in the top division.

Early on in the following season, Denis Smith sold Marco Gabbiadini to Crystal Palace for £1.8 million and subsequently signed John Byrne and Don Goodman. Little did any of us know that we would be on our way back to Wembley at the end of the season in the FA Cup final. Furthermore, we would have another man in charge after Denis was sacked just after Christmas. We had not started well and were positioned in the wrong half of the table.

Malcolm Crosby took over the reins in a caretaker capacity. We started to get some good results in the league and everything began to click into place in the FA Cup. After getting past Port Vale and Oxford United, we knocked out First Division West Ham in the fifth round.

We had drawn 1-1 at Roker Park against them. But we were absolutely superb in the replay at Upton Park and deservedly won 3-2. I didn't play that night due to injury but watched from the stands. John Byrne got two more goals and Tony Norman had an unbelievable match. But it was Kieron Brady who came off the bench to set up the winning goal for young David Rush.

Sunderland were in the FA Cup quarter-finals for the first time in 16 years and people now started to sit up and take notice. Byrney had started to get a taste for getting goals for us in the Cup – he had scored in every round – and that was making headlines. As was the fact that we still had a caretaker manager in charge of the team!

By now, Sky had started to show live FA Cup football and our quarter-final tie away at Chelsea was selected for a Monday night as a result. Our supporters obviously remembered our last cup tie there in 1985. But this Chelsea side was managed by Sunderland's 1973 FA Cup hero Ian Porterfield and Bob Stokoe even had a scouting job with them at the time!

Once again, we were given no chance. Once again, we proved the doubters wrong. John Byrne headed home a terrific equaliser with just minutes remaining after Clive Allen had scored for them in the first half. We earned a replay at Roker Park and it was apparently one of the greatest atmospheres the old stadium ever enjoyed.

The Roker Roar was no louder in my experience than it was

on this night. It was electric inside the ground. There is something about night games anyway. But this one was very special. Everybody who was there will still remember Gordon Armstrong's late, late header that won us the match. I was watching from the bench and when it flew in, the place erupted. To see how the Sunderland supporters celebrated that goal has stayed with me to this day. The joy on their faces was something else. It was another special night.

Our reward was a semi-final against Norwich City at Hillsborough. The Sunderland supporters were out in force again. They travelled down in their thousands once more. But I was still fighting my way back to fitness. I was named as a substitute for the match and I came on for the last 20 minutes or so. My instructions were to keep it tight and hold on to our 1-0 lead.

John Byrne had scored for us again in the first half and we were counting the minutes down to an unexpected and unbelievable trip to Wembley again. The scenes at the end of the match were quite emotional. Malcolm Crosby had performed something of a miracle.

But, just like seven years before, our league form had deteriorated as we had progressed in the Cup. We lost five league games in a row around the time of the semi-final and slumped to 21st in the table. Although we had some games in hand, it all began to get a little nervy again. No one dared to even think about the Third Division again. The difference this time was that the cup final came at the end of the season.

We climbed to up 18th in the table by the time we played Liverpool in the FA Cup final. We were massive underdogs. Although Liverpool were a team in transition, they were still strongly fancied to beat us. But we felt we had a chance of getting a result. We had knocked out three First Division sides to get there and on our day we felt we could be a match for them.

Liverpool had needed penalties to beat another Second

Division side, Portsmouth, in their semi-final replay. I wanted us to play Liverpool in the final. I think most people felt the same. It would be a proper cup final against them rather than two Second Division sides playing each other.

Team selection for the final was to be contentious again. Our right-back John Kay was injured, leaving a vacancy in defence. Kaysie held his hands up and said he wasn't fit to play which was a massive thing for him to do. Malcolm Crosby decided to go with Gary Owers in his place. I was selected in central defence alongside Kevin Ball and Anton Rogan switched to left back in place of Paul Hardyman, who was dropped to the bench after playing in every one of our matches in the cup run. He was understandably devastated, just like Colin West had been.

This was the biggest match of the three I played for Sunderland at Wembley. The FA Cup was the match of the season. We made a record called 'Ain't No Stopping Us Now' and we had the cameras with us for the full week ahead of the game; in the hotel, on the coach, everywhere. Everybody wanted to interview us. We were national news again. In fact, we were international news. The FA Cup final is shown all over the world.

The first half was close and we had a good chance through John Byrne, who frustratingly missed his kick from six yards out. We felt as though we were very much in the match at half-time. But Liverpool scored early on in the second half with a quality goal from Michael Thomas and when it went 2-0 it was no contest, really. They had quality players such as Steve McManaman and Jan Molby and they controlled the game.

We went up the steps as losers again. We collected our medals and noticed that we had been given the wrong ones! Sadly, we had to give the winners' medals back. At least we were FA Cup winners for five minutes…

We went back to Sunderland in another open-top bus

parade after the FA Cup final defeat and received another fantastic reception from our supporters. Who knows what it would have felt like had we come back with the FA Cup! It had been a truly remarkable cup run and brought back many memories of 1973 for older Sunderland supporters as we made our way to the final.

The chance for John Byrne would go down as another 'what if' moment for us, just like Clive Walker's penalty in 1985. Who knows what could have happened had we scored? Could we have gone on and won? Could we have been in Europe? It just wasn't to be.

It had been a hell of a ride since we had reached the League Cup final just seven years earlier: three Wembley finals, three relegations and two promotions. There was never a dull moment. There never is with Sunderland.

I was part of three Sunderland teams to play at Wembley. I am immensely proud to hold that record. But sadly we failed to score a goal in each of those matches and lost every one. We didn't do ourselves justice in the first two but the third was a fairytale to have got there in the first place.

People often ask me if I would have preferred to play football today? My answer is always the same: 'Yes' for the money but 'No' for the moments that I enjoyed. These were special times. In fact, I played 443 times for a special club. I couldn't have imagined what I was going to achieve with Sunderland when I signed for Len Ashurst back in 1984.

The Sunderland supporters have always made me feel special. They respect me and I respect them. This is my home. Without them, I don't think I would be here.

Gary Bennett is fifth-highest on Sunderland AFC's all-time first team appearances list. He holds the record for most appearances for the club at Wembley Stadium. He is now Sunderland AFC match summariser for BBC Newcastle.

5

Nothing beats a derby day victory over Newcastle United.

As Sunderland's run of wins over the old enemy went from one to two, three and then four, **Mike Grady** could scarcely believe it.

Exiled in London, he watched these games in the pub or at home, often with his sister for company.

Having never seen a derby win in the flesh, he thought twice about the risk of bringing bad luck with him to the Stadium of Light as the team set about making it Five in a Row…

He's very glad he decided to go.

FIVE IN A ROW

BY MIKE GRADY

'Why?' is the most common question. I always struggle to answer it honestly – it was a decision I made so long ago, I can't quite remember my reasons for being a Sunderland fan.

It is a question you face a lot in London; you are outside natural territory, your accent stands out a mile – even my mild North-Eastern tones – and your weekends are ruined by a perpetually rubbish football team. Being a Sunderland fan in exile isn't an easy thing.

Growing up, I was one of three Sunderland fans among my friends, so I was used to watching games in small groups. Most of my friends chose Kevin Keegan's Newcastle United as their boyhood idols. It was easy to see why – after all, supporting Mick Buxton's bottom-half of the Endsleigh Division One side wasn't exactly glamorous.

I always went to a lot of matches when I lived at home; that my first game – a 1-1 draw at home to Wolves in 1994 – proved to cultivate a long-lasting relationship should have been a clue about how much of a glutton for punishment I would be in the years to come. It might also have been what put my Dad off going to as many games as he might have done.

More often than not, I would go to games with my babysitter's husband, or my friend Tom and his Dad who have had season tickets in the north east corner since the Stadium of Light opened.

I moved away from home when I was 18 to go to university in Preston. It felt close to home for me – just down the A66 – but in football terms it was a million miles away. I lived with a group of lads who supported Bradford City, Blackburn Rovers, Leeds United and Manchester United. I was joined on my course by Bolton Wanderers and Manchester City fans while my then girlfriend – and her terrifying Dad – supported Liverpool.

Things didn't really change much when I moved to London. From jobs in bars, offices and as a sports reporter, I still haven't worked with a single Sunderland fan after seven years in the capital. I have been fortunate enough to get myself to some London-based away games and it is always odd hopping on a quick tube ride down to the Emirates or a few bus stops to White Hart Lane on my own. Fortunately, the London branch of the Sunderland Supporters Association stepped in this year and kept me company down at Selhurst Park.

It has always been tough getting friends along to watch games. Requests to spend Saturday nights watching Sunderland battle against West Ham United have been met with far-from-polite replies.

My match-day company tends to have been one of my sisters – Amy has been my shoulder to cry on many a time. She has joined me at midday on a Sunday to trawl the pubs of north London to find one with a foreign stream or perhaps an Irish pub more inclined to show Sunderland games than Liverpool or Manchester City.

I have never really counted myself as a particularly lucky fan; it took me about two years to actually see Sunderland win, while the only time I could afford a season ticket was the infamous 19-point campaign. I remember sitting behind the goal as Sunderland contrived to score three own goals in eight first-half minutes against Charlton Athletic, convinced it must be my fault. That season would also give me my first taste of a derby game, when Nolberto Solano's penalty gave Newcastle a 1-0 win, the first of four derbies I would attend without seeing a win. The next was the 4-1 defeat in which both Albert Luque and Michael Chopra managed to score after Sunderland took a 1-0 lead in what would be Alan Shearer's last-ever game.

A 1-1 draw followed at St James' Park in 2009 when I covered the game as a reporter. Remaining impartial was a true test of my professionalism. Luckily, I escape unscathed and my pockets were full after my bet of Djibril Cisse to score first and the game to end in a draw had paid off – a small consolation. In fact, the last derby game I went to was the last one Sunderland lost – the 1-0 home defeat to Ryan Taylor's flukey free-kick in 2011.

That was it for me. I vowed to stop travelling home for the games and bringing my hex onto an already hexed club. I would watch games in London from now on. Turns out, it didn't go too badly.

BUCKING THE TREND
April 14, 2013 – Newcastle United 0-3 Sunderland

Since I moved to London, I have always lived in the north – of course – specifically around Highgate, Tufnell Park and Kentish Town. It is jam-packed with pubs, from the gastronomic to the spit and sawdust ones you have been warned about. My pub of choice is definitely the latter: its cheap Guinness, bad crisps and a Norwegian feed of Premier League games making it the clear winner.

I had watched plenty of games in there before – I had even taken Catherine, my girlfriend, along to watch Darren Bent score for England against Switzerland. Our afternoon ended slightly earlier than expected, however, as we were kicked out of our seats as the women's darts team had a league match. Catherine hasn't been back.

I had watched Sunderland lose 5-1 in there, I had seen Asamoah Gyan score a last-minute equaliser with his backside in there, but I had never seen Sunderland win in there.

I am not sure if it is the same with all Irish pubs in London, but Geordies and Mackems seem to flock there on match days and you are always surrounded by some friendly – and some not-so-friendly – voices.

My family were down in London that weekend in April 2013, so I took my neutral Dad and Newcastle-supporting brother-in-law along with my Sunderland-supporting sister. Sunderland went into the game having just sacked Martin O'Neill after nine games without a win. Languishing in the all-too-familiar position of 17th with just six games left to play, a trip to St James' Park was the last thing we needed; Sunderland had not won there in 13 years since Niall Quinn and Don Hutchison overturned Gary Speed's early goal before Thomas Sorensen saved an Alan Shearer penalty, in one of the most dramatic derby games in recent memory.

This was to be Paolo Di Canio's second game in charge – his first being a 2-1 defeat at Stamford Bridge, remembered only for the worst jumper seen on the touchline. His appointment was a shock on Wearside; the fans had seen the volatile Roy Keane come and go, and experienced managers like Steve Bruce and Martin O'Neill replace him. Di Canio was a novice lower league manager with a reputation as a hot-head.

We took our seats in the pub surrounded by nervous Newcastle fans – they themselves were only five points above the relegation zone and needed a win to edge further away – and the teams were named. Sunderland started with Alfred N'Diaye, James McClean and Danny Graham. Not exactly Don Hutchison, Julio Arca and Super Kevin Phillips.

As the game started, we quickly realised something was wrong. Horribly wrong. The usually reliable Norwegian TV station was having technical problems – the coverage was buffering, the feed was delayed and the sound didn't work, filling the pub with nervous tension.

I resorted to listening to BBC Radio 5 Live on my iPhone, about 15 seconds ahead of the feed. So when I leapt to my feet and shouted at the top of my voice, the rest of the pub looked at me like I was some kind of idiot. I felt like one too, but little did I know that my celebrations would be eclipsed seconds later by the maniacal reaction from Di Canio – the Italian went bonkers, as did the rest of the Mackems in the pub when the TV coverage showed Stéphane Sessègnon's finish.

As people settled back into their seats, they soon realised that, yes, I was an idiot, but an idiot who was streaming the radio coverage of the match. For the rest of the first 45 minutes, half of the eyes in the room were on the TV, the other half were on me, watching for my reaction. I don't do well in the spotlight, so I tried to keep my reactions to a minimum.

The second half saw Shola Ameobi – the scourge of Sunderland teams in the past – come off the bench. This man, more than anyone in recent history, was Sunderland's Public Enemy No.1.

The second half plodded on and minutes after Tim Krul went off injured, Papiss Cisse caused me to look like even more of an idiot. 5 Live tells me he has equalised – smashing the ball past Simon Mignolet from a tight angle.

I slam the table and curse the skies while the TV catches up. I am too distraught to notice it has been ruled out. The pub erupts as the ball goes in, my usually stoic brother-in-law is on his feet when he finds his cheers cut short as the TV zooms in to the linesman's flag – he has given offside.

In an unusual stroke of good fortune, completely against

Sunderland's style, Cisse is shown to be a yard onside.

So far, it was just a normal derby game; few goals, plenty of controversy and Sunderland looking a bit shaky. It was all going to change soon enough. So far during his debut season, Adam Johnson had done little to justify his big transfer fee from Manchester City, but in a few seconds he curled a delicious left-footed shot into the top corner from 25 yards out. We go mental. The pub goes mental. And Di Canio outdoes us all.

If 2-0 was Cloud Nine, then we were about to go to dreamland as David Vaughan smashed in a screaming, curling left-footed shot. At this point, a noise came out of my mouth the likes of which I have never heard before. It was disbelief, joy and shock all rolled into one. *Grazie, Paolo.*

How many times have Sunderland scored three goals in a game, never mind away from home, at St James Park with just 34 per cent of the possession? That is a goal for every 11.3 per cent of the match. Wonderful. And yes, I worked it out.

Vaughan's goal turned a defeat into a humiliation and sent Newcastle fans teeming for the exits. In the post-game fallout, one Toon fan was involved in one of the most bizarre incidents ever to mar a derby game – he punched a horse. According to the *Guardian*, he 'began to clap in a horse's face before squaring up to one of the animals and punching it in the head'.

The Newcastle fans streaming for the exits must have also felt like they had been punched. It felt like a one-off, 'where were you?' moment – just like the 2-1 at St James' Park in 1999.

SECOND TIME AROUND
October 27, 2013 – Sunderland 2-1 Newcastle United

A lot can happen in six months, and at Sunderland it normally does. Di Canio was in charge as the Black Cats avoided relegation and set upon a summer of rebuilding with new director of football Roberto De Fanti, a former agent with contacts around the world.

We were all so optimistic: we had a young, hungry, passionate manager who didn't mind ruining a suit or two when celebrating at the home of our biggest rivals; a chief scout who (allegedly) discovered the likes of Alexis Sanchez at Udinese; and a director of football who came from Inter Milan. The world was our oyster. That summer, Sunderland signed the world. And its oyster.

When researching for this book, I came across one of the scariest sentences a Sunderland fan could come across: 'Maritimo defender Valentin Roberge, Basel midfielder Cabral and Lazio defender Modibo Diakité are also set to join the club next month.' (BBC Sport).

Five games into Di Canio's first season as manager saw Sunderland bottom of the league with one point, the players in revolt and a hotchpotch squad made up of obscure players. The Italian was given the boot and De Fanti recommended Gustavo Poyet as his replacement.

The Uruguayan would always be remembered for scoring a sumptuous volley at Stamford Bridge against the Mackems – but he had never lost to Newcastle.

Poyet carried on what would become a fine tradition of Sunderland managers by losing their first game in charge before facing Newcastle in their second. Di Canio had managed a remarkable result, but it couldn't happen again… Could it?

With the pub that served me so well back in April shut, I teamed up with my ever-reliable sister and we headed central, making a beeline for King's Cross to meet a Newcastle fan – after all, it had worked well having the enemy for company last time, it was bound to work again.

If you don't know King's Cross, it has a chequered past. As large swathes of London continue to become gentrified and awash with fancy cafes and artisan bakeries, it has become increasingly difficult to find a pub showing football around the area. We hadn't banked on so few options and as we legged it down Euston Road, we found a pub that was showing the game – never had The Euston Flyer looked so good. We are talking typical train station pub territory here – questionable Guinness and expensive cider.

Amy and I barged through the doors and found a tiny space on a table with a decent view of the match. Three minutes had gone and Sunderland had just won a corner thanks to Jozy Altidore. It was goalless. I exhaled, took my jacket off, sent Amy to the bar – all without taking my eyes off the screen.

Adam Johnson was all set. He played it short to Seb Larsson on the edge of the area who quickly returned the ball. Amy returned with a questionable Guinness and an expensive cider. Johnson turned back towards goal and dinked a lovely cross towards the back post. Steven Fletcher out-jumped Paul Dummett, headed downwards past Tim Krul and into the Newcastle net.

Five minutes in, Sunderland were 1-0 up. The pub, chocka with Sunderland fans went wild. All of a sudden, the Guinness was glorious and the cider tasted like champagne.

The first half came and went; a missed Altidore chance here, a Cheik Tioté foul there. Half-time was a chance to catch our collective breaths – Fletcher's goal seemed like a very long time ago indeed.

Now, there are two types of Sunderland fans: the optimists and the pessimists. I am an eternal optimist; players will always turn it around and Sunderland will always come good. The thing is, my mindset completely changes during derby day. When Sunderland take the lead, my gut churns waiting for the equaliser. When it comes, it almost feels like sweet relief.

It came, as it usually does. This time from Mathieu

Debuchy. An awful shot from Hatem Ben Arfa drifted aimlessly across the penalty area and seemingly out of the danger zone when an unmarked Debuchy tapped it past the helpless Keiren Westwood.

Defeat felt inevitable. A draw would be a point better than none. Winning was out of the question. It is hard to remember now, but at the time Sunderland had only won two derby games since the year 2000.

Newcastle started to take control of the game, pressing, passing and moving the ball better as Sunderland defended at the last and always managed to clear the ball. On 69 minutes, Poyet made the best managerial decision of his career up to that point: he brought on Fabio Borini in place of Adam Johnson.

Borini hadn't done a lot to endear himself to Sunderland fans to this point – he was another of the summer signings who seemed all filler, no killer. How wrong we were. He chased, harried and tracked back, hunting down the ball and trying to start attacks from deep.

As the game looked to be heading for another draw – five of the last ten had ended 1-1 – Fletcher won a soft free-kick on the halfway line. He took it quickly and played it inside to Ki – another of De Fanti's loan signings who would prove to be a success – who threaded the ball to Jack Colback. With a deft touch, he would present Jozy Altidore with the opportunity for greatness.

Now, as I said, I am an optimist. My telling of this moment may be vastly different from the rest of you. With anticipation and deftness, Altidore held off his marker and with the grace and skill worthy of the Brazil 1970 team, laid the ball off to Borini. The touch was perfect, Borini didn't have to break his stride or even look to see where it would go. It was, quite simply, the greatest assist in the history of football. What Borini did next was pretty special too.

Running across Altidore – and completely unmarked – the Italian picked up the ball, took a touch and fired an explosive shot past Tim Krul from 25 yards giving us the first sight of his famous hand-in-teeth celebration we would grow to love.

The Euston Flyer was flying. The noise in the pub at the time was unrivalled in London – Amy seemed to grow superhuman strength and picked me up as we jumped around like fools. This time she didn't spill a drop.

By the time we had settled down, the final whistle was upon us and Sunderland made it two in a row.

THREE AND EASY
February 1, 2014 – Newcastle United 0-3 Sunderland

'I think it's going to change the season,' said Gus Poyet on the 2-1 win over Alan Pardew's side at the Stadium of Light. By the time the return game came around, Sunderland had won just four games and were still in the bottom three.

Speaking of things which don't change, Amy and I headed back to The Euston Flyer to see if this could become our new good luck pub. We didn't have any Newcastle fans for company this time, more's the pity…

Poyet's Sunderland was slowly picking up points and behaving in traditional Sunderland style, losing to Hull City, Aston Villa and throwing away leads against Chelsea. What was that about change, Gus?

One thing that was different about this season was our cup form. If it was entirely predictable that we would be 2-0 down at home to MK Dons after 77 minutes, nobody would have had the optimism – not even me – to predict we would go on to win 4-2, even Jozy Altidore got on the scoresheet.

An unconvincing win over Peterborough, a close call against Southampton and the mother of all late winners against

Chelsea saw us go into 2014 with a League Cup semi-final against Manchester United to look forward to. The two legs of the semi-final were two of the most dramatic games in my time as a Sunderland fan. By the time the derby game had come around, my voice still wasn't at full-strength after that penalty shoot-out at Old Trafford.

We might have still been in the bottom three, but there was a sense of change at the club – the cup run had given us all hope. We thought that Things Can Only Get Better. In the space of a few weeks, Sunderland had received tweets from Nelson Mandela and Professor Brian Cox. With two derby wins under our belts and a cup final to look forward to, we went to The Euston Flyer with hope in our hearts.

This time around we were well prepared for the quality of the booze we were about to consume as we took our place perched at the bar as the teams were read out. All as expected with another loan signing, Marcos Alonso making his first derby appearance and Liam Bridcutt making his Sunderland debut. Newcastle, luckily, had top scorer Loïc Rémy suspended and had recently sold Yohan Cabaye. Needless to say, the moods in both camps were vastly different.

As the match got underway, I reverted to type and became a nervous wreck waiting for Alan Pardew's side to score the opening goal, bracing myself for Steven Taylor or Shola Ameobi to roll away celebrating as Amy tried to calm me down.

The game was tetchy, with both sides having their bright moments, but Sunderland soon settled with Phil Bardsley and Adam Johnson linking up well down the right. On 18 minutes, Johnson chipped a lovely ball for Bardsley to run on to. He charged into the box before being clumsily bundled over by Vernon Anita. I yelled out, totally unconvinced, but the referee pointed to the spot. Never mind, we would miss it… Fabio Borini stepped up – sharing a joke with the referee and looking totally at ease – and smashed in his fifth goal of the season. While the pub celebrated, for me it was just a wave of relief – like a nice whisky warming me up and relaxing my tense muscles. Barman, another…

It turns out it takes about the same amount of time for a pint of Guinness to be poured and paid for as it took Sunderland to double their lead. Jack Colback was in shudderingly good form that day and watching the match back, it is hard to imagine him now playing for Newcastle.

Just like the second goal at the Stadium of Light, this goal was made by Borini and Altidore, with the American playing a wonderfully cute flick behind himself and through to Colback who raced towards goal. Now, Jack was hardly the most menacing in front of goal and his shot was duly terrible. Lucky for him it took a deflection off Steven Taylor before Tim Krul palmed it to the feet of Johnson who tapped it in. Two goals in four minutes.

During Sunderland games, I always find it interesting to hear what Amy thinks – she knows her football, but will always offer reviews in plain language without the perspective of massive bias. To get a full sense of reaction, I always resort to turning on my phone and heading straight for Twitter.

Now, the north east is blessed with so many fantastic journalists and reporters – from George Caulkin at *The Times*, Simon Bird at the *Mirror* and Luke Edwards at the *Telegraph*, to Scott Wilson, Mark Douglas and Chris Young at the *Northern Echo*, the *Evening Chronicle* and the *Sunderland Echo*. Between them, the usual channels such as BBC Sport and the *Guardian*, and *Roker Report* and *A Love Supreme* you get a real sense of perspective. From the more biased views to smart, concise analysis of proceedings and explaining where the game has been won and lost, this lot always help me to connect with my team back home. However, it does not help me connect to my sister giving me daggers in the pub for spending the last 15 minutes on my phone.

After stocking up on reassuring Tweets which echoed the fact Sunderland had dominated, I returned the phone to my pocket and turned my attention back to the screen for the second half.

The Magpies bossed the second period and Sunderland did well to keep the scoreboard clear. In the closing stages, we seemed to find a renewed energy and could have made it three when Johnson curled a shot against the post and soon after when Krul saved at the feet of Altidore.

With a quarter of the game still to play, we were joined by my girlfriend. I loved it how she came along to watch at least some of the game – she was taken somewhat by surprise by the noises I made when watching the second leg of the League Cup semi-final in the house while she was on the phone to her Dad, so to find Catherine was willing to endure me during football was heartwarming – but I was filled with fear as the last time we had watched together it had ended with a Kevin Nolan hat-trick and an utterly humiliating 5-1 defeat.

With ten minutes left on the clock, Tioté played the ball into Ben Arfa on the halfway line. Colback, who was a man-mountain that day, shoved him off the ball and to the ground while Borini raced forward with the loose ball. The Italian played it to his left for the on-rushing Colback to race on to before smashing a left-footed shot past Krul.

Now, we went crazy.

It had happened again – 3-0 at St James' Park. Two years in a row. Three derby wins in a row. Immediate thoughts went out to the horses of Northumbria police. That win would mark the first time Sunderland had won three derbies in a row for the first time in 91 years.

I was beginning to like The Euston Flyer.

FESTIVE FOUR

December 21, 2014 – Newcastle United 0-1 Sunderland

It would be lonely this Christmas. Amy had gone back home for the festive season while I was preparing to spend Christmas with Catherine and her family in Kent for the first time. My friends weren't interested and Catherine had made herself scarce for fear of a repeat of the League Cup semi-final. The usual suspects were gone, so there I was, alone in my flat with mulled wine and mince pies to keep me company. It did mean that I got to watch the pre-match coverage – an unusual treat for a derby game – and revel in replays of the previous three wins, though. Not all bad.

If this was to be the first derby game I had watched on my own, it was also a game of firsts for a few of the main protagonists – Jack Colback would make his first derby appearance in the wrong coloured stripes while Gus Poyet would enjoy his first derby game not in the bottom three. Now, if only Christmas would come a few days early. It didn't seem likely as in the 116 years this fixture has been played, Sunderland had never managed four consecutive wins. They had only won two games all season and drawn a remarkable ten.

Before the match, Alan Pardew had confessed: 'I'm not from the area, I don't get so emotionally involved,' as he continued to endear himself to Newcastle fans.

The game kicked off with a late change to the Sunderland line-up after Anthony Réveillère was injured in the warm-up to be replaced by Sebastian Coates. As always, Sunderland fans found reason to be concerned.

One of the great things about derby games is the tackles and this goes for both teams. Players like Lee Clark and Steven Taylor, Kevin Ball and Lee Cattermole always turned it up a notch for a special occasion – the latter conceded his first foul in the opening minute. The away fans cheered from the rafters.

Newcastle started the game the better team, making my decision to watch the match alone a valid one. As I was sulking on the sofa, 17 minutes came up and the packed-out St James' Park stood as one and applauded in memory of John Alder and Liam Sweeney, fans who died aboard the MH17 plane en route to watch Newcastle in New Zealand – a truly touching moment that signified the on-going improvement in the spirit these games are played in.

A missed Connor Wickham chance here, a Tioté booking there, the first half seemed to be going as we all expected until Seb Larsson swept in a wonderful ball over the top of the Newcastle defence which was met by the deft left foot of Steven Fletcher. I leapt up, held my breath and prepared to celebrate the best goal ever seen – aren't they all? – when the ball crashed off the crossbar. All superlatives aside, this was inches away from being one of the finest goals in derby history.

Half-time arrived with the scores still level, and the opening 45 minutes was summed up perfectly by the *Guardian*'s Daniel Harris in which he declared: 'There has been almost no football in this football match, which is a hugely enjoyable football match.'

Ten minutes into the second half, I was furious. Jordi Gomez had just missed a sitter. John O'Shea executed one of those brilliant slide-tackle-then-pass manoeuvres which sent Gomez forward to play in Fletcher. Gomez continued his forward run and collected the return pass from the Scot in prime position to smash the ball home. It was already in before it had left his foot, I was on my feet and ready to celebrate… If only he had hit his shot as well as I kicked the cushions flying across the living room!

Sunderland were lucky to still be level, but as we have come to expect from recent derby wins there is always a chance for late drama. Never as late as this, though.

We all dream of scoring the winning goal in a derby game with a last-gasp winner at the home of our fiercest rivals – proper *Roy of the Rovers* stuff.

In the 89th minute Sunderland oh-so-nearly lost it when Moussa Sissoko lashed a shot at goal with incredible force before the tallest man on earth, Costel Pantilimon leapt across goal and tipped it over the bar. The corner was poor and easily cleared at the front post where it found Adam Johnson on the edge of the penalty area being manhandled by Sissoko. The winger shrugged off his rival and ran forward. He was then fouled by Paul Dummett, but again managed to stay on his feet.

Only when Johnson crossed the halfway line did I believe something might happen. We had almost lost the game a few seconds earlier, surely we couldn't win it in the 90th minute?

Newcastle had four men back as Johnson romped forward but Steven Fletcher, with hitherto unknown pace, was legging it up the left wing. He received the ball as the team pushed on and played a canny pass across the face of goal to Will Buckley. The former Brighton man laid it off first time into space where Johnson took a touch – it looked like he had all the time in the world here, I held my breath and it seemed like an eternity – before rifling a volley past Jak Alnwick.

I. Went. Bonkers.

All of a sudden, I was ecstatic with my decision to watch the game alone – this felt like a completely natural reaction, something unadulterated and in no way influenced by my surroundings. Sheer joy. The only downside was that when the final whistle went – after a terrible miss by Larsson, let's not let him off the hook for that – I had no one to celebrate with. My phone soon went and my Mam, Dad and Amy were FaceTiming from home – a truly 21st century way to celebrate a derby win.

By the time Catherine came home, my voice had gone, the mince pies had disappeared and the mulled wine was no longer. Merry Christmas.

FAMOUS FIVE
April 5, 2015 – Sunderland 1-0 Newcastle United

It had been a while since I had managed to travel home for a derby game. I tend to manage four or five home games a season, but it is rare that the stars align for a trip to a derby.

Finances and fitness have got in the way recently, but my family have always been on hand to help me out – be it keeping me company in the pub or calling me at half-time and full-time to make sure I had someone to vent to.

When the fixtures came out and I saw that the home game against Newcastle fell on Easter Sunday, I couldn't have been happier; after spending Christmas with Catherine's family, we were going back to South Shields for Easter.

My Dad always tries to stay impartial (as long as it is a north east team) when it comes to football – 'I like to see all of the north east teams do well,' he always says – but after taking him to the League Cup semi-final against Manchester United and the final against Manchester City, I think I had finally persuaded him to be a Mackem.

I bought a couple of tickets and headed home.

The thing was, I was due to run my second London marathon in a few weeks and that weekend was the peak of my training, with a 20-mile run on the cards. With that hanging over me, and the frustration knowing that my self-imposed booze-ban meant that I couldn't even recover with a pint of Guinness at the game.

My Dad had never been to a derby game before, and I had never seen Sunderland win a derby game in the flesh. The odd draw and a couple of thrashings didn't really lead me to believe I would be a good luck charm, but nevertheless we ploughed on.

We stuck to the usual pre-match tradition of a pint in The Old Ship on Sunderland Road in South Shields before hopping on the bus to The Grange, where we would usually soak up a bit of atmosphere – as well as some Guinness. Well, my Dad did – I was on the lime and sodas. Wracked with nerves, we headed towards the Stadium of Light.

At this point in the season, Sunderland were fourth-from-bottom with another new manager – Dick Advocaat. Gus Poyet had been sacked after a miserable run – Sunderland had won one league match since beating Newcastle in December. Advocaat fitted in with Sunderland's new-found tradition of losing your first game in charge ahead of a derby game, but could he follow suit and win his second?

A win for Sunderland was vital, with games against Crystal Palace and Stoke City coming up before a run of Southampton, Everton, Arsenal and Chelsea in the final five games.

We got to the stadium and took our seats. Only they weren't our seats. We were kicked out and moved to another pair nearby thinking there had been a mix-up. Then we were kicked out of those. We went down and chatted to a nice steward who told us he would sort it. It wasn't sorted. The game kicked off with us stood in the access gates and my Dad standing on his tip-toes to see the action.

'It's alright lads, I've sorted it,' said the steward at last. 'If you'd like to sit there,' he told me pointing up, 'then you can sit there,' he told my Dad, pointing to the left. Our first derby game together – my Dad's first derby game ever – and we weren't going to be sitting next to each other. I was gutted. I had waited years for this, and after finally turning my Dad into a proper Mackem, thought this would be my first derby win.

As we took our seats, we were three rows and fifteen seats apart – not exactly the opposite end of the stadium, but far enough apart. My Dad has always been a calming figure, especially at the football. His impartiality gives him a zen-like state of acceptance. While I am scoffing and sighing, he is assessing the passage of play.

Never mind, we would catch up at half-time…

The atmosphere was one of the best I have heard at the Stadium of Light, harking back to the days of Niall Quinn and Kevin Phillips – it was a guttural roar, urging the team on. My bones shook with every cheer and thunder of applause. After a furious start for Sunderland, I made eye contact with my Dad. 'Wow,' he mouthed, wide-eyed.

Now, my Dad and I always wait until the half-time whistle to head down back to the concourse, so as Costel Pantilimon readied himself for a goal-kick, people started heading for the toilets and bars. The Romanian's gigantic hoof found the head of Steven Fletcher, always one for bringing his best to a derby day. The Scot out-jumped Mike Williamson as he flicked the ball to his right.

As the ball began to drop, it looked harmless. We were at the other end of the ground so didn't see Jermain Defoe approach and watch the ball like a hawk. With better timing than the best Bob Monkhouse joke, the one-time England international swung his left foot at the descending ball and watched it connect perfectly before soaring, looping and crashing into the Newcastle net.

When Defoe hit the ball, it was looping so high that it looked like it was going way over the bar, as he had done against West Ham in the previous game. But the shot fell much quicker. The noise when it found the back of the net was nerve-tingling. The ground seemed to shake in the sunshine as Defoe ran towards us and collapsed in tears on the turf. Meanwhile, I was trying to reach across the celebrating hoards to give my Dad a high-five.

A sun-soaked Stadium of Light, a half-time lead and a goal of the season contender – not bad for my Dad's first derby game. We headed back inside the stadium for a half-time dissection – Dad was an Alan Hansen or Graeme Souness kind of pundit, overjoyed with the goal but utterly depressed with the poor quality of football on show.

It was the atmosphere he was really enjoying, the last few games we had seen were defeats to Arsenal and Liverpool while the opening-day defeat against Fulham under Paolo Di Canio would live long in his memory. The League Cup final was still a highlight, but that Fulham game wouldn't be erased easily.

The second half began and Dick Advocaat emerged from the tunnel with his lucky scarf on what was an unseasonably warm day for April. The fans were in their shirtsleeves and the manager was in his scarf.

Luckily for Sunderland, a second-half recovery from a John Carver-inspired Newcastle would never come. Across all four derby games before, this might just have been the worst performance from the Mags. No passion, no pride, no effort.

As the game went on, Sunderland showed signs of their good-old-selves, trying to throw it away. A succession of missed chances let the atmosphere change from bubbling cauldron to a gentle simmer of nervous tension.

Newcastle rarely threatened, with Papiss Cisse serving a ban for spitting, the Mags were toothless up front. It took until the 78th minute for them to give Pantilimon something to do, with nine of their ten shots off target.

When Ayoze Perez, the only Newcastle player to come out of either game this season with any credit, fired over five minutes from time, you knew it was going to be Sunderland's day.

As Tim Krul raced up for a corner – the final action of the game – the man-mountain that is Costel Pantilimon plucked

Ryan Taylor's corner out of the air and the final whistle blew.

One-nil. Five in a row. Who would have thought it?

As the final whistle rang out, the crowd roared once more, a cocktail of relief and ecstasy. The stands stayed full long after the match was over as the fans turned towards the upper north stand and gave the usual pleasantries to the away section.

Fifteen minutes after the game was up, I met my Dad and walked towards the bus stop for home. We had plenty to celebrate after all. Sunderland had won their fifth derby in a row, I had seen my first derby win out of five. Meanwhile, my Dad was celebrating a 100 per cent record. I am taking him every year…

So, why am I a Sunderland fan? Maybe it is the continuous search for success, maybe it is the drama or maybe it is because I am an optimist. Whatever it is, taking my Dad to the Stadium of Light – where we had been going since the opening day in 1997 – to watch Jermain Defoe score such a beautiful goal to beat our fiercest rivals made it all special.

Watching the game in the flesh and being there to soak up the atmosphere beats any pub hands down, and now my hex was lifted, perhaps it is safe for me to go back a bit more often.

Mike Grady has written for the *Guardian*, Channel 4, Eurosport and *In Bed With Maradona*. His head is in London but his heart is in South Shields.

6

Imagine being remembered for one moment in a football match.

Not just any football match, but a cup final at Wembley.

Your name is synonymous with one match-winning moment for the rest of your life, and probably beyond.

Except that moment was a mistake that led to a winning goal for the opposition.

And even though one of your team-mates missed a penalty in that same game, people remind you of your mistake 30 years on.

Jeff Brown puts David Corner centre stage to explain what that feels like.

CORNERED

BY JEFF BROWN

(Stage dark. PC David Corner walks into the spotlight).

PC David Corner: Evenin'.

Actually, that should be: Evenin' all.

Remember that? Every week, the first line of *Dixon of Dock Green*. Britain's nicest bobby. BBC One. Saturday night telly. About six hours of it, right the way up to *Match of the Day*.

It kicked off with *The Generation Game* straight after *Grandstand* – or maybe *Doctor Who*?

Then it was on. Ran for 21 years – 1955 to 1976. Jack Warner. Old British actor. Played PC George Dixon.

No?

Anyway, even if you don't remember him, you still might remember me?

'Specially' if you're from Sunderland... or Norwich.

PC David Edward Corner.

Born – Sunderland, May the 15th,1966, a couple of months before England won the World Cup.

You know, they were playing some of the games at Roker Park, about a mile from me mam and dad's, when I was just a bairn.

Chile, Italy, Russia – and their goalie, the great Lev Yashin. Y' never know – he might have gone past our house!

Amazing that: The World Cup – in Sunderland.

Maybe that's why I wanted to be a footballer?

Anyway –

Born Sunderland, May the 15th, 1966.

Died Wembley Stadium, March the 24th, 1985.

Not really. Cos I'm here, aren't I?

It's just... well... plenty of people wanted me dead...

Thousands...

Hundreds of thousands...

Millions, maybe! Except if you were from Norwich, obviously. Or Newcastle...

Mind, I could have come back from the dead – like Dixon of Dock Green. He got shot, you know. The character was in a film before it went on the box. *The Blue Lamp*.1950. Jack Warner playing Dixon – that's how he got the telly part.

Gunned down by a young Dirk Bogarde. Died in hospital. Came back to life five years later.

Lived on for another 432 episodes – until it got a bit far-fetched.

Why, he was 80 when they made the last one!

Imagine him chasing a hoodie up Murton Hight Street, or trying to sort out a domestic in Dawdon. Ha'way! He wouldn't have lasted two minutes!

Coming back from the dead, though? It would be handy, that (if he'd been a copper these days)...

Never thought I'd be a copper.

Never thought I'd find a job where I was hated even more than when I was a footballer!

Sucker for punishment, eh?

Of course, I never knew it was going to turn out like that.

Well, you don't, do you? Not when they're asking for your autograph, and your picture's in the paper, and the lasses are hanging round the door at the club, and the crowd's chanting your name.

'Living the Dream'. That's what they say, isn't it?

When you do something **loads** of other kids would **love** to do, if they'd been given half a chance and had the breaks, had the talent... had the luck.

I had all of that.

Didn't know it at the time, mind. It was just the way it happened. Good at footy: School team, town team, the lot... all the way to Wembley.

Living the dream...

Living the nightmare...

Mam set the video, so I could see myself on the telly when we got back from London.

You know how many times I've watched it? Correct – never!

Not once.

Well, you wouldn't, would you?

Worst day of your life.

Worst **moment** of your life.

Live on telly, in the days when there was hardly **any** footy on the box – apart from *Match of the Day*.

Only four channels back then, so if you were a footy fan, you'd be sat there with your lager and your crisps and your feet up on the settee. An audience of... I don't know how many millions. Ten? Twenty?

Doesn't matter, really. There was enough.

When videos went out of fashion, I thought that might be it, you know?

You could still read about it in books and that, but you'd never actually **see** it again – unless they put it on telly on some footy programme, or something like that.

Highlights of the 80s!

Let's have a laugh at what Davey did.

And all them old videos, eh? Packed away in boxes, stuffed up in the attic. Even the second-hand shops won't take them now.

Then came bloody YouTube.

Mind, you won't find it if you type in 'David Corner'.

Nah. You'll get David Beckham – scoring straight from a **corner**.

Golden Balls – that's what they called him.

You know what they called **me** on the telly?

Copper Top!

Seriously.

I'm standing with the lads, right near the end of the line, just before kick-off, waiting to shake hands with some posh bloke, when all you want to do is run away as fast as you can and get on with the game, cos it's a cup final, and you can feel your backside starting to go.

Anyway, he comes to me, and the camera's there, and Barry Davies – doing the commentary on BBC One – says: 'Copper Top – David Corner.'

That's racist. Gingerist. I could nick him for it, these days!

Mind, he didn't give me any stick for the goal. In fact, it was like he never saw it.

I did though.

I see it every night. When I go to bed. When I shut me eyes.

If you watch it again, the camera goes straight to me. **He** knew who cocked it up. The TV director. Cheers mate!

You can see Benno – Gary Bennett – who was playing alongside me at the back. He's waving his arm, telling me I should have stuck it in row Z.

Which I'd pretty much worked out for myself, like!

Barry Davies doesn't pick up on it, though. He just mentions the deflection.

'Own goal by Chisholm,' he says.

These days they would've been showing it from a hundred different angles, wouldn't they? Analysing it, back in the studio.

The lads were all right about it, mind. It didn't even get mentioned in the dressing room afterwards. Everyone was too sick to talk, really.

We drove back in the team bus the next day and as we got near home there were fans on the side of the road and on the bridges – shouting, waving their scarves and that.

It wasn't quite the same as '73, when they won the FA Cup – but there were still plenty about.

It was fantastic.

We'd done well to get there, to be honest. We'd been crap in the league, but for some reason we'd gone on this run in the Milk Cup and you just went out there thinking you were going to win.

First couple of rounds, it's just another game. But you get through and suddenly you think: 'Hey, we might do something here!'

Then you start talking in the dressing room, after training, and you find out a few of the lads are thinking the same. Then you start winning games you shouldn't really be winning...

Like Tottenham away, when Chris Turner saved a penalty and Chizzy – Gordon Chisholm – scored in the **right** end!

And Watford – in the quarter-finals – when Clive Walker takes a shot and it comes off one of **their** players and goes in.

And the semi-final against Chelsea – we got **two** penalties in the first leg.

Westy – Colin West – was the big lad up front. He even missed one of them, but it comes back off their keeper and he hacks in the rebound off his shin! Horrible goal, but you take them all day.

Chelsea fans went crackers that night. They were up in the old Main Stand. Lost, two-nowt. Probably thought: 'That's us knackered. Not going to Wembley now.'

And it was a big thing, that. No play-offs or cup semi-finals at Wembley in them days. You had to **get** to a final to play at Wembley – or play for England.

It was a massive day out: for the club, the players, the fans – everyone.

And they couldn't handle it. The fact they weren't going to get there. Started kicking the old wooden seats to bits, they did. Chucking them down on the coppers and the fans in the paddock.

There was hell on.

We should have known what to expect when we went down there, really.

This was the old Stamford Bridge: Terraces, The Shed...

Only this time they thought they'd come on the pitch.

We'd just gone 2-1 up – 4-1 on aggregate. No way they were coming back from that.

And then it kicked off.

They were smashing up the seats, ripping chunks of concrete out the terraces and chucking anything they could get their hands on.

I wasn't playing – I was in the stands.

Big Cockney guy looks over, says: 'You from San-lan?' I just shook me head! Didn't say nowt – not with **my** accent!

When we scored the third, there was a police horse on the pitch, chasing this kid through the penalty area!

Absolute madness.

We were lucky to get out alive.

We had about three-and-a-half thousand fans there, and on the way back a few of the buses had their windows put in.

Cos when you've got a convoy, the coaches don't move very

fast. So it's like a sitting target.

Me mate was on one of them. He said the lad in the seat in front of him got an eyeful of glass. There was blood everywhere.

But that's what it was like in them days.

All-seater grounds have made a big difference – 'specially for the coppers.

CCTV everywhere.

Anyway, it's great when the fans are **with** you.

And the day after the final we get back to the ground, and there's – I don't know – 500, a thousand of them waiting outside?

'Cos it was a big thing. Only the third time Sunderland had been to Wembley.

First time we'd lost, mind.

So the barriers were out, to hold back the crowds. But they're all hanging over them, wanting to shake your hand.

Lenny Ashurst, the boss, says to us: 'Make sure you say something to them, 'cos they're what the club's all about. They're pleased to see you!'

Aye, right.

So I get off the bus, sign a few autographs, get about ten yards down the line, and this big bloke leans over, grabs me by the collar, drags me over the barrier and screams in me face: '**You**, y' bastard! You lost us the **Cup Final**!!'

Lenny and a couple of the lads dive in, drag me away, shove me through the door into the ground.

And that's where it all began.

The first time I realised my life might be a bit different from now on.

You know how often I'm reminded about it?

Every day.

Every.

Sodding.

Day.

For the past 30 years.

It's like a life sentence – with no time off for good behaviour!

No remission.

No parole.

You've just got to live with it, son.

It's an open prison, mind, so I can come and go when I want.

It just means I can bump into more people who can dish out dog's abuse!

You'd think, wouldn't you, after all these years, folk might have got over it by now? Y'know – it's been a canny while!

But that's football for you. It's **part** of you. It's in the blood. At least, it is, up here.

And what I did's been passed on from father to son. Only, the story gets a bit mixed up – like it does, y'know?

Chinese whispers.

So when I was picking me kids up from school, it was: 'Dad, is **that** him – the one who scored the own goal in the cup final?' Nah – that was Chizzy.

Or sometimes it's: 'Dad, is that the one who missed the penalty at Wembley?' No – that was Clive Walker!

Aye, we missed a penalty as well! Hit the post. So it wasn't just **my** fault we lost!

But being a local lad and maybe being **ginger** – **nobody** forgets I did **something** I shouldn't have!

It was hardest on me mam and dad.

They got it everywhere they went.

It got so bad, sometimes they didn't want to leave the house.

We only lived a couple of miles from the ground, so I used to walk to training every day, with me boots under me arm.

Do you think Ronaldo does that? Or Messi?

I could hear it when people went past.

I could hear it when I went for me paper

Or at the garage.

But mostly in the pub.

It was like they took it **personally**.

Like I'd done it on purpose, just to spite them, y' know?

I had plenty of fights over it.

Maybe I should've just stayed at home and let it blow over – but 30 years in front of the telly?!

Nah, I didn't fancy that.

So I went out. I had a few beers. I had a laugh – which some folk didn't like.

'What's **he** laughing at? He cost us the Cup! Useless ginger get.'

That's usually how it started.

One of them ended up in Durham Crown Court.

Amateur boxer.

GBH.

Left me with a fractured eye socket, broken jaw and stitches in me lip.

He got off, an' all! Said it was self-defence!

I must have been hitting his fist too hard with me head!

That got in the papers, but most times, I just didn't bother.

Too much hassle to go to the coppers – and it would only give some nutter the idea of having a go.

Once, in The Londonderry – an old pub in the town centre... I'm standing there with a few mates when this bloke calls out: 'Davey?'

I turn round, thinking he wants to talk about football.

And he just smacks me right on the side of the jaw; smashes me teeth in. Then legs it out the door.

I mean, what can y' do?

The lads tried to run after him, but he got away.

It's just not **normal**, is it? To hold a grudge for 30 years?

I mean, ha'way – how many games have we played since then?

Thirty years. On average, about 40 league games a season. And, being generous, half a dozen each year in the cups...

Quick bit of maths: 30 x 46 = 1,380.

One thousand, three hundred and eighty football matches.

Someone must have done something worse than me in all that time!

I suppose you've got to be philosophical about these things, mind.

And who was the greatest football philosopher?

Bill Shankly?

'Football's not a matter of life and death – it's more serious than that!'

Only, **he** wasn't being serious when he said it.

What about Eric Cantona, after he jumped into the crowd and kung fu-kicked that kid who'd been giving him some stick, after he got sent off at Crystal Palace?

I know how he felt!

He got a nine-month ban, 20 thousand quid fine, two weeks in prison knocked down to 120 hours community service.

Would've been worth it, though.

I'd have settled for that.

And you know what – after he came back, they made him Footballer of the Year! Who says crime doesn't pay!

Mind, it was the press who voted for him, and that was only 'cos he filled their papers every day!

Remember what he said, when he had that press conference after he'd been banned?

'When zee seagulls follow zee trawler, it's because zey think sardines will be thrown into zee sea.' What a load of bollocks!

Nah – the greatest football philosopher was a bloke called Albert Camus.

Ever heard of him?

He played in goal for Racing University of Algeria, until he got polio and had to give up. He went on to write books and stuff, and won a Nobel Prize for Literature in 1957. Canny that.

His mate said to him once: 'Which do you prefer – football or theatre?'

You know what he said? 'Football – without hesitation!'

But it was a bit like a theatre, walking out at Wembley.

Just so much **noise**. From **everywhere**.

Rolling down off the terraces and crashing round your ears.

It was deafening.

I wasn't that nervous. You would have thought so, at 18, wouldn't you? But I was looking round, thinking: 'What's all the noise about? Who are they cheering for? It can't be for us. It can't be for me.' But it was...

It was incredible.

I mean, the **new** Wembley's good, y' know – don't get me wrong. About 80,000 seats and not a bad view in the house. No pillars, no girders, no one shoving you or pushing and pulling you from behind, trying to get past so they can see – or pissing in your pocket 'cos they're all squashed up and they've had a few beers too many and they can't get to the bogs in time!

Really – I've seen it!

Nah, it's not like the old days.

Not like the **old** Wembley.

There was a hundred thousand there in ’85. And about 70,000 of them were from Sunderland.

Well, not just Sunderland – I mean, from everywhere roundabouts.

From Murton, from Blackhall. All the Durham pit villages. From Ashington, from Bedlington. ’Cos when the miners went up into the Northumberland coalfields all them years ago – when there **was** coal – they never forgot their roots!

Aye – the Shields lot, the Jarrow lads, Billingham, Hartlepool.

And the London branch, of course. Second-biggest supporters club in London, behind Manchester United. And that’s only cos all the Man Utd fans were born down there!

Not like our lot. Follow the team for **love**, not glory. Just as well, mind. Nowt much glorious since ’73!

It’s that connection, y’ know? With home. Even though you can be a million miles away.

Maybe **lots** of places pull you back like that? I don’t know.

Sunderland does, though.

It’s in your blood.

Your DNA.

It was for me.

That’s why it took me years to leave.

I always wanted to be a footballer.

I only ever wanted to play for Sunderland.

I went to Oldham first, though.

Seventeen years old.

They put me in digs – but I only lasted three weeks.

Told the landlady I was poorly.

I was – I was homesick!

I jumped on a train and never went back.

Then Everton took me on after that – but I only lasted a week there!

That was a good decision, wasn't it? The year **we** lost at Wembley... The year I, well, y' know what I did, **they** won the League **and** the European Cup Winners' Cup!

It could have been me...

Anyway, back to Albert Camus.

His most famous quote was: 'Whatever I know about life, I learned from football.'

Sounds good that – if he wants to know about being kicked, or left out of the team, or being screamed at and spat at and having your lights punched out cos you **cost us the bloody Cup Final**!

Actually, what he said was: 'After many years, during which I saw many things, what I know most surely about morality and the duty of man, I owe to sport.'

Basically, he was talking about fair play. About having a bit of bottle. Sticking up for your mates.

Team work.

You don't get very far in football if you haven't got it.

And we didn't have much of it at Sunderland after the cup final.

We got relegated.

Last match of the season, y' know what the crowd was at Roker Park?

It was 9,000.

There had been 70,000 of them at Wembley. They'd gone all that way. Two months later, they couldn't even be bothered to leave the house and walk round the block to see us.

That's football fans for you.

And Lenny got sacked soon after.

They brought in Lawrie McMenemy. Or Lawrie Mackem-enemy as he later became known.

Highest paid manager in football.

Highest-paid flop.

Mind, he was good for me.

You only like a manager if he plays you. So I hated just about all of mine!

But Lawrie gave me my longest run in the team. And ended up being hated by the fans even more than **me**!

So that was good.

It took the heat off for a bit!

When he arrived he said he'd take us out of the Second Division. And he did.. He took us into the Third!

It was like he was on a kamikaze mission to ruin **us** and ruin himself at the same time.

He got run out of town in the end.

And what happened? A few months back, they put him in the Football Managers' Hall of Fame!

Some managers have made a canny living out of being sacked and walking off with a few years' salary. It's the only job where you can make a fortune out of being crap.

The best story about Lawrie...

Well, there's a few of them tell it, but I was there!

In fact, I was right in the middle of it.

We were training at Roker Park. On the pitch. The day before a game. Right at the end of the session, Lawrie has us lining up in formation and kicking off.

We're not playing anyone, mind.

No opposition.

Sounds daft, but it's just so's we can, like, go through the motions. Rehearse your moves, y' know.

So we kick off, and Eric Gates passes to Davey Swindlehurst.

He knocks it wide to Jack Lemon – Paul's his real name, but he gets Jack.

He plays it back to George Burley, and Lawrie shouts: 'Back to the keeper and we'll start again.'

So George gives it to me, and I turn to pass back to Hezzy – Iain Hesford – who's our keeper.

Only it bobbles, just as I'm playing it, and it loops up off me shin.

Hezzy's out of his goal and he has to jump backwards. He just manages to tip it over the bar!

And the lads are **killing** themselves laughing.

But Lawrie's going **crackers**!

He's shouting: '**Bloody hell** – we're playing no one and we're nearly getting beat!'

It still makes us laugh, that one!

But I don't think Lawrie would smile about it, even now...

He was from the north east. But he'd made his name right the way down the other end of the country, at Southampton.

Whenever he came back, it was like a big deal, y' know. They loved him. 'The Genial Geordie' – that's what the papers called him.

He thought he just had to turn up, and everything would fall into place.

So he comes here, loses his first five games and we don't even score a goal.

It was downhill from then until he packs his bags, clears his house and flies off to Florida.

Aye, that's what he did.

He also sold his story to *The Sun*.

So it was all over the back page the next day. By which time he was sunning himself on the beach! Even the club didn't know until they read about it.

That was **his** way out of a bad decision.

Wish I could've done something like that.

I suppose that every day you make decisions, don't you?

Am I getting out of bed?

What will I have for breakfast?

Do I need me coat?

What time do I have to be in today?

Most of them you do without thinking.

Just as well, really, else you'd never get anything done.

Some of them – the bigger ones – you need to weigh up.

If I do that – this'll happen. So maybe I won't do it. I'll do something else instead.

When I was a lad, they had these things on the telly. Public Information films, they called them. Common sense, really.

They don't have them now, 'cos folk don't like to be told.

'Specially not the kids.

Trouble is, **they** do things without thinking – and more often than not it's us coppers who have to clear up the mess.

'Don't be an Amber Gambler!' Remember that one?

'Don't jump the lights, in case you meet someone who's jumping them from the other direction.'

I've had to scrape a few kids out their cars.

Not nice.

'Don't go off with strangers!' Little bits of advice like that, just meant to stick in your mind. And help you make the right decisions.

Most of them were everyday things. But some things can change your life. Like mine did.

What you hear most, from football coaches, if the ball's running away from goal, down towards the corner flag, is: 'Hump it over the dead-ball line, far as you can.'

'If in doubt, put it out.'

Football's own little Public Information film.

Maybe I just wasn't listening...?

I'd not been well, leading up to the cup final. I had this disease. I can't remember what they called it, but me gums were growing over me teeth!

I know, it sounds horrible. It looked pretty horrible, an' all. And it felt pretty horrible. I couldn't eat properly. In four weeks, I lost about a stone.

I came back to training on the day they were taking the photographs to go in the cup final programme.

I thought I looked quite trim, y' know? Quite tidy.

You look at the pictures now – I look gaunt. Drained.

I said to Frank Burrows, who was our trainer: 'How d'y' think I'm looking, Frank?'

I'll never forget it.

He said: 'Son – you look **pathetic**.'

Y' know what? Of all the things people said to me about the cup final, that turned out to be the nicest!

I should've known, really. To be a centre half, you've got to be good in the air – y' know, jump up and head the ball away – and maybe have a bit of pace, be able to sprint when you have to, a bit of nous, so you can read the game – know what the guy your marking's going to do if he gets the ball, if you **let** him get the ball...

You've got to be a bit of a nasty bastard. Do just about anything to stop him putting that ball in the net.

I don't mean sticking the boot in. Just not letting yourself be bullied, y' know?

They call it: 'Getting your retaliation in first.' It sounds better like that!

Just letting him know y' there...

And you also need a bit o' beef – and I'd lost that in the weeks before the final, when I was ill.

What you do, when the ball's going out, you try to shield it. You stick out your backside, and use that as, like, a buffer.

That way, the ball will be over the line, out of play. The ref gives a goal kick, the keeper boots it upfield and you start all over again.

That's how it **should** have been.

You've seen it **thousands** of times before.

I'd **done** it thousands of times before.

I know what you're thinking: 'Cup final... hundred thousand there, watching... young lad... 18... trying to be a smart arse...'

But it wasn't like that!

It was **instinct**.

And I got it wrong. I just got it wrong...

So we've had philosophy. But football's more about kidology.

You can't get a degree in it. But it's about kidding yourself you're better than **them**. When you're **not**!

It's the same in **every** dressing room. From the dads with their bairns in the park on a Saturday morning to cup finals like ours.

Same old story, week after week... And we fall for it, every time.

'Come on, y' can beat this lot – they're **crap**!'

'Have y' seen the size of that skinny lad, centre half? A breath o' wind an' he'll be on his backside.'

'Look at the keeper! He couldn't catch a cold.'

'That lad, the midfielder everyone goes on about. I've seen him and he couldn't pass water!'

'On our day, we can beat **anyone**.'

Which is **true**. Mind, it's about the only thing that is...

'Let's get straight in from the off. Just keep it tight. Keep it simple. And don't forget: **nowt daft**!'

That was the bit I forgot.

We'd actually beaten Norwich at their place in the league, the week before the final.

3-1, it was.

I played in that one, so I had a canny idea I'd be playing at Wembley.

Me mam and dad couldn't be sure, mind. But they were fans, so they would've been going anyway.

They didn't drive. So they went down, early morning, on the supporters' bus.

Me? I only found out for real on the day of the match.

I was sharing a room with Jack Lemon – no, not that one, he was a film star. But if you don't remember Dixon of Dock Green, you won't remember Jack Lemon (or Jack Lemmon).

Some Like It Hot?

Never mind.

Anyway, Lenny Ashurst comes up to the room and tells him: 'Sorry, son.'

Jack's gutted. But deep down, he knew he wasn't going to get picked.

Then Lenny says: 'Davey – **you're** in.'

And I'm flying.

The thing was, I couldn't tell me mam and dad!

No mobile phones in them days. Or laptops. Or iPads.

Nowt like that.

If you didn't have a telephone in your house, you had to nip out to the nearest call box with a fistful of change. Tell that to the kids today, and they think you're off another planet!

So, my folks didn't actually know I was playing until they got to Wembley and they heard the names being read out over the tannoy!

Amazing, that, when you think of it.

And even now, after **all** the stick over **all** the years, they've never wished I **hadn't** been playing.

I mean – **your** son playing in a cup final at Wembley at 18!

I was the youngest player **ever** to play for Sunderland in a cup final at Wembley.

I still am.

Not many folk remember that.

I do, though.

I had a canny enough career when I **did** leave Sunderland. I went to Orient for a while, then won Player of the Year at Darlington. I helped get them back into the Football League, and then got them promoted to the Third Division. I played for England in the under-20 World Cup in Russia – kept Tony

Adams out of the team.. I wonder whatever happened to him!

They had a big party for me on the day I came back from Russia. All the family there for the homecoming hero, y' know.

And just as I stepped through the door, I notice that the telly's on, and it's *Football Focus*.

And I swear, I haven't even said 'Hiya,' when the bloke says: 'And England went out of the under-20 World Cup in Russia when they lost, thanks to an own goal from David Corner.'

It was like a balloon that someone's just stuck a pin in – and it's gone **bang**!

Let's just say I've been to better parties...

I finished up playing at Gateshead. Until me knees give out. I did me cruciate...

I didn't really know **what** I'd do, after that.

Then I'm on a stag do with some mates. One of them's a copper, and he says: 'Why don't you join the force?'

And I says: 'Me, a copper?'

The number of fights I'd had – or almost had, I didn't think they'd want me – or let me in!

But I went for an interview with Durham Police.

They said: 'What about this incident in 1991 – arrested for being drunk and disorderly?'

I said: 'It was a learning curve.' That's what they always say in football, isn't it, when they lose! 'We'll learn from it.'

And I got away with it!

So there I am – first day out on patrol on me own – about 18 months into the job, still a bit green.

And I'm in Seaham.

And there's a call to say there's been reports of a fight on The Avenue – big street, running right through the town.

So the blue light's on, and I'm straight there.

The thing is, I know I have to be quick, 'cos any second, there'll be 40-odd coppers charging to the same door to get a bit of the action.

Anyway, I'm first on the scene. And when I get there, there's this big bloke standing outside in the street – shirt off, blood all over.

And he's saying: 'I've killed him... I've killed him...'

He kicked off a bit, like, when he saw me – but I got the cuffs on and had him nicked before they all arrived.

I'd never seen a real, live – well, real **dead** – body before, so I was a bit nosey, y' know?

I wanted to see what he'd done to the other bloke.

So I says to the other guys:. 'Keep an eye on him, will you? I'm just going inside.'

And I goes in, and the paramedics are all there, and loads of other coppers. Only no one dares move.

And this bloke's just standing there in the middle of the room, absolutely **covered** in blood.

I mean, he's just **claret**.

There's this gash across his forehead, and it's so deep you can almost see his brains.

It turned me stomach.

But he's just standing there, like he's in a trance. Taking no notice of anyone.

And they're trying to talk to him. But he's just staring straight ahead.

And no one dares do anything, y' know, cos you don't know what this fella's going to do next.

I go in.

And his eyes just lock straight on to mine.

He just follows us around the room, and he's just fixed on **me**.

And then, suddenly, he says: 'Davey?'

And I says: 'All right mate?'

And he's still looking straight at me.

And he's shaking his head.

And he says, slowly: 'Davey Corner?'

And I says: 'Aye, that's me, mate.'

And he says: 'Davey, man... Why didn't you kick it out?'

Y' know, he's **dying**, and all he can think about is the **bloody Cup Final**!

And, it's like, 12 years after!

And I says: 'I don't know mate – but I do know **you** should go to hospital.'

And he says: 'Do y' think so, Davey?'

And I says: 'Aye.'

And he says: 'Well if **you** think so, Davey, that's what I'll do...'

And he walks straight out the door – blood dripping everywhere – and he climbs into the ambulance, and he's carted off to hospital.

And the sergeant sees him going, and he says: 'Well done, Davey – fine bit of policing, that!'

Course, he didn't know the full story... And I wasn't going to tell him!

But that day I **was** a hero – 'cos I helped save the guy's life.

Football, y' know – you lose a game and you hear them on the telly say: 'Tragic mistake, there, that led to the goal.'

But it's not, man. It's never **that** bad.

It **was** my life... but it **is** only a game.

What happened to me wasn't a tragedy.

Before the cup final, everyone's thinking: 'Beat this lot, we'll be in Europe next season.'

Which would have been a big thing, 'cos Sunderland have only been there once, after they won the FA Cup in '73.

I knew lads who'd been too young then to go abroad and watch the team.

They'd waited all that time. Twelve years. Seems like nothing, now!

Back then, in '85, they said if we won – passports ready – they'd go to the first game, wherever it was: Albania, Russia, back of beyond... It didn't matter.

The thing is, even if we'd won, we wouldn't have played in Europe. No English team did. Not for the next five years. Six for Liverpool.

Two months after Wembley, there was Heysel.

Strange, isn't it? People remember the Bradford fire, and

Hillsborough, of course. But Heysel's a bit of blur.

Maybe cos it happened abroad?

In Brussels.

European Cup final: Liverpool and Juventus.

Fans had been drinking all day – which was new to most of them. I mean, you couldn't do that at home. Not then, anyway.

1985: pubs opened for lunch, shut again about two. Back open, half six.

Most places, the shutters came down again, half ten. Twenty-five past, you'd get a stampede for last orders!

So lots of these lads are well tanked-up by the time they get to the ground, cos it's like being on holiday.

And you'd think, 'cos it's Brussels – the capital – you'd think it would be a canny stadium. Y' know, up-to-date. New seats. Fresh lick of paint. Make it smart, like.

You look at it – the pictures, from back then – it was an absolute dump. Terraces falling apart. Bits of concrete everywhere. Old-fashioned turnstiles... Old-fashioned coppers... They didn't know what to expect. Didn't know what hit them.

In them days, football fans were just like cattle. You herded them in, whacked them around with sticks to keep them in line. Treat them like animals – it's no wonder they behaved like animals.

And they just follow the leader. So when the trouble breaks out – and no one knows who really started it – they all just pile in.

There's a line of Belgian coppers. Sort of wire fence, stuck up between the Liverpool lot and what's supposed to be a neutral area – only it's full of Italians. There's a stampede. And this is a **real** one. They're not looking for the bar. They're scrambling for their lives.

Some of them got away.

But then the end wall collapsed...

When you're in that situation, you'll do **anything** to get out. So folk were climbing over the blokes on the bottom of the pile. **Standing** on them. **Real** people under their feet.

Horrific.

And they played the game afterwards!

I remember sitting at home, watching it on telly, and they're telling you the game's been delayed 'cos of the trouble and they're saying people have been hurt, but they're not saying folk have actually **died**!

They waited an hour-and-a-half, and they played the game 'cos they thought there'd be more bother if they didn't!

Unbelievable.

Did it matter who won?

Not really.

One-nil, Juventus, if you're really interested.

There **were** numbers that shouldn't be forgotten, though.

Six hundred.

That's how many were injured.

And 39.

That's how many died.

At first they said: '39 Juventus fans – 39 Italians.'

But that wasn't right.

It was actually 32 Italians, four Belgians, two French fellas and a guy from Northern Ireland.

Aye – Northern Ireland.

Called him Patrick Radcliffe.

Ever heard of him?

Thought not.

Look him up on the internet. You'll hardly find a thing – apart from his name on the list of the dead, in amongst the Giovannis and Lucianos and Luigis.

Apparently he worked for the Irish Public Records Office. He'd been sent over to Brussels on business.

He probably couldn't believe his luck, being out there when the European Cup final was on.

Being Irish – he might even have been a Liverpool fan?

He could've stayed in his hotel room and watched it on the box.

Maybe gone out to one of the bars in the town?

But he must've got a ticket from somewhere. Maybe off someone in the know? Maybe he paid over the odds to a tout? 'Cos he wanted to go to the game so much, 'cos it's a million times better than seeing it on the telly.

Right place, wrong choice.

Now **that's** a **real** tragedy.

Mine wasn't.

One minute into the second half at Wembley. Long ball down our right – their left – and it was going out.

I could have wellied it back down the line. But I thought I'd try to be clever: shepherd it out of play – get the goal kick. We'd then turn around, jog back upfield, and Chris the keeper would lump it back up to halfway and we'd start all over again.

Nil-nil.

Everything to play for.

I saw John Deehan coming towards me. Tried a dummy. Dipped me shoulder one way, so's he'd go the other.

Only, he came round on me blind side and nicked it through my legs.

Aye, a nutmeg.

He sprints into the box. Pulls it back. Chizzy gets a foot in but it comes off Mick Channon and drops straight to Asa Hartford.

Right foot shot, 12 yards out. It's going straight to Chris Turner. Easy save. No problem.

Only Chizzy gets in the way.

He's trying to block it, but it slides off his chest and into the bottom left hand corner.

Our keeper – no chance.

Own goal.

1-0, Norwich.

The goal that won them the cup.

All down to me.

And that's it. My life, changed forever, in just a few seconds.

Never be the same again.

'Cost us the **bloody Cup Final**.'

Simple as that.

And what would I do now?

If I was back near the corner flag with the ball rolling out and John bloody Deehan sneaking up behind me?

All them fans there.

The chance to win the cup.

The chance to be a hero.

Would I stick my foot through it?

Clear my lines?

Put it into row Z?

Nah!

If I'd done that – you lot would never have heard of me!

Evenin' all.

Davey Corner smiles, nods and leaves the stage.

Jeff Brown is a television presenter for BBC One North East and Cumbria, currently trying to find the time to finish a playwriting course with Newcastle's Live Theatre.

7

David Jones saw his first Sunderland match from the directors' box at Roker Park, as a guest of his dad's friend Alan Durban, who just happened to be the manager.

Today he presents Sky's coverage of the Premier League, a job which sometimes requires him to keep his allegiances in check and under wraps.

But his passion for the club is only ever buried just beneath the surface.

SUNDERLAND AND ME

BY DAVID JONES

I've considered myself a proud supporter of Sunderland AFC since I was eight years old but I didn't actually step into Sunderland city centre until a month before my 16th birthday – Saturday, March 24, 1990 to be precise.

You see, I had no family connections with the place, no real geographical link either: I was born in Shropshire and brought up in leafy North Yorkshire.

At least that's what I told people from the south… home for me was five miles outside Middlesbrough! All my friends were Boro fans but there was only ever one team for me.

Anyway, that sunny Saturday back in 1990 I set out from my little village on the 290 bus to Middlesbrough with my friend Julian, a big Boro fan, who I'd persuaded to come to the match with me.

Actually we'd done a deal: if he came to the match with me I would tag along on his date with this girl from Sunderland he'd met on holiday and look after her friend at the same time.

So we took the bus to Middlesbrough, walked through town and then boarded the slow train up the coast to Wearside. It seemed to stop everywhere and take forever but eventually we pulled into the city, full of excitement, nervous too.

We had that fear teenage lads do, especially those from little villages who didn't venture into towns much. Our heads were on the pivot, quietly aware of the dangers lurking from locals who might take offence at our accents, gelled hair, or indeed our spotty faces. And we were a long way from home. I'd pulled my red and white scarf out after the train had left the chimneys of Cleveland behind so I thought we'd be okay. But that wasn't the only reason we were anxious.

Julian was really hoping to impress this girl Emma and in reality I was going on my first blind date: I'd barely met a girl outside of my village before! We met at The Bridges and I remember thinking the Cleveland Centre in Middlesbrough wasn't so bad after all.

My date was very pleasant, Joanne I think her name was, but at 15 and living practically at opposite ends of the earth we both knew this was going to be a one-off. But we chatted, laughed even, while Julian was busy trying to ratchet up his relationship with Emma, which was normally confined to sprawling letters and late night phone calls.

We went to the bowling arcade after treating the girls to a couple of pasties but the minutes were counting down to the main event, and all I could think about was football…

We waved goodbye to the girls, and walked along to Roker Park to take our places behind the goal, halfway down the Roker End where we met my brother who'd managed to borrow my mum's car and would be giving us a lift home.

In truth I'd had second thoughts about dragging Julian along to the game.

Marco Gabbiadini was injured and with this team, watching him was half the fun, actually probably more than half.

Gabbiadini had long been my hero: a devastatingly simple yet effective centre forward; built like a bull with bulging thighs which could propel him beyond most centre halves, and a rocket of a right boot to match.

Time after time he'd burst through the inside left channel, run back across the edge of the box and then with barely any backlift smash the ball into the bottom corner of the net.

At times he was carrying our club but not on this day. There was a young kid in the starting line up against West Ham United, barely older than me but old enough to hypnotise the Hammers. His left foot seemed to have the ball on a string, he shimmied with the balance of a ballerina, swerved like a rugby wing. We were hypnotised too, scarcely daring to believe this kid was wearing red and white and he was ours.

It was one the best Sunderland matches I've ever seen: seven goals and a 4-3 scoreline which didn't really reflect our dominance that day. We looked like we would score every time we went forward, especially when the ball was on the left wing.

My first ever blind date ended up with me falling in love… with Kieron Brady: I'd long since lost my heart to Sunderland. By the time of that first foray into Sunderland city centre I was old hat at visiting Roker Park…

From my first timid steps into that magical old stadium as a wide-eyed youngster in 1982 to Brady's debut eight years later I'd already experienced two relegations, one promotion and a cup final.

This was what football supporting was about, or so I thought; lurching from one extreme to another without rhyme or reason; triumph one year, failure the next.

But it was never dull.

I felt the sense of history around the club, in the wrinkled faces of working men whose soft Sunderland lilt I loved from the first moments I heard the chatter on the terraces.

The stadium never seemed particularly full, we never seemed to win very often but none of that really mattered.

After my first game, I was hooked.

For me it came out of the blue but my dad had probably been planning it for sometime, in much the same way I waste too much thinking time plotting my son's life as a football fan. Perhaps the love will just rub off, but it wasn't the case in our family. My dad was a cricket and rugby man primarily. He'd grown up around Northampton and watched the Saints one week, the Cobblers the next, but as soon as the cricket season started football was forgotten.

And that's how my brother and I were brought up.

I had a bat in my hand as early as I can remember; my dad was only too happy to ferry us around for cricket coaching when he felt we'd outgrown his advice. Rugby too, at Middlesbrough, where Rob Andrew had been schooled in the game – though if he'd been shoved into the front row on a freezing January morning and emerged with a bloody nose and frostbite in his fingers maybe he'd have been lost to the sport like I was?

Football was never forced on me; I found football.

Like all kids we played in the street; epic games that went on for hours, ended by darkness in winter and the call of parents through the summer months.

We lived at the end of a cul-de-sac so the intervention of cars was rare: Jack Charlton lived there too while he was managing Middlesbrough. They would have been the obvious choice of team to support – it was just 15 minutes down the road to Ayresome Park – but it was never an option for me.

I was born in Shrewsbury in 1974. My mum was a teacher there and my dad a civil engineer. He played cricket for Shrewsbury CC; a good team, league winners countless times and while he was there he shared a dressing room with a talented all-round sportsman who had at one time been a very successful footballer.

Alan Durban was a Welsh international, a Football League championship winner at Derby County under Brian Clough and the reason I support Sunderland.

We left Shropshire in 1976, moving to the north east for my dad's work, and five years later Alan followed to manage Sunderland AFC…

The Durbans chose Yarm, just off the A19, as a home. It was 30 minutes to the office at Roker and ten minutes from us.

My dad quickly re-established the friendship and before too long they were turning out for the same cricket team again, but this time in my village, Great Ayton.

It was towards the end of Alan's first season in charge at Roker Park, when I was eight years old, that my dad decided the time was right to take us to our first game of football. It wasn't an ordinary introduction but we weren't really aware of just how privileged our debut was.

Arriving at Roker Park at 1pm on match day we were swept into Alan's office where we were offered a glass of coke; we were already in treat territory here. Alan appeared from somewhere deep in the stadium's bowels and instantly took us off on a tour of the dressing rooms where one or two of the players had already started to arrive.

We walked out through the tunnel onto the pitch and at that moment it dawned on eight-year-old me just how special a moment this was.

(Even now, after walking through dozens of tunnels, that feeling hasn't died, it still feels special be it at Bury or Wembley).

Sunderland were playing Southampton. Their manager, a beefy chap called Lawrie McMenemy appeared when we were back upstairs, pleasantries were exchanged in the manager's office. Perhaps he was sizing it up…

The match seemed to go on for a long time but the sandwiches at half-time went down well and Dad had brought midget gems along for the second half.

The view from the directors box was pretty good, and I knew it must be the best place to sit because the chairman had the entire stadium to choose from and he had decided to sit a couple of rows in front of us.

It was a 1-1 draw but I don't remember either goal; the only thing I remember was the roar. I'd never experienced anything like it. I'd been to a county cricket match at Acklam Park before and enjoyed the cheer of a falling wicket or a lustily hit six but this was on another scale.

It was physical, and not just because everyone around me leapt to their feet. The terrace behind the goal to our right (which I later learned was called the Fulwell End) seemed to come alive as a twisted heap of bodies lurched in rhythm of the celebration.

And the noise. The noise you felt deep in your chest, a great guttural explosion of joy that seemed to hang in the air long after the goal had been scored.

That was it for me. I was hooked.

From that day on my brother Robert and I begged to go to Sunderland as often as we could. Visits became more frequent through the following season and always took the same pattern: Alan's office before the game, sandwiches at half-time, seats in the directors' box.

Our knowledge grew of what it was and who it was we were watching: Gary Rowell, Colin West, Nick Pickering, Chris Turner the names are as familiar to me now as they were then.

My dad's friendship with Alan grew as well.

One New Year's Eve we all went to stay at the Durban house in Yarm. Our parents were going out for dinner, I think at the Tontine, a legendary local eatery, and one of the Durban daughters was tasked with babysitting my brother and me.

I remember being allowed to stay up to watch *Match of the Day* and I'd promised Alan I would keep a close eye on Sunderland's next opponents to see if I could spot anything. Now ten years old, I sat there in front of the TV with pen and paper in hand making notes from the highlights.

I don't recall the opposition I was supposed to be scouting but I do remember watching clips from the Sunderland game and noting down, 'Rob Hindmarch – too slow.'

The next morning Alan received my scout report with good grace and I thought no more of it.

When Hindmarch was sold to Derby the following summer a pang of guilt hit me, had I been to blame? Tragically, when the same Rob Hindmarch died after a battle with motor neurone disease 18 years later I felt it again.

But Alan was no longer at the club by the summer of 1984.

As fate would have it, I was off school sick on March 1 of that same year. With my mum and dad both at work a family friend, George, was tasked to babysit me.

I spent most of the day in bed so I must have been quite sick and I remember nothing else about that day apart from the moment George, who was a sombre, elderly man, came into my bedroom to deliver the worst news imaginable.

'David, are you awake? How are you feeling? I've got some bad news. I've just seen on Teletext something I thought you'd want to know: Alan Durban's been sacked.'

Those words left me hollow, void of thought or feeling; then anger and incredulity followed by tears.

I sobbed and sobbed; first for Alan and his lovely family who'd shown us such kindness and then for me. Did that mean we couldn't go to any more games? What about our seats in the directors' box? Sandwiches at half-time? The tears came again.

I'm sure George was chuckling to himself: like everyone else in Great Ayton, he was a Boro fan.

And so we entered the wilderness years: Alan and his family eventually moved away, as he took a job at Cardiff City and then drifted out of management into scouting for Stoke City and briefly for Sunderland under Peter Reid.

He and my dad lost touch as Alan's main focus became a tennis centre down in Telford, where I'm told even now in his seventies he puts young pretenders to the sword.

I met him again, briefly, about six or seven years ago. I was hosting a Championship game at Coventry City's Ricoh Arena for Sky Sports and our presentation position was down by the pitch.

Up in the stands behind the dugout I saw an elderly man with silver grey hair; a boxer's nose framing that ruggedly handsome face. It was the first time I'd seen Alan for the best part of 25 years.

This mythical figure who'd unwittingly played such a big part in my life, who'd planted the Sunderland seed in my heart and never seen it grow.

I walked up the stand and introduced myself to him, briefly explaining who I was and what I was doing now for Sky.

I don't think he remembered me. The connection in his mind was probably all too vague. If only he knew all the heartache and pain he was responsible for. If only he'd landed the top job at Arsenal, Chelsea or Manchester United, life would have been so much more simple, and probably half the fun.

Regardless of who was in charge, my passion for Sunderland was undimmed. The visits were less frequent and we found a new home in the Clock Stand; wooden seats, less comfy, and certainly no half-time treats, apart from watching the police dog maul pretend victims on the pitch at the interval.

Our new manager Len Ashurst was certainly testing my loyalty. Out went Gary Rowell and Colin West along with another of my favourites Paul Bracewell.

And, cup run apart, it was a season to forget.

Chris Turner performed heroics in goal to drag Sunderland to a Wembley final with Norwich City.

By this time, spring 1985, we were in between houses and gathered around a tiny portable TV in a rented place to watch the Milk Cup final against Norwich.

It was a surreal experience. Watching Sunderland play on

national television was not a regular occurrence, in fact it was probably the only time it happened until Sky surfaced the following decade.

There's a five-minute clip surviving on YouTube: Barry Venison's puffed out chest leading them out; David Corner's aberration (you can hear someone shout 'Away' just before he's robbed of possession); Gordon Chisholm's deflected own goal; and Clive Walker's missed penalty. Gary Rowell would have scored.

For me watching at home, the afternoon ended in tears: this was becoming a theme but I knew even then how rare trips to Wembley were for my club.

To make matters worse, Sunderland were relegated with a whimper. The last home win of the season was in February and just 9,000 turned up at Roker Park to witness the final game of the season. People forget how bad things used to be.

But that was the just the start of it. Lawrie McMenemy was installed to bring the good times back and promptly served up the worst season in Sunderland's history. I got a cuddle from the big man though, turning up to one midweek game in full kit, scarf and hat, we were at Roker as the manager arrived.

He signed my programme, told me he loved my outfit and in that big booming voice promised to win the game. I'm guessing he didn't but I don't recall.

As results got steadily worse the following season Lawrie left but not even Bob Stokoe could save us from the indignity of the Third Division for the first time in our history.

My first play-off experience was listening to a remarkable commentary on the radio, 12 goals shared with Gillingham and losing out thanks to the away goal rule; my second relegation in five years as a football supporter. It felt like the end but it was actually just the beginning.

I loved Division Three: it was the first time in my time as a

Sunderland supporter that the team I adored won more games than we lost.

We were brilliant. The team and the supporters came together. We took thousands wherever we went, handed out thrashings on a weekly basis and romped to promotion.

Two games stand out for me and both were against my dad's team, Northampton.

December 12, 1987: It was my brother's birthday and our first away game as Sunderland fans at the old County Ground, which was tiny in comparison to Roker Park. It stood alongside the cricket pitch, where I'd already witnessed the brilliance of Allan Lamb with a bat in his hand: thankfully their football team wasn't quite in the same class. My dad took us into the home end, don't ask me why. I'm guessing he was probably a little wary of the more excitable travelling supporters around his impressionable boys. It all seemed very strange, The Lads wearing the away kit, the likes of which we'd only previously glimpsed them in during 30-second highlights bursts on Tyne Tees TV with Roger Thames. The locals had really funny accents and sang funny songs about how rubbish Peterborough were. We won 2-0, Marco scored, we celebrated quietly and there wasn't a whiff of danger on or off the pitch. Somehow winning away from home, at somebody else's stadium, felt even better.

By the time the Cobblers arrived at Roker in early May our promotion was inevitable.

How proud we felt taking our places among the 29,000 – by far the biggest crowd I'd ever been part of. The atmosphere was incredible and the team responded, winning 3-1; the Roker Roar had been cranked up to another level. We were heading back to Division Two and for the first time as a Sunderland fan I could start to boast about my club; it was bigger than I had ever realised.

Denis Smith had got us going again and Marco was my hero

but there were others I loved in that era too: Colin Pascoe could open a defence with a clever turn, Brian Atkinson always had time, Gordon Armstrong and Gary Owers were making their mark and Paul Hardyman was catching the eye as a dependable left back with an unstoppable penalty.

By this point I was a very impressionable teenager who fancied himself as a footballer: captain of the school team, playing for the district and with one or two teams around the area showing an interest. And as captain I was also designated penalty taker: always right foot and always slid into the bottom corner to the keeper's left.

That was until Paul Hardyman came along…

I wanted to take penalties like him, a shortish run up and then powered with the side of the left boot into the top left-hand corner. Even if the keeper knew which way it was going there was no chance of him keeping it out given the force with which the ball was struck.

It became my party piece for a while. I practiced and practiced with a run up from straight behind the ball so the keeper wouldn't know whether I was going to hit it with right foot or left. Sometimes I wouldn't even bother with the run up and just step slowly up to the ball concentrating on the Hardyman technique… side foot… slam… top corner. When my schoolmates asked where I learnt it from I would always reply, 'Paul Hardyman.'

The problem was no one around my area had even heard of him… until the Division Two play-off semi-final first leg against Newcastle United.

Perhaps the enormity of the occasion got the better of him but he seemed to change his technique, opting to place rather than power the ball past John Burridge.

Newcastle's keeper couldn't believe his luck; he knew which way it was going, we all did, but he must have expected the ball to sail past his ears rather than nestle in his gloves. Perhaps that's why Hardyman lost his head and tried to remove Burridge's head with his follow-up!

It should have been the turning point in the tie. Roger and his friends at Tyne Tees replayed the incident over and over and by school on Monday everyone knew who Paul bloody Hardyman was. I went back to taking penalties with my right foot after that.

The magic moments at Roker live on in my mind: Gary Rowell's raised arm celebration, countless Marco Gabbiadini goals, Gary Bennett's marauding runs upfield and his tangle with David Speedie under the lights.

A backflip from Peter Beagrie, Don Goodman's hat-trick, Terry Butcher whipping up the crowd; Barnes, Beardsley, Gazza, Scholes breaking our hearts.

And Chris Waddle's delicious free kick to say goodbye to the crumbling old stands.

We watched from the bottom of the Clock Stand that day, rooting around at the final whistle to see if there was anything we could take with us, but it seemed to be the perfect way to say goodbye.

I'd never seen more than 32,000 in that stadium but I'd never heard a noise anywhere like the one to greet Gordon Armstrong's header against Chelsea in the FA Cup quarter-final replay in 1992.

It meant a semi-final date with Norwich at Hillsborough and we had to be there.

The FA Cup has always been special to Sunderland: I was too young for '73 but '92 I will never forget: not so much the final itself, which passed our lads by, but everything that led to that day under the Twin Towers.

After Armstrong's spine-tingling moment against Chelsea the club had to come up with the fairest possible way to distribute their ticket allocation for Hillsborough. The only way, they decided, was to let the fans queue, and queue we did… in our thousands!

My friend Dan had a car and a plan. He picked me up at three o'clock in the morning and we sped north in his Mini Metro to Wearside.

Parking the car around the corner from the ground, our hearts sunk as we arrived at Roker Park to see the mass of bodies already gathered, smothered in hats and scarves, and snaking around the old stands.

It took us about half an hour to choose a queue: none seemed smaller than another but every minute more people were filling the roads around the stadium and panic was rising. As light dawned, to great relief and excitement, the turnstiles started to crank open.

Our queue didn't seemed to be moving and word reached us that behind the Clock Stand a new gate had opened. We gambled. Having stood for hours in one place we left our spot with heavy hearts to chance our arm elsewhere.

Frustration was starting to boil over for some who'd chosen the wrong queue or whose alarm clocks had failed them and realisation dawned that they weren't going to be at Hillsborough; the atmosphere, which had been jovial overnight, was turning sour.

We kept our heads down, kept our non-Sunderland voices quiet and edged closer and closer to the ticket door, finally emerging from the stands clutching a pair of tickets for the FA Cup semi-final. It had all been worthwhile.

Hillsborough itself felt like a dream; the long journey down, the dizzying climb up the towering kop from where the players seemed like red and white dots below, and the emotion of another celebration. Unforgettable.

Later that year, 1992, I left the north east, first for university, which seemed an awful long way away down in Gloucestershire, four hours from home by train.

Matches then became few and far between for me. I had the occasional trip to Molineux with my best mate from college who was a Wolves fan, where we always seemed to do well. Apart from that it was during the holidays and I recall a night at Oakwell after my brother had driven down to Cheltenham to pick up me and all my worldly belongings.

In March 1994, we lost 4-0 to Barnsley but what stands out most is that the bloke standing next to my brother on the terrace had his head split open by a brick thrown into the away end from outside the ground. We were 4-0 down, blood was pouring down this bloke's face, but did he leave? Did he heck.

Next stop for me was Sheffield where I won a place on a post-graduate journalism training scheme, and then Chesterfield, where I took my first steps as a newspaper reporter on the *Derbyshire Times*.

It was a weekly paper, published on a Thursday, so I rarely worked Saturdays. My brother would often drive down from Teesside and ferry us to away games at the likes of Stockport County, Bury and Sheffield Wednesday.

These were good times. This was my favourite Sunderland team playing under my favourite manager – Alan Durban apart, obviously – Peter Reid.

We used to win almost every week: 31 games in one season under Reidy, 26 the season before.

They were a joy to watch, spearheaded, of course, by Niall Quinn and Kevin Phillips but supplied by Nicky Summerbee and Allan Johnston from the flanks.

We were spoilt for choice in midfield with the steel of Kevin Ball and Alex Rae complemented by the craft of Lee Clark, controversial I know, but one of the most sumptuous players I've ever seen in a Sunderland shirt.

Our full-back pair, Chris Makin and Mickey Gray, still haven't been surpassed and nor has Thomas Sørensen in goal, who helped us develop an aura of invincibility.

I got to a lot of games in those two seasons but by the time Sunderland were on the verge of promotion in 1999 I'd moved to London to start my television career at Sky Sports.

April 13, 1999, a Tuesday night at Bury: the night we sealed our return to the Premier League and the night of my 25th birthday. Sunderland were back at Gigg Lane and I'd have loved to have been there too but thankfully the game was live on Sky.

We had become the darling of the channel that season: scoring goals for fun and filling grounds to capacity home and away.

The only thing to dampen my mood was the chronic gastric flu, which had left me bed bound, sweating profusely and losing weight at an alarming rate.

Oh, and it was also the night my Sky was on the blink. So while Super Kev was plundering goal after goal – four in all in a 5-2 win – I was relying on updates from my dad, who after years of sending me local newspaper cuttings, was now resorting to text messages.

It didn't matter that I couldn't see it in the end. I was happy enough lying back on my bed, staring at the ceiling and imagining the joy in those away stands, packed to the rafters and full of people, who through no connection beyond a football team in red and white, had become my people.

Sunderland's journey up the leagues had coincided with my own at Sky; a journey for me which had begun writing scripts at Sky Sports News and culminated in me becoming a Premier League presenter.

Joining the company in 1998 I began to immerse myself in football beyond the north east so that every team would become almost as familiar as my own. It wasn't enough to be passionate about one club, at Sky Sports News you had to be passionate about news from every club. I applied the principles of my studies for a history degree to my journalism: forensic, detailed research which meant that on the road as a TV reporter, which was my next step, I would know the answer to any and every question that came my way.

That news background from the *Derbyshire Times* gave me the skills to spot a story, ask the right questions and then file a report clearly and concisely.

Opportunities kept on coming, first as a rookie touchline reporter and then later in front of camera as a presenter on Sky Sports News.

But the job kept on taking me back to my roots. Ironically, given how much I'd always championed his cause, I was the last TV reporter to interview Peter Reid after a game as Sunderland manager.

It was at Highbury against a rampant Arsenal and the game was live on Premiership Plus, a Sky/ITV collaboration which charged for matches on a game-by-game basis.

Sunderland were expected to lose but perhaps not surrender in the manner they did; two down within minutes and it was over as a contest.

Afterwards Reidy told me he felt like he was speaking to the players in Swahili because they didn't listen to any of the instructions he gave him: the message he received from the board shortly afterwards though was delivered in very plain English.

There followed a New Year's Day game at Old Trafford when a Sunderland team led by Howard Wilkinson had somehow found themselves winning 1-0 with ten minutes left on the clock.

Standing in front of the dugouts at Old Trafford, my stomach was churning, and not just because of the previous night's revelry. Could Sunderland possibly hold on to pull off a mighty upset? And if so, how would Alex Ferguson react to his team losing live on TV to inferior opponents? But this was Manchester United of a different era: David Beckham equalised before Paul Scholes won it at the death. Rather than hand the champagne to Jurgen Macho for a heroic effort in goal I had to interview Beckham as 'man of the match' instead.

Alex Ferguson, Sunderland and me weren't finished there though. There was the infamous game at the Stadium of Light when Jason McAteer wound up our future manager Roy Keane about telling tales in his book. McAteer got an elbow in the head for his troubles while Keane picked up a red card.

On the Monday morning I was sent by Sky to Manchester United's training ground for a pre-arranged interview with Mr Ferguson on the implicit instruction to get his reaction to Keane's latest transgression.

Fergie didn't do small talk before the cameras rolled, certainly not with young reporters like myself. Before we started the interview he looked up at me, fixed me with that stare and said: 'No questions about Keane… right?' Right.

Another game in that same season took me back to Sunderland on touchline duty for the home match with Manchester City. Our team were awful, spanked 4-0 and the Wilkinson experiment was becoming an embarrassment.

Howard took an age to emerge from the dressing room but we'd stayed on air because our producer felt there was another story brewing around Sunderland managers.

I gave Howard a hard time, as any reporter would in those circumstances, but I suppose there was an extra edge to my questions given how much the performance had shamed me as a supporter as well.

Mick McCarthy arrived soon after but couldn't stop the rot: relegation was inevitable. But Mick, who I was very fond of, had the recipe for success in the Championship – he still does – and took us back up at the first attempt.

By now I was a frontline presenter on Sky Sports News and we dedicated an entire afternoon to the open-top bus parade which saw thousands turn out to celebrate the latest promotion. By this stage I'd lost count of how many! It was a lovely moment for me to return to Wearside again to host the coverage.

After four glorious years working alongside Georgie Thompson on Sky Sports News I left the channel in 2007 to become the face of Sky's Football League coverage.

Peter Beagrie, backflip expert himself, was my resident expert and we travelled the length and breadth of the land covering games from the Championship and beyond, always avoiding Sunderland, who by this time had made their way up to the Premier League again and stayed there…

The number one reason for that was Niall Quinn. The club and its fans had penetrated his heart as it once had mine. He'd pulled together the Drumaville Consortium to drag us from the mire, and given us Roy Keane who put the pride back in Sunderland hearts.

As chairman, Quinny had made Sunderland an attractive enough proposition to tempt American billionaire Ellis Short to dip his toes into the murky waters of football, and before long Short was up to his knees.

Since 2011 I've been concentrating solely on the Premier League for Sky Sports. I've seen at close hand the shifts in power between London and the north west fighting it out for the honours whilst always hoping that Sunderland could start to punch above their weight.

As coincidence would have it I've continued to host big games involving my team, always hoping they'd come out on top, but always striving to maintain a level of professionalism that wouldn't offend a non-Sunderland supporting viewer, of which we have many.

The game at Stamford Bridge under Gus Poyet for example, live on Saturday Night Football, when no one gave the visitors any hope against a Chelsea team never beaten at home in the league with Jose Mourinho in charge.

It was the result which really saved Sunderland that season and ended Chelsea's hopes of winning the title but it was my job to maintain neutrality throughout for our viewers.

I managed it just about but I'm sure my voice went up an octave at the final whistle.

Same again towards the end of the 2014-15 season, when Dick Advocaat stepped up into the breach at West Ham, again as fortune would have it, live on Saturday Night Football. The defeat was disappointing but my questions had to be considered and detached from the emotion.

So when, at the end of the 2014-15 campaign, Sunderland, now sensing some reason for hope under Advocaat, needed a point at Arsenal to survive, and I was presenting the Sky coverage in the studio at the Emirates with Thierry Henry and Niall Quinn himself and with a countdown from 20 seconds to off air in my ear, with the programme wrapped up and Sunderland safe for another season, you can understand why I took a split second to collect my own thoughts about what I'd just seen and the impact that would have on Wearside, amongst people, who through football I consider my own. You can understand why I afforded myself a sigh of relief and a smile.

For 33 years I've shared their joy and their pain, and hopefully I will for at least another 33 more.

David Jones presents *Saturday Night Football* on Sky Sports. He is also a *Sunderland Echo* columnist and an ambassador for the Sunderland AFC Foundation of Light.

8

The stresses and strains of football management doesn't so much build character as reveal it.

In his time covering the club for BBC radio, **Nick Barnes** has dealt with nine Sunderland managers.

All of them have had to lead the Black Cats to the Premier League, or battle to keep them in it.

And all of them have proved to be very different characters.

Prepare to meet the men who have led the club from the training ground, the dressing room, the dugout and the touchline.

HOT SEAT

BY NICK BARNES

Nine! There have been nine full-time managers – three of whom were technically 'head coach' – since I began commentating on Sunderland's matches for the BBC in 2003. Nine very diverse characters, ranging from the 'call a spade a spade' Mick McCarthy to the letter-writing Gus Poyet and in the intervening years the cerebral, the fiery, the ebullient and belatedly the openly emotional. One thing remains constant covering Sunderland AFC: It's never dull.

To begin with I will list them. I could leave you for a few minutes of course to let you rack your memory and see if you can name them in the correct order but to use the oft-quoted phrase on the news ahead of *Match of the Day*: 'Turn away now if you don't want to know the results.'

Mick McCarthy; Niall Quinn; Roy Keane; Ricky Sbragia; Steve Bruce; Martin O'Neill; Paolo Di Canio; Gus Poyet and Dick Advocaat. There is a caveat to the list. By the time you read this it may be longer but that is for another chapter…

I found them all good to deal with and none can be faulted in terms of co-operating pre- and post-match. Some, inevitably, were better than others and if I had to grade them in those terms the list would be as follows, from the worst to the best: Paolo Di Canio; Ricky Sbragia; Mick McCarthy; Niall Quinn; Gus Poyet; Dick Advocaat; Roy Keane; Martin O'Neill and Steve Bruce. In Quinn's case there is some mitigation for being middle of the list. Had he stayed in charge and not passed the baton on to Keane he may well have been top of the list, but while he was manager I only dealt with him for a handful of matches and so that particular area of our relationship was short lived, but as chairman he was a natural communicator and more at home in his skin. That is also true of Dick Advocaat. He has been at the club such a relatively short time I haven't been able to build a meaningful working relationship with him but as the weeks passed he was warming to our weekly pre-match press briefings and I have a suspicion he will edge himself closer to the top of my list in his first full season.

The most eccentric was without question Paolo Di Canio. So let's start with the 'madness' of his reign and work our way through to the relative sanity of Steve Bruce's time in charge of Sunderland. Di Canio is not a big man but he has a big presence. He is a whirling dervish and I use the oxymoron purposely. One can't emphasise enough quite what being in the presence of Di Canio for 45 minutes feels like.

Once a week the lads from the *Sunderland Echo* and *The Chronicle* and I would sit down with the diminutive Roman and face a verbal assault. My three or four questions would elicit roughly 20 minutes of impenetrable quasi-English which once even included an impression of a squawking crow. I kid you not. I would get back to my BBC editing kit and have to sit through it all again and try to interpret Di Canio's answers. The crow was uninterpretable. There was no switching off when I had asked my questions either. Di Canio had the habit of turning to me when answering the questions from the newspaper lads as if he was seeking confirmation or approval of something he had just said and so the overwhelming desire for a rest was denied me.

Don't get me wrong. He often had interesting and pertinent points to make and it was clear his footballing ideas were, as far as they went, good on the whole. He was tactically astute and certainly lived and breathed football. His introduction to Sunderland was inevitably coloured by the racism row sparked by his 'Roman' salute in support of Lazio but once that storm had blown over he was able to concentrate on the football. He dressed as you would expect an Italian to dress and could make even shorts and a training top look sharp.

There was an overriding sense though that everything revolved around Paolo Di Canio. He even referred to himself in the third person and never as 'I' or 'me'. In a way that was quite endearing but it was clear his loyalty was to him and everything else was secondary. There was one particularly telling episode: A student from Edinburgh was trying to make a film about Di Canio and to round the piece off was hoping for an interview with the Sunderland head coach. The student tried all the usual channels but with no luck so his last resort was to try and doorstep the Italian at his hotel. This he duly did. Di Canio arrived late in the evening, after another long day at the Academy, surrounded by his coaching staff all of whom incidentally had loyally followed him from Swindon Town. The student apologised for interrupting Di Canio while he was with his friends to which Di Canio replied tellingly: 'These are not my friends. These are my colleagues.'

One change in recent years reporting on football has been the relationship between the media and the manager. Gone are the days – and they weren't that long ago – when you would have the manager's phone number and you could happily call him anytime and he would willingly talk to you off the record. An exception in the last decade at Sunderland was Steve Bruce, but I will come to Steve later. Di Canio was, if the truth be told, not interested in the media. His sole focus was football and he was diligent and conscientious and would spend 16 hours a day at the Academy, often there by 8am and not leaving before 11pm. On that he couldn't be faulted but his man management skills clearly needed work. The stories about his regime are legion and are indicative of why his relationship with his players broke down. For me the true extent of the unravelling came at the Hawthorns following Sunderland's defeat by West Bromwich Albion which, as it turned out, was Di Canio's last in charge. I already had question marks over Di Canio's behaviour when at Crystal Palace he publicly criticised John O'Shea who, while he had made mistakes in the match, to my mind didn't deserve the humiliating humbling of him by Di Canio. A player of O'Shea's standing deserved a little more respect.

In the tunnel following the match at The Hawthorns, Di Canio himself appeared to be unravelling. He had already marched across to the away end and stood stoically in front of the angry Sunderland fans remonstrating loudly behind the goal and the memories of his slide along the pitch at Newcastle United seemed distant and irrelevant. The fans were angry after a poor start to the season and while Di Canio will forever be remembered for overseeing a 3-0 win at St James' Park, which was as unexpected as it was triumphant, he will be remembered more for the seeming madness that followed. His post-match interview that afternoon was rambling and incoherent. Or I should say more rambling and incoherent than usual. The writing was inevitably on the wall.

I do Ricky Sbragia a disservice placing him low on my list. Ricky couldn't have been a more obliging or genial manager but he was clearly uncomfortable with the role and interviews were, I suspect, a necessary chore for him. After a bright start to his tenure he too saw Sunderland become mired in yet another inevitable relegation fight. Much like Niall Quinn, and I will bracket the two together here, he was far more comfortable as a coach as Quinn was as a diplomat, than as a football club manager.

Mick McCarthy was the first manager I dealt with at Sunderland. I have always got on fine with him and to this day if I see him he will say hello and stop for a chat. Salt of the earth as they say. He disliked – and I daresay still dislikes – the media. He distrusted the written press but was more tolerant of radio, judging it was harder to twist his words. He was blunt but fair though and had a tendency in post-match interviews to disagree with most of the things you said. He was to my mind under-rated at Sunderland. History is treating him more kindly, but at the time he was heavily criticised while in reality he was trying to keep the team in the Premier League with not one arm, but both arms tied behind his back. Quite naturally, towards the end of his time as manager, with the team losing match after match, he became tetchy and indignant but in the circumstances that is highly understandable.

The most memorable episode though occurred in a pre-match press conference ahead of a game with Watford. My colleague Simon Crabtree was interviewing Mick ahead of me for Metro Radio and Simon did at times knowingly push the boundaries. On this occasion he mischievously asked Mick if 'he liked Cox', a reference to the Watford centre-half Neil Cox but asked in such a way that left no misinterpretation to the imagination, as he, I, everyone else in the room and Mick well knew. Mick was apoplectic. His reply to Simon was peppered with expletives. Actually, it wasn't peppered it was laden with expletives. Simon and he didn't speak to each other for some weeks but Mick eventually held out the olive branch at the Withdean Stadium ahead of Sunderland's match at Brighton. Mick doesn't suffer fools, but knowing that you accordingly treated him with respect and he, in turn, would reciprocate. The same applies to Roy Keane, more of which later.

The Ides of March probably have more meaning at Sunderland than any other club as it is around that time the axe seems to fall. Gus Poyet's reign spiralled out of control in the spring of 2015 but his year-and-a-half in charge was not without its moments.

He was passionate and focussed and unpredictable. He was not dissimilar to Paolo Di Canio with his approach to the media but embraced it more than the Italian. I am not sure the Uruguayan was ever comfortable with his title but one can't afford to be too fussy for the chance to 'coach' in the Premier League. He was certainly more comfortable with his 'locals session', which I alluded to with Paolo Di Canio, than when he first arrived at the club, but then that is the benefit of building a bond of trust with the manager/coach.

I have to deal with the manager week-in, week-out and it is inevitably a rollercoaster. It certainly was with Poyet who careered from the heights – a League Cup final and two successive wins at Newcastle United – to the lows of an 8-0 defeat at Southampton and an FA Cup exit at League One Bradford City and a few uncomfortable points in between. I think it is fair to suggest his fan base at Sunderland was always shaky and one of the reasons he hadn't been given as rocky a ride as he could have was because the supporters accepted the club was in dire need of some stability which has arguably been lacking since the departure of Mick McCarthy.

Poyet brought a fresh vibrancy to the club largely because he is himself larger than life and it is arguable that while he may have alienated many, his ambitions were underpinned by his desire to be a winner. It was painful for Sunderland fans and the football was at times laborious and pedestrian but ultimately Poyet targeted an ideal along the lines of the model adopted by Swansea City, and that template is still the model for Dick Advocaat.

These things don't happen overnight and there was always a major question mark over whether Poyet would stay at the club long enough to see his plan through? He was an endearing character to deal with. He can be humorous and indulgent and his love of football shone through. He generally dealt with any question or issue addressed to him. His tendency to go on the defensive though proved to be an Achilles heel and was, to a greater degree, the catalyst for his 'open' letter to the fans following the club's defeat at Bradford. I applaud that. I liked his refreshing candour and I think it would be a step backwards if he was forced to rein in his heart on his sleeve approach.

Encouragingly he himself says he is too old to change his ways and we were assured of further outbursts while he remained in charge at Sunderland. His antics on the touchline at Hull City at the culmination of which Steve Bruce had to be restrained by the assistant referee are a case in point. His reign unravelled following Sunderland's draw at Swansea with the first signs of his personal unhappiness evident in the home defeat by the hitherto luckless Queens Park Rangers who, until their match at the Stadium of Light, had not earned a point away from Loftus Road all season.

Poyet's failure to address Sunderland's tactical shortcomings during that match were rubber-stamped in the subsequent home game with Aston Villa – 4-0 down at half-time and Poyet seemingly unwilling rather than unable to halt the tide in the first 45 minutes his tenure was hanging by a thread and his demise was all but certain following the pantomime at the start of the second half when Seb Larsson appeared three minutes into the second period having been receiving treatment for a foot injury in the dressing room. Sunderland chairman and owner Ellis Short admitted that incident was the final straw. Ultimately the Latin American temperament doesn't appear well suited to life on windy Wearside.

So why if Poyet was good to deal with does he come behind Roy Keane, Martin O'Neill and Steve Bruce on my list ? It is a fine line and purely personal. I got on with and liked Gus Poyet but if push came to shove I would prefer to deal with the others before him on my list.

Dick Advocaat. Well he came out of the blue, or to quote Sir Bobby Robson when he saw a former colleague of mine who he barely tolerated: 'Your questions come off the moon!' Advocaat may as well have come off the moon. No one saw his appointment on the horizon but he had been sounded out some weeks before, when Poyet's grip on his position was clearly loosening.

Advocaat was the recommendation of Hans Gilhaus, a former Dutch international and now Sunderland's co-ordinator of their European scouting network. 'Give Dick a call,' he told sporting director Lee Congerton. So Congerton did. Dick expressed his interest and availability and within days of Poyet's departure was appointed head coach for Sunderland's nine remaining matches of the 2014-15 season.

The 67-year-old's first press conference appeared to set the tone. He arrived with his long standing assistant Bert Van Lingen and his first team coach Zeljko Petrovic in tow and he answered the questions fired at him curtly and peremptorily, but politely. He clearly wasn't a fan of the media. My first meeting with him followed suit. Very much his own man he bucked the tradition of conducting the television interviews first and newspapers second and reversed them, apparently a bid to get what he perceived as the most awkward session out of the way first. The 'locals' are last so what does that say about us?!

Actually being last in the press conference pecking order brings its benefits as Dick, like his predecessors, always appears more relaxed in the company of less than a handful of reporters. As the weeks passed he became more relaxed and his demeanour reflected that in his interviews. He always avoids direct questions about individuals but openly discusses tactics and the team as a whole. That is all part of the process of getting to know the man in charge. You poke and prod and eventually you establish the profitable areas and the areas not to pursue, although that doesn't preclude one from ever asking the question.

It was rare he would be unaccompanied by Bert and Zeljko, but I enjoyed their presence. Bert will inevitably chip in here and there and he and Dick unquestionably have a very close working and personal relationship. Advocaat was without doubt falling in love with Sunderland as every match passed. The fans, the players, all got under his skin.

The derby win laid the foundations. It was the best derby atmosphere at the Stadium of Light in some years and Jermain Defoe's goal, breathtaking in its execution, inferred a status on both him and Advocaat that whatever happened would mean their names would always be spoken with affection. Advocaat built on that. His drive and focus remained stubbornly on Sunderland staying up and he never once wavered from his belief he would pull it off. He exudes an air of benign calm and confidence and that filtered through the club. Every player I spoke with talked warmly of him and unusually, as players notoriously toe the party line, all publicly said they would love Advocaat to stay.

I was enjoying our weekly pre-match jousting, which reached a zenith following Sunderland's 0-0 draw at Arsenal which secured Premier League football for another season, when having watched Advocaat cry on the touchline at the Emirates, I reduced him to tears again ahead of Sunderland's final match at Chelsea. Sunderland had got under Dick Advocaat's skin and Advocaat has got under mine.

There is no question my voice was shaky in what I assumed would be our last interview at Chelsea and Advocaat, without saying as much, was undeniably torn. If his initial appointment had come off the moon the news he was going to stay came from Mars. It made mine and I suspect every Sunderland fan's summer.

From the benign magnificence of the Little General to the seemingly simmering heartlessly fearsome… how appearances can be so deceptive, even if he was once infamously quoted as asking if Clive Clarke had a heart…

Roy Keane.

Roy Keane is an enigma. Feared, reviled, admired in good measure, the jaundiced, these days hirsute, Irishman was a total pleasure to deal with in the time he was at Sunderland. The first beard was grown when he was at Sunderland in the weeks leading up to his departure and has now become synonymous with an assumption that beard equals problems. To an extent I think that may have been true to start with but now I think Keane grows it because he knows it stokes speculation and one thing became clear in his time at Sunderland, he loves a joke and he would be highly amused by the reactions to his beard.

I, like everyone else I am sure, greeted his appointment with some trepidation as his reputation preceded him. However, from the very first he was nothing but polite and respectful. He was a stickler for time-keeping so at the end of his first season, when he kept me waiting an hour for an end of season interview for the club, he was mortified and very apologetic. He was not one for making 'friends' of the media. I don't think he referred to me by name in all the time he was manager and he certainly didn't use anyone else's names in the media pack.

I was amused several years after he left Sunderland when rather randomly I was waiting to meet someone outside Carlisle Civic Centre one cold December afternoon. From the corner of my eye I saw someone walking down the road with a young woman and sure enough my suspicions were confirmed when he got closer. Yes, it was Roy Keane. I was some 20 feet away across the concourse and he barely broke stride but he did smile in recognition. That is as close as you would get to what could in any way be described as having a relationship with Roy Keane. The young woman was clearly his daughter before you start jumping to all the wrong conclusions.

If Roy Keane was in a good mood at his pre-match press conference, which he generally called for an 8.45am start and was rarely late, he would, in the small room where he met me and the other local lads, crack jokes and then laugh at them. I think we were all too scared not to laugh along with him but on the whole he was actually quite a good comedian. Without question I am sure he enjoys a good laugh.

He always kept you on your toes and I revelled in the weekly joust. There was no question of turning up to interview Roy Keane on a wing and a prayer. You had to know your stuff and there were occasions when your mettle was tested. Following Sunderland's 2-0 defeat at Newcastle United, Keane was subjected to a great deal of criticism through the week from supporters using social media and message boards to deride his tactics at St James' Park. I had no choice but to challenge him when we next met on the Friday morning ahead of the following match. I raised the issue and said his formation had come under much scrutiny and criticism. His immediate steely-eyed response was: 'What were my tactics?' It is at that point you feel your stomach muscles tighten and your face beginning to flush, but it is also the point at which you know you have to respond. There was no question of mumbling and fudging some half-hearted excuse of an answer. I had to man up as they say.

'Well…' was my nod to a fumble, 'You played Kenwyne Jones up front with Andy Reid just off him…' and there followed a moment's silence, which felt like an eternity with Keane just staring at me, before he quietly replied: 'Yes.'

From there the interview flowed like any other. Keane used

the technique often away from home in particular to unnerve reporters. He loved to challenge a question he didn't like and I think he quietly respected any journalist who was prepared to fight their corner. It was the tradition of mutual respect.

Roy Keane never shied away from controversy or, as happened on a few occasions, heavy defeats, notably at Everton and Chelsea, though at Goodison Park it took him a good hour to surface from the dressing room. When he did so he was cool, calm and collected and as is so often the case the manager has more to offer following a defeat than following a win. There is more to talk about.

His weakness, Keane's Achilles heel? Without question, in my mind, was his lack of a strong right-hand man. Both at Sunderland and at Ipswich Town, Keane relied on his close friend Tony Loughlan, who with the greatest respect seemed to garner little or no respect within the dressing room and wasn't strong enough to stand up and make the decisions that Keane needed to be made. There were clearly times, especially in the Premier League, when Keane needed the level headedness of an experienced older coach at his shoulder and it is interesting that he became a number two at Aston Villa to Paul Lambert which I wondered was an acknowledgement he needed to explore the importance of the role which is a key one at any club. He is of course number two to Martin O'Neill with the Republic of Ireland.

Martin O'Neill was the dream ticket at Sunderland. He was the manager the club had always seen as the perfect fit. He had turned down their overtures once before but eventually the temptation for the Ulsterman who had supported Sunderland as a boy was too great. He was instantly likeable and charismatic. I warmed to him immediately and his pre-match press conferences in particular were a pleasure to attend. He would address you by name and he, not unlike Roy Keane in this respect, was a challenging interviewee, happy for a riposte and to challenge my questions, which believe me he often did. Martin O'Neill is an intellectual giant among football managers, though he is not the sort to patronise or wear his intellect on his sleeve as some sort of badge of honour. Where O'Neill came into his own was with his 'off the record' chats in which he would talk football, crime, music and literature and those conversations were a highlight of every week. Like Keane he is also a very good comic and would have us in stitches with many of his stories of his time as a player at Nottingham Forest. His music knowledge is extensive and his love of criminology fascinating. He would talk of all and there was always an air of disappointment when he had to take his leave of us. To this day Martin O'Neill still has my copy of Seamus Heaney's *Collected Poems* and I cannot think of a better or more suitable home for the tome. If you are reading this, Martin, it is an honour for me for you to keep the book.

So why did Martin O'Neill fail at Sunderland? The argument continues to this day that had he not been sacked he would have won the two matches Sunderland needed to win to stay up and, with hindsight and Wigan Athletic's involvement in the FA Cup, it is a persuasive argument. Sunderland were actually no better off when the season ended as they had been when Paolo Di Canio took over and while O'Neill's football had become laboured and boring to watch it is not inconceivable he would have engineered those two wins.

Of course we will never know but it is interesting to compare O'Neill and Poyet in terms of their progression at the club and where they both were or are after similar lengths of time in charge. The accusation levelled at Poyet was his football had become similar to O'Neill's but most Sunderland fans would accept the club needs stability and Poyet seemingly offered that. If that is the case then it is a fair argument that

Martin O'Neill was harshly done by but that is football and we have to move on. Steve Bruce could argue he too was harshly treated, sacked in November with barely a third of the season gone.

Steve Bruce is what we football reporters would describe as 'old school' but none the worse for it. In fact we embrace the fact. By 'old school' I mean he knew us all by name and was happy for us to call him anytime and he would give me the team before every match secure in the knowledge he was safe to do so. It is all about building trust and Bruce was and still is, canny enough to understand the nature of the relationship between the media and the manager.

Bruce was renowned for mixing his metaphors and we would all take great delight in laughing at his corruption of the English language but by so doing he was not only happy to laugh at himself but he was building a long lasting relationship with the reporters. I don't think there were any of us he fell out with, and if he did it was short lived. His time-keeping wasn't the greatest and that one day prompted my eight-year-old daughter to write him a letter reprimanding him for keeping us waiting and to admonish him for not wearing a tie and looking smart. Steve Bruce is the kind of manager who you could happily give such a letter and he would take it in the spirit in which it is was intended.

In fairness Roy Keane was similar in that respect and that reminds me of a morning when an endearing colleague from Metro Radio called Jenny, who always appeared dressed as if she had come straight from a nightclub and had body piercings in places you and I wouldn't dream of piercing addressed Keane with: 'I understand you've had a narky letter from Jack Warner?' Even Roy Keane couldn't suppress a smile.

It is also worth remembering that Steve Bruce took Sunderland to their best top flight finish since Peter Reid's two seventh placed finishes and there have only been a few occasions since the 1950s that Sunderland have finished in the top ten. His critics will argue the tenth place he engineered was by default as on the final day of the season at West Ham results elsewhere conspired in his favour and that 13th or 14th would have been more realistic, but even if that was the case 14th place in the context of where Sunderland has finished in recent seasons is not to be sniffed at.

Steve Bruce is an avuncular good-natured ebullient character. It is easy to forget when you see him now squeezed into a tracksuit on the touchline that he was one of Manchester United's finest centre-halves. Being a Geordie it was said from the minute he was appointed as Sunderland manager that at some point it would become a stick with which to beat him.

Cruelly that is exactly what happened, though Bruce hasn't helped himself with his comments subsequently directed at the club, even though they were entirely understandable in the light of the abuse he suffered when he stood alone on the touchline in charge of his final match at home to Wigan Athletic. No manager should be subjected to the vitriol and hate that seemed to pour down on the hapless Bruce that afternoon and I know it hurt him intensely.

I was reminded watching Sunderland's match at Hull City last season in which Steve Bruce uncharacteristically lost his temper and tried to attack Gus Poyet that many of the Sunderland team that evening were signed by Bruce. Lee Cattermole, Seb Larsson, Wes Brown and John O'Shea – four of Sunderland's best players – were brought to Sunderland by Bruce.

The fact they all remained at the club four years after he left is testament to the quality he brought to the club even if all have their critics. Bruce also brought Darren Bent, Danny Welbeck, Asamoah Gyan and Niklas Bendtner to Sunderland and not since Niall Quinn and Kevin Phillips had Sunderland had more effective forwards. It was through no fault of Steve Bruce's that the club were unable to hold on to any of them.

History, I suspect, will treat Steve Bruce and Mick McCarthy more kindly and both deserve the revision and recognition, as to an extent does Martin O'Neill. I think we would all agree the appointment of Paolo Di Canio was a mistake. We can look back at his tenure now and laugh but at the time he blew through the club like a tornado and arguably left as much collateral damage.

No blame can lie at the door of Ricky Sbragia and Roy Keane has since written a very interesting record of his time in charge and what stands out is the clear affection he still holds for Sunderland and his admission he made a mistake in leaving. Keane was perceptive enough to realise the club has enormous potential and to realise that potential needs stability. The very fact that in 11 years I have overseen nine managers and a couple of caretaker spells under Kevin Ball, suggests that stability remains elusive. I also find it interesting how the club shifted from being very British under Mick McCarthy to a very cosmopolitan continental club under Gus Poyet, but back again now to a very experienced pair of hands, eschewing the path the club were going to go down in probably appointing the inexperienced Paul Clement, assistant to Carlo Ancelotti at Real Madrid, as head coach.

It is encouraging that Sunderland have been a Premier League club for nine successive seasons *but* it has done so by the skin of its teeth when Sunderland should be a club well established every season in mid-table. The reasons for that are myriad and for another chapter of a future volume of this series, but clearly stability is a key factor.

The appointment of Dick Advocaat was, in my mind, a breath of fresh air and gives the club more stability than it has had in some seasons. Advocaat is the first close season appointment since Steve Bruce and offers the club the breathing space to find his successor and build on the legacy that Advocaat has already left in the space of a very short time. Ellis Short and Lee Congerton are to be applauded for 'harrassing' Advocaat to stay. Both realised they had at the club the ideal candidate, especially when it became so glaringly obvious there was a dearth of suitable replacements and they stubbornly refused to let their little bit of Holland off the hook. As it is Sunderland it won't be a smooth ride, that goes without saying, but I do believe Dick Advocaat will deliver a more stable season and the Ides of March 2016 shouldn't be feared.

All the managers and coaches I have worked with at Sunderland have brought something different to the table and I can honestly say not one of them has been difficult to work with. In stark contrast to Ruud Gullit when he was the manager at Newcastle United. Having experienced working with Advocaat's compatriot, those I have had the privilege to work with at Sunderland have been a breath of fresh air, yes, even Paolo Di Canio.

In conclusion, I don't think any of the other eight – apart from arguably Niall Quinn, who managed through absolute necessity rather than any career ambition – were or are bad managers. Inexplicably it seems the problem is managing Sunderland. But have we finally got a man in Dick Advocaat who has the handle on that?

Nick Barnes has been Sunderland AFC commentator for BBC Newcastle since 2003. He loves to adorn match days in a tweed jacket and carries a matchbook which, through the conduit of social media, has become a viral sensation.

9

Doug Weatherall knew Brian Clough when he was a centre forward who scored almost a goal a game.

Long after he was forced to retire early after sustaining a terrible injury, Clough was held up as the number nine all his successors were compared with – almost all of them unfavourably.

Clough really was that good as a player, and, as he liked to point out, when it came to football management, he was in the top one.

Several opportunities to appoint Clough passed Sunderland by and, as Doug argues here, it's very likely he's the greatest manager the club never had.

CLOUGHIE

BY DOUG WEATHERALL

My brief for this Sunderland book is to focus on Brian Clough. So I must confess at the outset that, to many readers, it won't be too objective a view. It will be as biased as can be – for the simple reason that I believe he was a genius as a player and an even greater genius as a manager.

The older I get – and I am 82 at the time of writing – the more I am convinced he could have managed at his age when I first interviewed him; he was 20. His strongly held opinions hardly altered.

It was early in the 1956-57 season. He had played a few first-team games for Middlesbrough the previous season, but manager Bob Dennison still started the new campaign with Doug Cooper at centre forward. Fortunately for me and, of course, Middlesbrough, by the time I saw Brian play, Mr Dennison had had the sense to give him the number nine shirt.

My first viewing of him in action was on the night of Wednesday, September 12, 1956. I was so taken with him that I reported for the old *Daily Herald* that 'he was the most exciting player to enter a penalty area I had seen in years.' Almost needless to say, he scored in a 2-1 Boro win that night.

I was so convinced Brian would become one of the greatest finishers football has ever known that I arranged a few days later to do an in-depth interview with him. How could I ever forget that first long chat?

One of the predictable questions for a reporter to ask a

young footballer – and over my long career I have asked it hundreds of times – is: 'Who has helped you develop as a player?' The Clough answer was anything but predictable. Yet, as radio listeners and TV viewers were to learn in his later years, it was stingingly honest and unambiguous.

'First,' he said, 'I'll tell you who hasn't helped me.' Then he listed three well-known names. He didn't say the comment was off-the-record. But to protect him and to safeguard the reputations of the professionals he mentioned I didn't use those names in my piece. (They're all dead now but, for the feelings of their descendants, I won't use them now, either.)

Brian did go out of his way to stress who had helped him: Mickey Fenton, the former Boro centre forward who coached the reserves, and Jimmy Gordon, the former wing-half who inspired the juniors. He thought so much about Mr Gordon, indeed, that he was to employ him as the first-team coach at clubs he later managed.

Happily, that first major interview with Brian was a prelude to a friendship which lasted to the day he died. But, my goodness, did he make headlines! Initially through phenomenal scoring, tragically through the injury which was to end his playing career, excitingly through winning trophies and, shamefully on the part of the Football Association, through his being ignored when our country needed a manager.

First, though, to Brian's actual play. I just loved watching him. The object of a team is to score goals – and he was just fabulous at achieving that object. Some years ago, as I was clearing stuff from my desk, I came across old notebooks. My note-taking style was always to print in capital letters the scorer's surname in my description of a goal.

There, on page after page for Boro and later Sunderland matches, I saw in bold:

CLOUGH. CLOUGH. CLOUGH.

Hat-tricks were frequent. Still fresh in my memory is what happened 57 years ago. On the first day of the 1958-59 season. Brighton and Hove Albion, newly promoted to the Second Division for the first time, had the misfortune to start at Ayresome Park. 'Just our luck!' said Brighton manager Billy Lane, after Boro had won 9-0, Clough having scored five times.

In those days, I used to collect my father – a true Sunderland supporter – from his home in Seaham, and drive him to Ayresome Park. My Dad almost invariably saw a Clough hat-trick and Brian said: 'Keep bringing him!'

Such was the consistency of Brian's scoring that, despite Boro's league status, I was among the first observers to urge his recognition by England. He had represented England under-23s and England B but I believed firmly there was no greater English centre forward then than Brian Howard Clough.

It was on a day an England team announcement was due that I decided to be with him as he heard whether he would be chosen for the first time.

This brought a new experience for me. After they had trained, Messrs Clough and Boro goalkeeper Peter Taylor went game-shooting. The great marksman proved pretty useful with a rifle too. The odd partridge didn't live to tell the tale, but I was delighted to report he had been chosen to lead England's attack as the number nine against Wales at Ninian Park, Cardiff, in October 1959. Unfortunately, for him and his country, England managed only a 1-1 draw. Still, he retained his place for England's next test 11 days later, against Sweden at Wembley. Again he didn't score and England lost 3-2.

He was not to be chosen again for England. Yet I believed the middle three of England's five-man attack selected for both of his appearances didn't make sense. The inside-forwards to his right and left, Jimmy Greaves and Bobby Charlton, were, of course, superb players, but both were themselves more like orthodox centre forwards. A schemer like Johnny Haynes or George Eastham would have been more logical in my opinion.

Still, Brian's goals continued for Boro and you would think someone who scored so often would be loved by team-mates. Well, Brian was by a few Boro lads, but certainly not all. He was the team's captain, so you can imagine how he felt when a majority of the regular 11 signed a letter to the club's management, asking for Clough to be skipper no longer. 'That's broken my heart,' he told me before asking for a transfer. Never have I reported a more poignant quote, but, coming from anyone with normal sensitivity, it could be expected.

Brian's patience was sorely tried. You would think a Second Division club with a scorer averaging nearly a goal a game would be red-hot favourites for promotion, yet that was never achieved in Brian's time, mainly because, despite the high numbers in the goals for column, there were too many under goals against.

Witness a game at Charlton Athletic. Again you would think a team scoring six away goals would win, yet Boro managed only a 6-6 draw! The following week, as Brian put on his boots at Stoke City, he asked Boro centre half Ken Thomson, 'If we score seven do you think we'll get a point.' Boro lost. The late Thomson, like players for other clubs, was later jailed for match-fixing.

Clough's request for a move was turned down, but repeated ones eventually led to a £55,000 transfer to Second Division Sunderland in July 1961. Wearside supporters were delighted. So were his new playing colleagues and the manager who bought him, Alan Brown.

There was no stricter disciplinarian than Mr Brown. As I soon discovered, when I wrote something which upset him, he could be devastating with his condemnation. But Brian respected such discipline so much that he would try to repeat what Brown preached when he himself entered management.

One of the Clough stories I enjoyed writing most followed a drawn game at Home Park, Plymouth, on November 10, 1962. Sunderland, striving for promotion to the top division, had trailed by a goal to Argyle until near the end when Brian snapped up a half-chance and scored the equaliser.

That was a fair match story, anyway, but what made it better was what Charlie Hurley, Sunderland's revered centre half and captain, had to say after the match. As the players relaxed in the communal bath, Charlie told Brian: 'It's great having you in the team.' Remembering the dressing room trauma of Middlesbrough, that was music to Brian's ears.

I collected that match angle as Brian and I travelled in a car driven to a country pub by a contact of Peter Taylor, who was to be Brian's illustrious managerial right-hand man. But not before I had been mightily embarrassed in front of the formidable Alan Brown.

It was the custom on those away trips for Mr Brown to have dinner in the team's hotel with the travelling north east pressman. So the late Bill Butterfield (*Sunderland Echo*), Alf Greenley (*Newcastle Journal*) and Len Hetherington (*Evening Chronicle*) and I were having our meal when Brian appeared at the dining room door to announce in that firm tone of his: 'Hurry up, Doug!'

Now managers aren't keen on pressmen consorting with players but Brian didn't mind anyone knowing he was a friend of mine. I bolted down the last of my meal, mumbled my goodnight and exited far less boldly than Brian had entered. Still, the patter with the particularly happy Brian that night was terrific and I knew I had that lovely Hurley-Clough angle to pen the next morning.

Over the years I have been asked what was the greatest goal Brian scored and, of course, the choice is wide. Yet I could never forget a League Cup one he notched against Norwich

City at Roker Park. Sunderland lost the tie 4-1, yet his goal was probably his most spectacular. He was near the grandstand outer angle of the Roker End penalty area when the ball arrived to him. With back to goal, he promptly volleyed right-footed over his left shoulder and into the top far angle of the goal. It was so good that years later his Norwich marker in that match, Welsh international Ollie Burton, told me he just couldn't believe it had happened.

Brian, in fact, was more noted for – and more proud of – goals he popped in from inside six-yard boxes. 'That's where real finishers get their goals,' he would say. And that was my argument after Newcastle United supporters said after successive Tyne-Wear draws at St James' Park: 'He just had to tap in his goals.'

It was then I would cite the wicket-taking of Brian's fellow Yorkshireman, Freddie Trueman, whose critics would say many of his wickets were of tail-end batsmen. 'If taking their wickets is so easy why don't other bowlers claim them?' I reasoned.

I was amused when a young winger, Tommy Mitchinson, about to make his debut, suggested to Brian that he be at the near post if he got to the byline and was ready to centre. Brian, noted for near-post chance-taking, said quietly: 'I'll be there.'

Brian undoubtedly had the ability to make final scores unfair on the opposition. Two games come quickly to mind. In a Middlesbrough match at Anfield, Liverpool attacked for almost the whole 90 minutes. Final score: Liverpool 0 Middlesbrough 2, thanks to Brian converting Boro's only two chances.

I also recall vividly a remarkable Sunderland match at Huddersfield Town. In one of the most one-sided first halves I have ever seen Huddersfield did everything but score. Even by his own outstanding standards Sunderland goalkeeper Jim Montgomery was utterly brilliant.

As we enjoyed our tea and pork pies at the interval,

colleagues speculated it was only a matter of time before Huddersfield scored. I asked what more could Huddersfield produce that they hadn't already shot and headed at Monty? But I certainly didn't anticipate what was to come.

Early in the second half, George Herd put Brian in possession and, bang, the Red and Whites led 1-0. Not long afterwards, a Herd repeat and, bang, a repeat from Brian. Then George Mulhall made the final score Huddersfield Town 0 Sunderland 3. It was crazy – but that was Clough.

The great scorer went out of his way to pay tribute to what Monty had done. 'It was Jim who kept us in it,' said Brian, who never forgot the keeper's brilliance. Seasons later he was to sign him for Nottingham Forest.

It was in that Huddersfield game that Brian completed the quickest 200 goals in Football League history. The result took Sunderland into second place in the table. They were now red-hot favourites for promotion. Little did I or anyone else guess that only three games later the fabulous reign of the finest Sunderland centre forward I had ever seen would be over.

Ironically, Brian's last pre-injury away match would be at Middlesbrough. Watched by a crowd of 43,509 – huge by Boro standards – it was drawn 3-3, Brian almost inevitably scoring, this time between strikes from Mulhall and Herd. It would be his last pre-injury goal and the penultimate one before his eventual retirement as a player.

After a 2-1 home win over Leeds United, Mulhall and Hurley scoring for Sunderland, the Boxing Day visitors to Roker Park were Bury. Their centre half and captain was Bob Stokoe, later to be the managerial FA Cup-winning 'Messiah' of Sunderland.

Because of ice and snow, match postponements were common on December 26, 1962, but referee Kevin Howley, from nearby Billingham-on-Tees, declared the match on although the surface was far from ideal. Sunderland surprisingly lost the game 1-0 but remained second in the table.

The haunting memory, though, remains of Clough's injury. The long forward pass from Sunderland's left towards the Fulwell End was followed in the air by Brian, his right-leg stretching, the main weight of his body being backwards, he being unaware that Chris Harker, Bury's north east born goalkeeper, was advancing to collect. Most of Harker's body weight was directed forward.

As Sunderland trainer Arthur Wright raced on to the pitch to attend to Brian, Stokoe suggested to Mr Howley that Clough was 'just foxing'. I knew instantly Brian was seriously hurt; he hardly missed a match for any reason. Now, in his agony, his right hand was pounding the pitch.

The football world and the Sunderland public in particular awaited the medical verdict with fingers crossed. I got it exclusively – from Brian himself. Such are the strictures of modern football, it wouldn't happen these days, but I got into Monkwearmouth Accident Hospital in Newcastle Road, Sunderland, and Brian's room.

'How are you, bonny lad?' I asked. No messing, Brian replied: 'I'm told everything in the knee has gone.' I had a good idea what that meant and I reckoned I would never see my pal play again. That same night I told Alex Mutch, the Newcastle United physiotherapist, what Brian had told me. 'Then he's finished,' said Alex.

When the news was made official Sunderland supporters were devastated. Their hero had scored 24 league goals by the time of his injury. Their fears for the club were only too dramatically justified. Sunderland stayed well enough in the promotion race to go into their final game of the season needing only a point to be sure of going up but rivals Chelsea won 1-0 at Roker and 7-0 in a re-arranged Stamford Bridge match with Portsmouth to squeeze Sunderland down into third place.

I was certain that, but for Brian's injury, Sunderland would have been promoted long before that final match. And goodness knows what his final goals tally would have been.

Brian, 27 at the time he was injured, was at the peak of his playing career. The blow was to have a lasting effect on the club. Sunderland were to be promoted in the 1963-64 season, but, subsequently, key members of the side, not least skipper Hurley, were leaving their best days behind.

Meanwhile, Brian was trying to rescue his football career. To the day he died he insisted that he was not the person to say he was finished as a player. He battled so well to return to action that, after scoring a hat-trick in a reserve match, he was given the chance to play in the only three First Division games of his career. Not surprisingly, he also managed a goal. He was prepared to risk a further injury which was likely to make him a cripple. Sunderland wouldn't take such a risk. They announced his playing career was over and took the insurance money.

Brian was lost, wondering what he could do. George Hardwick, now managing Sunderland after Alan Brown's departure, almost gave him a new life. George put him in charge of the club's juniors.

They were the youngest group of players ever to represent Sunderland in the FA Youth Cup. But Brian's influence was so strong that they reached the semi-finals of the competition.

Youngsters like Bobby Kerr and Billy Hughes, both of whom were to enjoy that historic senior FA Cup final day in 1973, featured in the side. But when I asked who was the juniors' top performer, Brian replied simply: 'Number four.' He was referring to the previously unheralded Colin Todd, later to be bought for Derby County by Brian for a record fee for a defender and to be the Players' Player of the Year in 1975.

To my astonishment and that of most Sunderland fans, the

club's directors decided Brian was not for them after they parted with George Hardwick. He was out of work, but Len Shackleton, one of Sunderland's all-time great players, launched his record-establishing managerial career. Shack, by now a sports journalist, rang Mr Ernest Ord, chairman of Hartlepools United, and advised him to appoint Brian as his team boss.

The volatile Mr Ord had many critics. These were to include Brian himself and Peter Taylor, whom Brian made his right-hand man. But Ord rightly claimed he was the man who gave Brian his first taste of management.

The club had applied for re-election to the league more times than anyone else, which made them the butt of jokes for years. The late Charlie Summerbell, Hartlepool born, *Hartlepool Mail*-trained and the *Daily Mirror*'s top sports man in the north east, once opined that a ground improvement at the Victoria Ground meant a new candle in the press box.

Though Pools were in the lowest league grade, I could still count on Brian to make news. He and his team often made long bus trips for away fixtures, so it occurred to Brian, 'How would we cope if the bus driver took ill and couldn't drive?' The answer: he took coach driving lessons and was pictured behind the wheel.

After his first part-season with Pools, I did another feature with him. 'What,' I asked, 'had he learned from his first spell as a manager.' 'Not so much learned,' he explained, 'My experience has confirmed what I always thought – that management is mainly about judgement of players; those you have and those you want.'

Brian and Peter did such a good job for 'Pools that Len Shackleton recommended them to new employers. He rang Sam Longson, chairman of Derby County. Mr Longson was flattered that such a footballing name as Shack had contacted him, listened to what the former England forward had to say and from 1967 Brian was in charge at the Baseball Ground.

Little wonder that Brian is so hallowed around Derby: the Rams were struggling against possible relegation to the Third Division when the Clough-Taylor partnership arrived. The progress was breathtaking. Derby, exciting to watch, won the Second Division championship in 1968-69 and the Football League title for the first time in their history in 1971-72.

After each achievement my late wife, Edna, and I had the joy of attending the celebration dinners. There, too, were colleagues Shack, Vince Wilson (*Sunday Mirror*) and Bob Cass (*Sunday Sun*) with their wives. In a tremendous speech at the first party in the Midland Hotel, Derby, Brian told directors, players, officials and wives: 'You may wonder why those people from the north east are here. Well, they're my friends and I like to be with friends when I'm happy.'

Brian also emphasised that his speech would be lengthy since he had 'many people to thank'. His tributes to each member of his side were riveting. No platitudes. All different. And – typical Clough – no punches pulled.

He saved to the last an eloquent thank-you to captain Dave Mackay, the former Scotland international wing-half many had thought was way past his best when Brian signed him from Tottenham Hotspur. Mackay had been Clough's voice on the pitch; an inspiration for team-mates, particularly youngsters like fellow wing-half Colin Todd and centre-forward John O'Hare. Todd had cost £170,000, a record fee for a defender; O'Hare, another of Clough's former Sunderland juniors, was a bargain at £22,000.

Brian and Peter were to keep proving the lasting value of good judgment of players. Before Brian swooped for Roy McFarland, for example, there had hardly been a mention of the Tranmere Rovers centre half, but, as a Ram, he was also to wear the number five shirt of England, a defender of great quality but also a fine ball-distributor.

Since Brian knew I was dying for him to succeed he invited me to Derby for the final match of the season with Liverpool, strong contenders themselves for the crown. Before the match Brian, his Mum and Dad, and I had tea in the Midland.

From her handbag, Mrs Clough produced an old newspaper cutting she had found. It was from the *Evening Gazette* and pictured a hat-trick of goals from Brian against Charlton. Delighted to see it, Brian asked: 'What do you notice about those goals?' 'All scored from inside the six-yard box,' I said.

'Quite right,' said Brian. 'That's going on the dressing room wall tonight with the message: "Be there!"'

Liverpool were beaten 1-0, but not by a six-yard box effort. John McGovern's winner was a cracker from the edge of the penalty area. On the night I was a privileged fan with a directors' box seat.

It had been a good May Day, but we couldn't yet celebrate since Liverpool would still top Derby if they won at Arsenal on May 8. Brian's squad were holidaying in Majorca when their title was clinched, Liverpool having drawn 0-0 at Highbury. Brian, with wife and family and his parents, was holidaying in the Scilly Isles. Derby could look forward to a first season of European Cup action.

By now, there wasn't a bigger football personality in England than Brian. He was so accepted as the uncomplicated voice of the common man that my daughter, Julia, was able to buy a 'Cloughie' at a burger bar near Brunel University. It was a plain burger without trimmings.

I knew that Brian would have preferred to be managing Sunderland. That was where he had been happiest, where he and Barbara had started a family. He would have crawled on broken glass from the East Midlands were the call to have come from Roker Park.

Instead, while Brian's Derby were winning the top division title in 1972, I was sitting among pathetically small Roker Park crowds of, say, the 8,273 who watched a Second Division match with Portsmouth and the 8,981 who bothered to see Alan Brown's team play Watford.

I campaigned regularly during Brian's Derby days and in his subsequent stints for that call to be made for him to return. My message did not go unheeded by Sunderland supporters. Two of them, Michael Peers and Alan Endean, printed 'Bring back Clough!' car stickers. They could be seen throughout the north east. I set it up no fewer than three times for Brian to manage Sunderland while they looked for a new man. Three times the directors preferred someone else.

I was urging Sunderland to appoint Brian from early in his Derby reign, but the club preferred to take back Alan Brown from Sheffield Wednesday when they sacked Ian McColl in 1968. My case for Brian was even stronger after Brown was dismissed in 1972 – but Bob Stokoe got the nod.

I am assured that before Jimmy Adamson was given the Sunderland job in 1976, Brian was only the runner-up in a close boardroom vote. It was after the Adamson appointment that Brian told me: 'That's it – I wouldn't go if another chance came.'

Another chance did eventually arrive. Having taken control of Sunderland, Sir Tom Cowie couldn't have been more determined to land the people's choice. He handed Brian a signed cheque, inviting him to write his own amount. The figure was never entered. Brian stayed in Nottingham.

Brian's feelings for the area were always strong. One Boxing Day morning, despite there being much snow on the roads, I was amazed, on leaving Christ Church, Seaham Colliery, to see him arriving by car: 'You've just missed the service,' I hurriedly told him, 'but follow that hearse!' He did – and didn't miss the cremation of the mother of sports reporter Vince

Wilson. Thoughtful? Certainly, but his thoughtfulness is underlined when, after the cremation, he motored back to Derby and, despite the elements, made it in time for a home kick-off that very day. Brian had always appreciated one of Mrs Wilson's culinary specialities, leek puddings.

When I have heard criticism of so-called brash Brian, I often also relate what happened after my late wife, Edna, had major heart surgery on the eve of the 1972-73 football season. When she woke up in intensive care a beautiful bunch of roses was at her bedside. They were from Brian. Nice touch? Not half! But even more impressive when you consider that very day he was paying a then record fee of £225,000 for the transfer of Leicester City full-back David Nish to the Baseball Ground. That is class. I wonder whether most of us would have been as thoughtful while having such football responsibility on our minds.

Would Derby directors have been so considerate? Amazingly, even though Derby reached the European Cup semi-final, relations between manager and his employers became soured. Mr Longson was often embarrassed by Brian's strong words on TV, radio and in newspapers. Brian had always been, well, Brian. Only now he had a bigger profile, a much bigger platform. Sam had been so taken with him at one time that he carried a picture of him in his wallet. Now he had to put up with anti-Clough comments from influential football administrators.

There were plenty. And Mr Longson buckled. He grabbed his chance when, against Peter Taylor's wishes, Brian, without another job to go to, offered his resignation. Longson and his colleagues, sensationally in the eyes of the football world, accepted it.

Roy McFarland and the rest of the Derby dressing room, as well as the Derby public, were outraged. There were anti-board demonstrations. Strikes were threatened. But the establishment eventually won the argument. It was not the greatest consolation for Brian to have occupied the higher moral ground. He was looking for a job. Later he was to advise other managers to negotiate a good contract – and not to quit.

Brian's standing in the public eye was mighty. But he had a wife and family, and needs must, he had to earn a living. After his great record at Derby his next appointment was humbling. He joined Third Division Brighton and Hove Albion. With him, too, went Peter Taylor and County's scouts and backroom staff.

The truth is Brian failed at Brighton. I felt for him as he won only 12 of his 32 games in charge. I certainly felt for him as Brighton lost 4-0 at home in an FA Cup replay to non-league Walton and Hersham. That was only eight months after he managed Derby against Juventus in a European Cup semi-final. I wondered what else could hit him after his side lost 8-2 at home to Bristol Rovers.

Yet, in the summer of 1974, the buzz was that Brian could leave Brighton for the home of the league champions, Leeds United, Don Revie having become England's manager. Hence the *Daily Mail* sent me to Majorca where Brian was having a family holiday. Assigned there, too, was Vince Wilson, the journalist who regularly ghosted meaty Clough columns for the *Sunday Mirror*.

We were the only two British newspapermen to be on the story. We were long-standing friends of Brian, but we didn't expect an easy ride. That was confirmed when he told us at our first confrontation that he didn't want to be disturbed. That was on Thursday, July 18. Imagine my near-horror, then, when I got an overseas copy of the *Daily Mail*. There was I trying to eke a few words from Brian and I was reading a very critical piece about Brian from the late and great columnist Ian Wooldridge.

I was tempted to try and buy every available copy of the

Mail in the area, fearful that Brian would read Wooldridge. I assume that Brian never did, for later that day, taking pity on us, he invited Vince and me for lunch. As I write, I am looking at my diary entry for Friday, July 19, 1974. It says: 'Clough breaks silence (with pic)'. It wasn't my greatest despatch, but it was exclusive. Vince's publication would be printed two days later. (The picture of Brian and me in the Spanish sun, taken by a Majorcan snapper, is one I treasure).

I didn't know how long I would be staying in Majorca, but when Brian broke his holiday to return home on the Sunday, that was my cue to book a flight to England. Later that day, I was able to report that Brian was to manage Leeds and Peter would stay with Brighton as manager.

To those of us who knew of the bitter relationship between Messrs Revie and Clough, Brian's move was all the more surprising. Leeds were big-time winners, but Brian had told anyone who was interested that he didn't like their tactics. They were brilliant, but they were well-known to be a dirty side. They had also been linked with attempted match-fixing. Bob Stokoe went on record in a sworn affidavit for the *Daily Mirror* to say that when managing Bury he had been approached by Revie with a cash offer. Stokoe claimed that Revie wouldn't take no for answer – until Stokoe threatened to report the exchange.

Before Newcastle United met Leeds, Derby's championship challengers, at St. James' Park on April 19, 1972, Brian, fearing that the match might be fixed, telephoned me and asked whether I thought Newcastle could be 'bought'. I was convinced they wouldn't be. 'Why?' Brian wanted to know.

'I'll go through the team,' I said. 'First, goalkeeper Willie McFaul – I would stake my mortgage on him. Right-back David Craig – I would put my house on him as well. Left-back Frank Clark ditto. Do I have to continue?" Brian took my word for it. And, thankfully for more than one reason, Newcastle improved

Derby's chances of winning the title by beating Leeds 1-0.

Brian knew there would be resentment in the dressing room at Leeds. But – again typical Brian – he met it head-on. He said to the champions of England: 'Wouldn't it be nice to win the league cleanly?'

I won't go into further detail. Those of you who watched the splendid, though fictional, film *The Damned United* will get the thread. Sufficient to say that Don Revie was still very much in touch with his former players and Revie and Clough had a memorable right set-to on Yorkshire Television.

Like Clough, Revie was born in Middlesbrough and he, too, had played for Sunderland. Indeed, he had captained them in their first relegation season of 1957-58. Don and I had been friendly enough for him to be my guest at a Football Writers' Association's Footballer of the Year dinner in London. That friendship withered somewhat after my reporting of fierce Sunderland-Leeds and Leeds-Newcastle matches in the 1960s. The playing careers of Sunderland's Willie McPheat and Newcastle's George Dalton were ended by legs being broken in Elland Road games.

Leeds' results, under Brian's management, were nothing like what was expected of league champions. He bought players like John O'Hare whom he knew, of course, and Duncan McKenzie. But things still didn't work out. So Brian was fired after 44 turbulent days. To the credit of Leeds chairman Manny Cussins and his board, Leeds honoured the terms of Brian's contract to the penny with a pay-off estimated at £98,000, a fortune then. Financially, Brian was made for life – and that, I believe, was obviously good for him but also for his next, and final, employers. If possible, it made him even more positive, even more decisive.

Nottingham Forest were 13th in the Second Division when Brian replaced Allan Brown on January 6, 1975. His first game in charge was an FA Cup tie with Tottenham, a 1-0 win. Obviously Forest fans were pleased, but, not in their wildest dreams, could they have imagined what lay ahead.

Neither could even his most declared journalistic backer. In his first full season Forest finished eighth. Significantly, though, Peter Taylor rejoined him in July 1976 and promotion was won in Brian's second full season, 1976-77.

As at Derby, Brian made spectacular buys for Forest, but he didn't ignore talent which preceded him there. This included Northern Ireland international inside-forward Martin O'Neill and outside-left John Robertson.

Robertson looked nothing like a typical winger or, indeed, a typical footballer. He was short and almost portly. But he was crucial in victory after victory for Forest in all competition. It was he, indeed, who hit the lone-goal winner against Hamburg to retain the European Cup in 1980.

Brian loved him, but had a strange way of showing this. His nickname for him certainly wasn't flattering. In a posh Jersey hotel restaurant before Forest met Wolverhampton Wanderers in the 1980 League Cup final, Brian shouted from our table to Robertson on another: 'Hey, Fatso, have the Dover sole!'

Normally, I would have been working on my north east beat, but I was covering Forest's preparation for that final since Jeff Farmer, my Midlands colleague, had two clubs at Wembley. He had opted to report the Wolves' end and I was chosen to travel with Forest because of my friendship with Brian.

Not that Brian had put down the welcome mat when I reported his final press conference before flying to Jersey from East Midlands Airport. He made it clear that he didn't want any pressmen in Jersey. I reminded him that the *Daily Mail* paid my wages and they had instructed me to go to there. It was up to him whether he tolerated me. I couldn't have guessed one of the reasons he didn't want me around. He explained he knew

I would be extremely anxious for him to succeed and he didn't want to sense my tension. He wanted to relax. I suppose it was just my luck that I didn't see Forest beat Wolves. Brian's team went down to an Andy Gray goal.

The most important of Brian's earlier mentioned spectacular buys was that of Peter Shilton. For someone who scored so many goals, Brian put greater value on keeping clean sheets. Hence his determination and that of ex-keeper Peter Taylor to land the England man who made a total of 125 full international appearances. Brian paid Stoke City £250,000 for him in 1977. Frank Clark says without hesitation that he was Forest's trophy signing. With Forest he won the league title, League Cup, FA Charity Shield, the European Cup twice and the European Super Cup.

He was outstanding as he kept two clean sheets in the 2-0 aggregate win over European Cup holders Liverpool. So was another of Brian's great signings, Kenny Burns, the Birmingham City centre forward converted by the Clough-Taylor pairing into a magnificent centre half. On the day he signed for Forest in a £150,000 deal, Taylor told him: 'We have taken you from the scrapheap. You'll go back to it if you don't do your stuff.' He was the Football Writers' Association's Footballer of the Year at the end of the season.

Brian's main headline signing, though, was Trevor Francis since he was the first £1million man. He, too, arrived at the City Ground from Birmingham, yet was treated the same as the rest of his new club-mates. There was no chance of him getting too big for his boots.

Francis was to head the winner in Forest's European Cup final victory against Malmo of Sweden in 1979, but I remember seeing him being introduced by Brian to the all-time great inside-forward of Middlesbrough and England, Wilf Mannion: 'Meet someone who could really play,' said Clough to Britain's most expensive player. Clough, as a boy, had idolised Mannion.

While Brian was winning the top honours in the game with Forest, Sunderland remained in the Second Division. At least, when Forest retained the European Cup in 1980, Ken Knighton's team did clinch promotion back to the top flight in the same month with a 2-0 victory over FA Cup winners West Ham in front of 47,129 at Roker Park.

Consolation? For me, hardly. Sunderland should never be out of what is now called the Premier League...

I hope I have done Brian Clough proud. I haven't gone into detail about the drink-inflicted illness from which he died on September 20, 2004 or the accusations after he retired that he took transfer-deal backhanders. I prefer to think of the words of Martin O'Neill whose tribute at a Pride Park memorial occasion still resonate. 'Without him, we'd have won nothing.' I prefer to remember seeing Brian statues being unveiled in Albert Park, Middlesbrough, and Nottingham city centre.

If only the late Sir Tom Cowie, chairman of Sunderland, had been successful when the Red and Whites at last offered their job to the greatest manager Sunderland and England never had. Sir Tom invited him to write the figures of his own salary. But, by then, Brian and his family were too settled in the East Midlands.

How many trophies would Sunderland have won with Brian? I believe success would have been routine!

Doug Weatherall was born in Seaham in 1932. His first football-related memory is his father's message to him before he went down to London to watch Sunderland beat Preston North End in the 1937 FA Cup final: 'Listen to the wireless and I'll give you a shout from Wembley.' Doug was nine when he attended Roker Park for the first time. He entered journalism as a 16-year-old cub news reporter with the *Sunderland Echo* and later worked for the old *Daily Herald* in Manchester and the *Daily Mail*, based in the north east. He has a column in the Sunderland matchday programme.

10

The striking partnership between Niall Quinn and Kevin Phillips was the classic combination of a big man to win the headers and a small, pacy man to feast on the flick-ons.

They were the footballing equivalent of Morecambe and Wise or Lennon and McCartney.

But, as **Graeme Anderson** explains, there was so much more to it than that. The relationship Quinn and Phillips developed led Sunderland to promotion and successive seventh place finishes in the Premier League.

They dovetailed perfectly, they brought out the best in each other and the quest to find a partnership as potent has continued ever since.

SUPER KEV AND THE MIGHTY QUINN

BY GRAEME ANDERSON

The prolific partnership of Niall Quinn and Kevin Phillips holds a special place in the history of Sunderland Association Football Club and the hearts of its fans.

Just the mention of it has club statisticians salivating as much as supporters drooling and watching the strike pair in action was one of the highlights of my time as chief sports writer of the *Sunderland Echo*, which took in the beginning, blossoming and ending of their partnership.

What was it that made that pairing so special? Why has affection for it grown, rather than ebbed over the years? And why have successive Sunderland sides not come close to matching it since?

These are questions that I have heard many times and in this chapter I will offer my own answers.

But perhaps the first thing we should remember is how inauspiciously it all began and how close the Quinn-Phillips partnership came to not happening at all.

When Quinn joined Sunderland in August 1996 – a year before Phillips' arrival – it was not a signing which set Roker Park alight.

Peter Reid paid a club record £1.3m to bring the former Arsenal and Manchester City forward to a newly-promoted side but although all of Quinn's football had been played at the highest level and he was a regular Republic of Ireland international, he was not seen as the answer to the club's strike problems by the vast majority of fans.

Sunderland's promotion to the Premier League had been based on an utterly miserly rearguard and a consistent goal-scorer capable of unlocking Premier League defences was desperately needed. The club's leading finisher the previous season had been 22-year-old Craig Russell with 13 league goals but he was unproven at the highest level. Fellow forward Paul Stewart was slow and ponderous; David Kelly, prolific previously at Newcastle United, struggled to score at all for Sunderland.

Quinn was a name but he was approaching 30 and his last campaign had seen him score eight times for a Manchester City side which had been relegated. By a lot of fans he was seen at best as a superior version of predecessor big men Sunderland strikers Brett Angell and Lee Howey, neither of whom had been able to find the back of the net regularly.

He could also be put in the same bracket as Stewart and Kelly, as players who had earned recognition at other clubs but whose best days were behind them.

The signing therefore required the fans to trust in the judgement of Sunderland's manager.

Thankfully, that did not present a problem. Reid had been voted Football League manager of the year after earning Sunderland promotion on the back of saving them from relegation to the third flight on his appointment the previous season. Supporters, even the uneasy ones, were prepared to give him and his summer signings a chance.

In the event, both Quinn and Sunderland made a slow but steady start. The Irishman scored three goals in eight games – two in a 4-1 win over Nottingham Forest and one in the League Cup – as Sunderland took a solid nine points from the first 21.

But in September, Quinn suffered the second cruciate knee ligament injury of his career. Half-an-hour into a game against Coventry City which Sunderland were to win, reinforcing their early season progress, Liam Daish fouled Quinn leaving the Irishman in a heap on the turf.

As sometimes happens when serious injuries are sustained on a pitch, the perpetrator did not realise the damage done and called his fellow Republic of Ireland international a cheat.

But by the time Quinn appeared in a Sunderland shirt again it was April. A month after the striker's cruciate had been torn, Tony Coton, another former Manchester City player now plying his trade at Roker Park, had suffered a leg break at Southampton which ended his career.

In the final analysis, Reid was to point to the loss of these two key figures early in the season as the main reason Sunderland failed to sustain momentum as the campaign wore on. The club was in free-fall when Quinn returned – clearly not fully fit – for the final few games.

During that long spell on the sidelines, Quinn still had club duties to perform, of which probably the least engaging for him was the weekly *Sunderland Echo* column. There used to be a joke among the players at the time that whoever did the column was taking a risk because every season that player seemed to get crocked. The 'Curse of the Column' was the least of Quinn's worries though, he was more concerned about a frustrating rehabilitation.

The column was at least helping his image with Sunderland fans. Everyone knows now – but fewer did then – how intelligently and eloquently he speaks. With respectful apologies to all those players I have interviewed before and since, Quinny was undoubtedly the most articulate footballer I ever met.

He was effortlessly professional in these chats, always able to keep his observations interesting and well-expressed without deviating too much from the party line. Midway through one straightforward answer about his rehab though – maybe it was the boredom that got to him – he suddenly blurted: 'Look, I'm not kidding anyone, least of all myself, and the truth is that the injury hasn't responded as I would have liked. I've got another appointment with a specialist next week and if there's no good news I'm going to retire. I don't see the point of taking the wages if I'm not likely to make a full come-back. And I don't think I would be being fair to Sunderland or Sunderland fans if I just hung on to take the money trying to see my contract out.'

Wow. Pick the bones out of that.

I had a major scoop on my hands.

'Quinn poised to quit!'

'I'll hang up my boots' – Quinn.

'D-Day for Quinn'

'Quinn faces the end!'

All of those potential headlines rolled through my mind.

But there was the unspoken convention with the club that an interview for a column was supposed to be only used for the column – not for the back page.

Besides, I was still new to the job in 1996, and sport is a world away from news. As an experienced news journalist with over a decade's experience, I was at ease talking with ministers of state, magistrates or chief constables.

But as a novice, slightly star-struck sports reporter, I was conscious I was getting to grips with a whole new way of going about the job.

The journalistic basics in news and sport may be the same but they are chalk and cheese in the way they work. I recalled advice from my predecessor at the *Echo*, Geoff Storey, who said: 'Remember, you're the local reporter with the job of covering this club for decades to come so you're in it for the long haul. You might have a good story that will get you pats on the back from your mates down the pub now and then. But it's chip paper tomorrow and if you've broken a trust or put something at risk, doors might close that you need open. You always have to weigh things up because if you're not careful you'll find yourself with no stories and unable to do the job you're being paid for.'

I called the sports editor: 'Hold the back page!' I weighed it up. I considered my options: Journalistic glory but leaving Reid's office for the last time with testicles in a sling? Or play the long game, confide in the manager, build trust and look to work with him?

In the end it wasn't a difficult decision to make. Not when your balls are on the line!

'Hello Peter, Quinny says he's ready to quit'

'What!!!!!?'

'I've just done a column with him and he says he's ready to retire if it gets no better.'

'Jesus! Have you written anything?' he asked.

'No, not yet. I thought it best to come to you first, to see how you want to play it.'

'Brilliant,' he sighed. 'Look, do me a favour and don't write anything for the moment – I can tell you now, he's not finished. The big man's head's up his arse! He's all over the place. But he's not finished. He'll play again. He's just really down. I'll have a word with him… And son? You're learning, eh?'

In the end it was the right decision all round – apart from selling a few extra newspapers I suppose. Quinn was not finished, and mine and the manager's relationship went up a whole new level of trust. From my point of view it was an example of the value of playing the long game for a local sports reporter.

But the story illustrates just how close Quinn was to packing it in – how, in a *Sliding Doors* world, the Quinn-Phillips strike force might never have been – and just how much Reid stood by the striker, protected him and ensured he would go on to the best spell of his entire career.

Though Quinn came back for the final five games of the season he was clearly far from fit – a last throw of the dice from Reid in a relegation season – but the Irishman made an instant impact after a summer's rest.

During that summer of 1997, Reid made a raft of signings – Lee Clark was the big name but there was Jody Craddock, Chris Byrne, Chris Makin and a barely-known young striker called Kevin Phillips who arrived from Watford for £325,000.

The buzz in pre-season was about how good the new arrivals looked but only Clark was really regarded as a shoo-in to the starting 11 at the time.

Their moves to Wearside coincided with the end of a 99-year association with Roker Park and the move to a new home.

The first home game of the 1997-98 season marked the opening of the brand new Stadium of Light on the banks of the Wear. The game was played on a Friday evening and the darkness only added to the atmosphere surrounding the club's shining new home.

It was a wonderful occasion for the club and a wonderful result for the team. Quinn had the distinction of scoring the first goal ever scored at the stadium and Phillips joined him on the scoresheet in a stirring 3-1 win over Manchester City.

It was a sign of things come, though in the weeks that followed it seemed like a false dawn. Quinn's knee was still not right and Phillips suffered a knock which sidelined him.

And Sunderland suffered a slump in performances and results which culminated in an awful result at Reading – beaten 4-0 – with Sunderland players suffering awful abuse from fans as they waited to board the team bus home. It was a horrible thing to witness, standing alongside as shell-shocked players endured the anger of fans feeling their club was sliding towards another relegation.

Reid had stood loyally by players who had been so narrowly

relegated in the previous campaign but at this moment of crisis he reacted by promoting faster, younger legs that had been eager for their chance.

In came the energy of Jody Craddock, Darren Williams and Michael Bridges, supplementing the youthfulness of players like Michael Gray, Allan Johnston and Martin Smith and a fresh, energetic, attacking side began to emerge. That was only given fresh impetus when right-winger Nicky Summerbee was signed from Manchester City, with Craig Russell going the other way.

November was also the month that Quinn, now restored to full fitness, finally returned.

Exploratory surgery had shown that although previous cruciate ligament surgery had been successful the problem had been two fused bones in the knee. It was those fused bones which had been holding the big man back, depriving him of full and painless extension. Once they were free, so was Quinn.

Coming on as a late substitute in a game against Nottingham Forest, he laid on an equaliser for Kevin Phillips in a 1-1 draw. In the following game, a 4-1 win at Portsmouth, the Irishman was back on the scoresheet.

A corner was being turned. Before the Forest game, Phillips had scored four goals in 12 games – three of them in games where Quinn had been on the pitch. Now, four months into the season, this remodelled team had begun to click and the goals started to flow.

Beginning with that goal against Forest, Phillips went on to score a staggering 31 goals in 35 games. In one purple patch, he scored 11 goals in seven games. His last goal of the season broke Brian Clough's post-war record – which had stood since the early 1960s – for most goals in a season by a Sunderland player. Quinn, meanwhile, was to finish with 17 goals and Sunderland ended up on 90 points – an amazing result after their indifferent start.

But it was not enough. Not enough for automatic promotion despite the exhilarating style of football. Reid's side fell at the final hurdle, losing an epic play-off final to Charlton Athletic – a 4-4 draw at Wembley concluding with penalty shoot-out defeat.

Goals were not Sunderland's problem – Phillips and Quinn had seen to that – naivety in defence was. Reid made more signings in the summer, the vital one being superb young goalkeeper Thomas Sørensen, and the Black Cats went up as champions the following season with a then record 105 points.

From the Irishman's return against Forest until the end of the 1998-99 season, these were golden times for the flourishing Quinn-Phillips partnership. In the promotion season, they lost just three games out of 46 – another record for English football.

Even before that staggering season got underway, Phillips' position as hero and favourite of the fans was established. Young striker Michael Bridges had seemed certain to be the coming man but Phillips came from nowhere to become the main man almost immediately.

Just a few weeks into the ex-Watford man's first season at Sunderland, Bridges said to me, with a smile but also a heavy heart: 'He's nicked my song!'

Bridges is one of the nicest and most genuine people you will find in football. Eventually he had to accept he needed to leave in order to fulfil his own undoubted talent. And but for horrendous injuries, he too could have been a major star of the Premier League. But it tends to be forgotten now that the iconic Sunderland chant of 'Super, Super Kev…', used to be 'Super, Super Mick…'

Phillips came flying out of the traps at the start of the season, notching eight goals in the first ten games but still didn't feel he was playing as well as he could. That led to a fateful decision to play in a League Cup game against Chester City in September for the chance of easy, confidence-boosting goals. He did get a goal in a comfortable 3-0 win but he also picked up a foot injury which was to sideline him for four months of the campaign.

He still managed to get 25 goals by the season's end – which included ten goals in a seven-game burst – but it is worth speculating on how many more he might have got had he not missed a full 22 games of the season! Quinn, meanwhile, scored 21 goals as Sunderland were promoted with four games to spare.

It meant that between them, the duo had scored 98 goals in just two seasons. The big question was whether they could do it in the Premier League. Reid was in no doubt they would flourish: 'Quinny's done it before and Kevin will score goals at any level,' he sniffed.

Meanwhile, Lee Clark, who had been such an important contributor to Sunderland's Championship rise, laughed when he told me: 'People talk about Quinny struggling in the Premier League because he lacks pace. What a joke. He's NEVER had pace! But he was a great team player when he was in the top flight last time around and he'll be even better for all that experience and having Kevin alongside him this time.'

Clark was not to be there to enjoy Sunderland's Premier League impact – he, Allan Johnston and Michael Bridges all departed that summer: Johnston because he could not agree a new contract, Bridges because he needed first team football, Clark because of a daft moment with Newcastle fans which made him look hugely disrespectful to Sunderland supporters. Once again, this was a 'what if?' moment for the club.

Reserve team coach Adrian Heath had been relishing the damage that the partnership of left-winger Johnston and left-back Gray would do to Premier League defences. They had traumatised Championship rear-guards in the preceding two seasons, thanks to Gray's astounding stamina and Johnston's ball control and natural right-foot on the left flank.

Heath enthused over their telepathic understanding: 'Johnston carries the ball forward, Mickey overlaps and the opposition full-back can never be sure which one to go for, if he goes for Johnston, Allan finds Mickey with a pass and a cross comes in from near the byline; if he goes for Mickey, then Johnno can cut inside on his right and either chip in a cross or go for goal himself.'

It was a partnership much appreciated by Quinn and Phillips themselves, as was the service coming from the other flank from the much more direct Summerbee.

Recently, Phillips told me: 'People talk about mine and Niall's partnership and how many goals we got but in some ways we were an attacking four rather than two. I would have to say the two wingers we had in that era – Summerbee and Johnston – I loved playing with.

'And to that mix, I'd have to add Mickey Gray bombing on from left-back.

'Although Mickey was supposed to be the left-back in that team he had such a good engine that he was always catching up Allan or more often than not going past him. If anything, Mickey operated as a wing-back even when he was supposed to be a left-back. And I used to love to turn towards goal and see him overlapping on the wing and usually ready to hit a first-time cross.

'All strikers thrive on crosses simply because a good ball in automatically turns defenders and gives you more of an opportunity and although they were two very different types of players, Johnno and Nicky Summerbee were among the best in the business in delivering a fantastic cross. I scored loads of goals off their crosses, so for a striker it was a dream to have two players like that in the team.'

It was a blow to Sunderland's whole attacking set-up to lose Johnston, not to mention the natural Premier League ability of Clark and the attacking promise of Bridges. Given those departures, it was some achievement by Reid and Sunderland that the club managed to be second in the Premier League at Christmas and seventh by the end of the season.

But it was nothing short of remarkable that Phillips should also score 30 goals, from a diminished attack, in his first season in the Premier League.

Unlike his previous achievements in the Championship, Phillips' goal haul was more attritional in the top flight, a steady relentless accumulation rather than scored in bursts.

Not only did he finish leading scorer, ahead of more exalted names like Alan Shearer (23), Dwight Yorke (20) and Andy Cole (19), he also won Europe's Golden Shoe award as the top scorer in all of the continent's major leagues that season.

Phillips remains the only Englishman ever to have won the honour.

Not bad for a lad who had cleaned Shearer's boots as an apprentice at Southampton. Not bad for a lad who had been stacking shelves at Dixons as a non-league player a few years later.

Quinn, meanwhile, and as ever, made his contribution – scoring 14 goals. The Irishman scored in the 2-1 win in the rain at Newcastle and in the amazing, still talked about, 4-1 win over Chelsea at the Stadium of Light. As did Phillips. The big forward scored twice in a 2-1 win over Spurs, he scored against Manchester United, he scored against his old club Arsenal in a season that brought so many highs and fully vindicated Reid's decision to push the veteran forward on.

Reid's continued tenure as manager had also been an endorsement of chairman Bob Murray's faith in him. Reid repaid him with a good transfer window after promotion – in particular the shrewd acquisition of Steve Bould, who locked down the defence, and Stefan Schwarz who added solidity and guile to a Sunderland side looking for balance after Johnson's defection.

The side's strength, though, lay in the team spirit fostered in the previous two seasons and the understandings between players. There was also the fact that Quinn's team-mates loved playing with a target man enjoying the most amazing Indian Summer to a career it was possible to imagine.

'You see Quinny?' Alex Rae said to me one day after training, in a conversation about Sunderland's success. 'He's the catalyst for it all. The wee man scores the goals and he's brilliant at it – as good as I've seen – but the big man is the catalyst. He's what makes it all tick. He'll always provide you with an 'out' when you need to pass the ball, he's the one who gets us upfield and his head is like a third foot – he can pass it with his head as well as others can pass it with their feet!'

That was all true, but it was not as if Phillips was exactly a junior partner.

'It's quite interesting when I talk to people that everyone seems to think that Niall did all the hard work and I did the easy bit of tapping the ball into the back of the net,' Phillips reflected recently with a smile.

'But the hardest part of the game IS putting the ball in the back of the net and that's what I was there to do.

'Niall was no slouch at it either, mind you. And it was only because I was scoring so many alongside him that he didn't get more credit.'

Phillips had now been on a long upward trajectory ever since his arrival at Sunderland.

He had been voted Nationwide Player of the Year in his first season at Sunderland and had won both the club and the supporters' player of the year award in his debut season,

1997-98, and his first season in the Premier League, 1999-2000.

Quinn had won both awards in the season in between, and also won the North East Sports Writers' Player of the Year award in 1999 – the year before Phillips was presented with the same trophy.

In the season he scored 30 Premier League goals, Phillips was also runner-up to the PFA player of the year and the Football Writers' player of the year – only pipped to the post by a certain Roy Keane.

Now happily settled with his wife and young family near Durham, life just seemed to get better and better for the former Baldock Town striker who was thrilled his talent was being recognised after being so long overlooked. I first met him when we shared a seat on the team bus during the club's pre-season tour of Ireland, a few weeks after his arrival, and we got on well from the start.

In his first season, he took over Quinn's duties as *Echo* columnist and the arrangement worked so well he continued doing it all the way up to his departure six seasons later.

No player had ever done the *Echo* player column anywhere near that long and no one ever will do again. Apart from that four-month spell on the sidelines in his second season, he broke the 'Curse of the Column' and we built up a friendship that lasts to this day.

It was me who rang him in April 1999 to break the news that Kevin Keegan had selected him for England duty – he and Mickey Gray were the first England senior call-ups from Sunderland since Nick Pickering 15 years previously.

And when Phillips and Gray took the field against Hungary in Budapest – a game I was privileged to be at – they became the first two Sunderland players to appear in an England shirt in the same game since 1926.

The honours that came his way were many and always

appreciated by the player himself but they were topped by those England call-ups and that unique achievement among Englishmen of winning the Golden Shoe.

The good times continued in Sunderland's second season in the top flight when once again they were second at Christmas but unable to sustain their surge, finished seventh once again.

There were still plenty of glory days to be had, right from the off, with a 1-0 win over Arsenal at the Stadium of Light where Quinn scored the winner. There were to be only eight goals for the Irishman that season but one of them was the winner in a second 2-1 triumph over Newcastle United at St James' Park. The goal – a perfect header past Shay Given into the 'postage stamp' in the top corner of the goal ended a move which illustrated precision teamwork and wonderful team spirit – was Sunderland at their very best.

And Quinn's last goal of the campaign came in a 3-2 win over Charlton Athletic – a game in which his strike partner also scored – offering a tiny modicum of revenge for that play-off final defeat.

Phillips scored 18 goals in the 2000-01 campaign, notching a hat-trick against Bradford City, to go with the hat-trick he had scored against Derby County in the previous season and the four goals he had scored in an FA Cup game against Rotherham the campaign before that.

It was broadly agreed at the end of it that Sunderland's overall display that second Premier League season was better than their first one. That was because – even if Europe had narrowly been missed for a second campaign in a row – the Black Cats had prospered in the traditionally 'difficult' second season.

Reid had been fighting off approaches from Premier League rivals for Phillips' signature.

After two goal-laden seasons, the striker was now an established hot property but Phillips was happy to stay at

Sunderland, reasoning that the club where he was happy would only go from strength to strength.

Everyone was in for a shock though as Sunderland slumped the following season. For the first time since his arrival, Reid had a genuinely disappointing transfer window. Unable to gain value for money at home in the transfer market, he had largely looked abroad and the signings he brought in didn't succeed – they failed to gel either on the pitch or in the dressing room. On top of that key players were being lost, Don Hutchinson, seeking another contract rise, departed; Alex Rae was allowed to leave and, most crucially of all, Quinn was now physically on the wane.

But if the writing was on the wall, we didn't see it at first. Sunderland started the season solidly and when they beat Bolton Wanderers 2-0 at the Reebok in September they leapt up to fifth in the table. This game was also memorable for Phillips' 100th league goal in Sunderland stripes – albeit the two-tone navy blue stripes of the away kit that season. It was the only time I ever asked anything from the striker – the shirt off his back – which I still have. It is autographed 'Top 100'.

A chastening decline was around the corner but at the time it felt like Reid might still successfully evolve a squad struggling to accommodate change. Chief among his problems was how to ease the burden on Quinn, who was now in his 34th year and finding it harder and harder to mitigate the wear and tear. The knees had just about held out but his back was now giving him severe problems and Reid fumed regularly at the lack of protection given to the 6ft 4ins forward by officials.

Quinn had proven himself unplayable at times in his two seasons back in the Premier League. His heading ability was superb and he had the height to out-jump defenders. He was also incredibly hard to knock off the ball and with his back to goal, he could use that head or those telescopically long legs to lay the ball off well to advancing team-mates.

Eventually, opponents found the best way to contain him – they simply roughed him up, realising that more often than not they would get away with it.

'It's ridiculous what he's having to put up with,' Reid said. 'He's getting fouled all the time, defenders are jumping on his back, leaning on him, dragging him… There seems to be this unconscious attitude from referees that he's a big man, that he can handle himself, that it's a man's game.

'Now all those things are true but a foul is a foul. And teams are getting away with it, especially in the box where he's being pulled all over the place but he's trying to stay on his feet, because refs don't like giving penalties. He needs protection because he's coming off in most games now with his back in agony.'

It was true that Quinn was taking longer to come up for any post-match interviews with a regime of after-care in the physio's room now taking place as standard.

Reid and his coaching staff appreciated that the burden needed to be eased on Quinn and an eventual successor found. But who? And where?

Quinn tells the tale in his autobiography that after successfully coming back from his cruciate ligament injury and producing a match-winning performance at QPR, assistant manager Bobby Saxton said no centre forward in Europe had played better for his team than the Irishman had that day.

'I don't know how he knew it, but I loved hearing those words,' Quinn said, with a note of amusement.

But maybe Saxton had not been entirely exaggerating. Several years later, Sunderland still couldn't find a replacement for the big man.

Reid looked and looked. His scouting team searched Europe and top of the list of strikers was Anderlecht's Jan

Koller. But Reid was not impressed by the Czech when he checked on him or any of the other European candidates. He didn't think any of them were as good as Quinn had been.

There was one young prospect he fancied, a young player called Zlatan Ibrahimovic at Malmo. But the teenager could not be dissuaded from joining Ajax.

Phillips, meanwhile, had long since reached the stage of his Sunderland career where records were beginning to tumble at regular intervals. The shirt he handed to me after the Bolton game had been for his 100th league goal. But his 100th goal overall had been reached in some style – the final goal of a hat-trick in a 4-1 Boxing Day 2000 drubbing over Bradford. In beating the Bantams, Phillips joined club legends Len Shackleton and Gary Rowell as the only Sunderland players to have triple figures next to their goals tally since the end of the Second World War.

He was still climbing though, and at one stage we joked that he was being interviewed for another record being approached or broken almost every other week. After reaching 100 goals just after Christmas, he passed Shack's 101 on New Year's Day and Rowell's 103 by the end of January. By the time he was signing the shirt after the Bolton game in September 2001, he had eclipsed Patsy Gallacher's 108 and had Arthur Bridgett's 118 in his sights.

But the goals were drying up now. That other great supplier of crosses, Nicky Summerbee had also moved on, after just one season in the Premier League. Claudio Reyna might have made a difference but the gifted American was injury prone and made just 28 appearances in two seasons. At least he had class, even if he was made of glass. Several other signings simply proved not up to the job while up front a succession of players were paired with Phillips without success.

Sunderland finished a lowly 17th in the 2001-02 season.

They secured the last day point they needed for survival when Phillips took a pass from Quinn and advantage of a mix-up between Derby County's Danny Higginbotham and Mart Poom to slot home in a 1-1 draw.

It had been a sobering, cold slap of a campaign. Reid needed a good transfer window, especially with it being clear Quinn might be no more than a bit-part player the following season.

The manager was patience itself in pursuit of the big prize but he missed out, agonisingly, on a summer-long pursuit of free-scoring Irish international Robbie Keane. That meant Marcus Stewart and Tore Andre Flo were panic buys and they, and the emergent youngster Kevin Kyle, proved as ineffective a replacement for Quinn alongside Phillips, as Lilian Laslandes, David Bellion, Patrick Mboma or even Danny Dichio had done previously.

In a panic and fearing mutiny from the fans, Sunderland sacked Reid just a few matches into the new season with the club on eight points, fourth-bottom and a run of easier games to come. He was given the bullet after just nine games of the new season. Quinn played his last game for the club in the tenth.

If chairman Bob Murray was hoping for a new manager bounce, he didn't get it. Sunderland were dreadful in Howard Wilkinson's first game in charge – a home game to fellow strugglers West Ham – when, trailing 1-0, Quinn was introduced as a substitute on the hour.

Magically, it was the Quinn of old and suddenly Sunderland were a team transformed. They went close to equalising and might even have won. But Wilkinson told Quinn in the days that followed that he was really only interested in players who could play a full 90 minutes. The striker, now having passed his 35th birthday, got the message and retired immediately from football with a combination of sadness and relief. No more need to put himself through the agonies and the post-match recovery routine.

At the end of a torturous season in which a relegated Sunderland, shorn of its leaders on and off the pitch, had imploded, Phillips left. He finished top scorer – as he did in every season at the club – but this time with just nine goals to his name. Months before the end, it was painful to watch him trying to carry the attack of a side which was a shadow of its former self, feeling the pressure to always be the one to get Sunderland out of jail.

Phillips left the club, in the summer of 2003, with a tally of 130 Sunderland goals. He was joint-sixth highest scorer in the history of the club – alongside 1930s hero Raich Carter, remembered as arguably the greatest player ever to don the red and white stripes. Not bad company to be in.

Although Sunderland's Premier League adventure ended badly and sadly, as many footballing stories do, the end of the affair could not diminish how glorious an era the Quinn-Phillips years had been for the club.

When memories are cast back now by fans, it is never to remember the Howard Wilkinson, Mick McCarthy months in which Quinn quit the stage, Sunderland slumped and Phillips headed for an ignominious exit. It is to recall a time when the sun always seemed to shine on a Sunderland side playing wonderful football and constantly surpassing expectations.

That is perhaps why Gus Poyet, at the end of his time as head coach of Sunderland, attracted such anger from fans when he criticised them for harping back to the 'Route One' football of Quinn and Phillips. He misjudged what Sunderland were about in that era and how entertaining their football had been.

The little and large combination of those two Sunderland strikers might have presented a very straightforward, traditional challenge to defenders but that didn't make it any easier to defend against. It was one thing to know the challenge and another thing altogether to counter it. What Poyet really misunderstood was that Sunderland did not play Route One football in that era.

The totem-pole Quinn might have been the fulcrum of many of his side's attacks but Sunderland played some breath-taking football on their way to promotion and successful seasons in the Premier League. Poyet should have known better than to hand that side such a label – particularly when he was part of a Chelsea team utterly disassembled by Sunderland in that famous 4-1 victory at the Stadium of Light in December 1999.

Phillips was 30 years old when he left Sunderland in August 2003. He too was to enjoy an Indian Summer. And then some! After moving on, he was to score well over 100 goals for a diverse range of clubs. He played on until he was 40, helping Crystal Palace into the Premier League via the play-offs before ending his career at Leicester City.

It is perhaps idle to speculate on what he might have achieved had he stayed at the Stadium of Light and had Sunderland been able to sustain their early momentum after promotion.

But certainly he would have passed Raich Carter, Johnny Campbell, George Holley and Dave Halliday in the list of prolific Sunderland hitmen. He might even have troubled all-time top scorers Charlie Buchan and Bobby Gurney, who reached the 220s.

Phillips went on to prove he could be a lethal striker in any decent team. He had plenty more good times ahead when he left Wearside. But now, especially since hanging up his boots, it is his time at Sunderland and that marvellous partnership with Quinn that he looks back with most fondness. And what he marvels at most is that the amazing understanding they both shared on the pitch was something which was natural to them from the start.

'Probably the most interesting thing about the way we worked on our partnership was that we never really worked on it at all!' he told me.

'Yeah, we would do shooting together – where strikers practice their shooting – literally just Bobby Saxton or Adrian Heath setting you up and you firing at goal. We did that. But we never worked specifically on training ground routines as a partnership. We talked – you have to talk – but we never went through possible match scenarios on the training ground.

'It just seemed to happen for us.

'These days, I'm working with the strikers permanently doing sessions, trying to get the pairs working together making the right runs and so on.

'But at Sunderland, me and Quinny just never, never did it.'

Phillips pointed out that some of the best Premier League partnerships have been arrived at without a great deal of work or closeness between the pairings involved.

'It would be interesting to speak to Dwight Yorke and Andy Cole from when they were at Manchester United because I don't think they particularly worked on it either,' he said.

'From my brief conversations, they never really practiced at it over and over again on the training pitch but they still had a great rapport.

'When you go back to Teddy Sheringham and Andy Cole, they famously never even talked to each other off the pitch but it still didn't stop them forming a great partnership on it.

'Mind you, I did have a good friendship with Niall – I still do, to this day. But what worked for us was just speaking about stuff, rather than practicing it on the training pitch.'

It is tempting to borrow one of Reid's favourite phrases: 'It's not rocket science.'

And Phillips would probably agree with that...

'Hey, listen, when you play up front alongside someone who is 6ft 4ins, it pretty much irons itself out,' he smiled. 'He's going to be the focal point and I pretty much play off him.

'But it helped at the time that we all got along so well.

'Quinny was the ultimate team spirit man and if we were to do anything as a group, he was usually at the heart of it – him and Alex Rae and, of course, Kevin Ball, the skipper. The team spirit was second to none and Quinny was a huge part of that – on and off the pitch. We were very together as a team and when it was at it's best, it was incredible.'

Phillips agrees with Reid's viewpoint that the problems started when the club had to continually look abroad hoping to buy talent that was too expensive in this country.

'There's a lot in that,' he nodded. 'The squad was mainly made up of British players at the time – and I'm not having a dig here at foreign players – but we did have that British mentality that we all stuck by each other. If one of us were in trouble the rest of us would get behind him and try to help. Gradually we started to lose that but sometimes things happen so gradually that you don't realise until it's too late that you have big problems.

'Of course it affected us when we began to see less and less of Quinny in the side – it affects any side when a top class player goes out of the team,' he added. 'You could look at Liverpool in the past season in losing Luis Suarez and Daniel Sturridge – it had a massive effect on them. We felt it when Niall was no longer playing so much and was struggling to be fit, because he was such an important element in that team.'

Phillips though, like many of his team-mates of that era, subscribes to the famous notion that you shouldn't cry that it is over, but smile that it happened in the first place.

'You consider Quinny,' he said. 'And he had actually done

really well in the first place to come back from the knee problems that looked as though they were going to finish him. These were bonus years in a way for him because he thought that he would be finished with the cruciate even before I arrived.

'In the end, we both helped each other tremendously and we'll always be grateful to each other for that. I probably gave him an extra two or three years on his career and he was instrumental in really helping launch mine. You wish it could go on forever – but it did go on for a few great years.

'Ultimately though Niall is such a big guy that the back is always likely to be a problem and so it proved. There's no doubt though that it was the best partnership of my career. I'd struck up a couple of decent ones early in my career but the one with Niall really helped make my name.'

As well as his many assists to his team-mates, Quinn scored 69 goals in 220 appearances for Sunderland – close to one in three. And his ex-strike partner says his ability to find the back of the net should not be obscured by his other qualities.

'He had a very respectable goal ratio and was a very good finisher,' Phillips said. 'I remember a goal away at Leicester when he produced a great bit of skill and another one against Port Vale which was stunning – lobbing the keeper from distance and then turning away to celebrate before the ball hit the back of the net. For such a big guy his feet were incredible. People underestimated that Quinny could really play some delicate football for such a big man. He was a big help for me as a player and a person and I felt I was getting better and better alongside him. Niall fading out of the team definitely affected me because I just couldn't produce quite the same partnership with Dichio or Flo or Laslandes or Stewart or whoever,' Phillips added. 'Don't get me wrong, I wasn't a bad striker – I scored goals wherever I went – it was just that partnership with Quinny: we were tailor-made for each other.'

Indeed they were.

But, personally, I think it was down as much to design, as it was to accident.

Players prefer good partnerships and thrive on simple systems – Reid and Saxton provided both and found players who would bring the best out of each other. They knew there was no one better in the business for holding the ball upfield, bringing team-mates into play and supplying his fellow striker than Quinn.

They also knew they were wasting a precious resource if they did not support him properly.

In his first season at the club, Quinn had been labelled a carthorse by those who simply saw a big man, back to goal, who didn't look the part of the natural finisher.

But he was surrounded by players who simply weren't natural goal scorers at the highest level and was continually being asked to hold on to the ball a few seconds longer than was practical while team-mates, usually intent on defence, struggled to get up with the action.

Recognising that, Reid and Saxton built the perfect team to exploit Quinn's qualities and the plan worked a treat. Johnston and Summerbee, in particular, but many others to follow, thrived on his intelligent flick-ons and lay-offs, while Phillips buzzed around him and benefitted.

Quinn, for his part, was eternally grateful for those extra years granted by Reid's belief in him and the company of players who enjoyed playing to his strengths.

And maybe Phillips and Quinn worked at that partnership more than Phillips realised. It was no accident that the two strikers were made room-mates on their first pre-season tour together.

Saxton was always a believer in the need for players involved in being partners on the pitch to get to know each other off the pitch too. He was certain that the more attuned minds were to each other generally off the pitch, the easier it would be for them to work together on it. Maybe that was one reason why the relationship worked so well. But there must have been others…

Sometimes, I amuse myself with the thought that it was because when the ball came into the box, both players had just one thought on their minds. Kevin was thinking: 'How can I score here?' And Niall was thinking: 'How can Kevin score here?' Two minds in complete harmony! But that is simplistic. And unfair.

Quinn was often under pressure with the ball coming into the box and it was only natural he should be thinking of the lay-off and Phillips was elusive and always on the move in the area and it was only natural he should be finding a space that his partner could nod the ball into. Besides, Quinn would admit he scored some of his goals because terrorised defenders were trying to track Phillips' runs. And the big striker also got more than a few goals when he reacted quickly to shots from his strike partner being blocked.

I think it is closer to the mark to say that a huge part of their success was down to a mutual understanding and respect of each other's strengths. Phillips knew that if the ball was coming anywhere near the area and reached Quinn, his partner would invariably be able to find him with a flick on or a header. He simply tried to take up a position from where he could most likely score.

Quinn for his part, instinctively looked for Phillips, when a ball was played up to him. He knew that the gift for goalscoring that Phillips possessed was a rare thing and he knew that if he could provide enough service to his partner, Sunderland were likely to win the game.

The Quinn and Phillips combination was one of the

greatest strike partnerships in the history of Sunderland AFC. Something to be copied and emulated. So why hasn't it been duplicated since? Well, probably because great relationships don't come along that often. That ability to read each other's play, to completely understand each other's game is a rare thing.

Sunderland fans appreciated that then.

And their affection endures because they appreciate it just as much now.

One of the hardest tasks in life is to fully recognise and appreciate the good times when they are happening.

I did at the time.

And the lucky ones were those that similarly enjoyed the golden days rather than fretting about the coming tomorrows.

In the end there is a host of golden memories to be re-run of a time when Sunderland were on the charge and Phillips and Quinn provided as potent a strikeforce as could be found anywhere in the land.

That would be a fitting sentiment on which to end this chapter.

But maybe the last word on the issue should go to Super Kev himself: 'We had an understanding, a telepathy or something… I don't know,' he shrugged. 'It just seemed natural to us – like that was how it was meant to be. It was simple really. But then you try to replicate that with someone else and it just doesn't happen and you can never quite work out why… That's when you start to realise you've got something special.'

Graeme Anderson has written more words on Sunderland AFC than any other journalist in the club's history. He was one of only four *Sunderland Echo* chief sports writers to cover the club in the 20th century, reporting on Sunderland's fortunes from 1996 to 2015.

11

Gary Rowell was an apprentice when Sunderland set out on the road to Wembley in 1973.

He missed some of the FA Cup matches because he was playing for the youth team at the same time but the cup run nevertheless inspired him.

Watching from close quarters, he learned so much about the game as the first team players set about making history.

Within a couple of short years, he transformed from a star-struck kid into a first-teamer himself.

And he credits the lessons he learned that spring for helping him get his own career off the ground.

1973 AND ALL THAT

BY GARY ROWELL

The 1973 FA Cup final between Sunderland and Leeds United is universally acknowledged as one of the greatest in the competition's history.

In my view it is *the* greatest.

Given the publicity the amazing story attracted at the time and over the weeks, months and years that have followed, you would think there was nothing fresh to be said.

If there was, then author Lance Hardy – the driving force behind the publication you now hold in your hands – surely covered it all in his critically acclaimed book *Stokoe, Sunderland and '73* a few years ago.

Maybe though, I can add one last, fresh perspective, because the tale has never been told from the viewpoint of a starry-eyed teenager who had the incredible luck of being a fan on the Roker Park terraces during those cup ties *and* was also a fresh-faced apprentice at Sunderland Association Football Club as the dramatic run unfolded.

It gave me the happiest moments of my Sunderland-supporting life, as well as spurring me on to make a success of my own career. And looking back all these years later I can assure you it still feels as much like an astonishing privilege to me now as it did to me then.

In the summer of 1972 – six months before that marvellous FA Cup run began – I signed a two-year apprenticeship with the only club I have ever supported.

I put pen to paper in front of the then Sunderland manager, Alan Brown, which shows you how long ago it was!

But it was hardly a signing to make headlines – just me and a group of other hopeful 16-year-olds filing meekly into the boardroom, following the well-trodden path of countless others in daring to dream.

It was not a glamorous time for football and not a glamorous time for me either. Getting to training involved a bus from my home in Seaham to Park Lane bus station in the town, another bus from Park Lane to Washington and then what felt like a 15-mile walk to get to the club's Washington training complex! It was a bit of a pain – but I couldn't have been happier.

At a time when my friends were leaving school and most were looking for jobs in the pits or shipyards, I could put my place of work down as: Roker Park.

What could be better for a young lad dreaming of becoming a professional footballer?

More than that, the apprenticeship meant I was now rubbing shoulders with my boyhood heroes, albeit at a distance, because the youth team only really got involved with the seniors during warm-up runs. They were all there though – Jimmy Montgomery, Dennis Tueart, Bobby Kerr, Billy Hughes – and I was getting to watch them close-up as a perk of my working week.

There used to be a viewing platform at the Washington complex and if I wasn't training, I would more often than not be up there watching them, enjoying and trying to learn from them.

There wasn't much in the way of mixing – they had their jobs and we had ours – but I was lucky enough to be involved with a great group of lads who all got on well with each other. One example of that was boot-cleaning.

Part of the job of an apprentice was to clean the pro's boots and at a lot of clubs, an apprentice would be allocated to each pro's boots – but we preferred just to pitch in altogether, get all the boots poured out of the skip, and work on them as a team.

If we had a leader, it would have been Peter Stronach, an absolutely brilliant young footballer who was head and shoulders above the rest of us. He had it all and was training with the first team in his first year but he was to break his leg twice and never went on to fulfil the potential he so clearly had.

When Peter suffered the injuries he did, it was not a tragedy for him personally but also for Sunderland AFC because he would have been a great player. He made just a couple of first team appearances.

I remember little of Alan Brown – a stern, head-masterly sort of figure – but I remember a lot about Bob Stokoe taking over from him at the end of November 1972.

Bob could be quite a forbidding character himself when he wanted to be but he was a complete breath of fresh air at the time. He loved to be on the training ground enjoying himself with the lads and straight away the atmosphere changed and there was a vibe around the place.

Looking back, I think Bob simply released the players from a very restricting environment and all of a sudden they started to feel freer to express and enjoy themselves and performances and results began to improve.

Even so, there was hardly a buzz of anticipation when that famous cup run started on January 13, 1973 with a 1-1 draw in front of just over 15,000 fans away at Notts County.

I was in the crowd that day and Dave Watson got us an equaliser late on but what everyone who was there remembers was an astonishing save from Jimmy Montgomery just a minute before Dave drew the side level.

It was on a par with Monty's FA Cup final saves. It came from a powerful Les Bradd header which looked a goal all the way but out of nowhere he produced one of those amazing reflex saves and clawed the ball away. It could have been over for us but Monty's save kept the scoreline at 1-0 with ten minutes to go. Notts County were seen off at Roker Park in the replay thanks to another goal from Dave Watson and one from Dennis Tueart.

That was a routine win for Sunderland – unlike the first game between the two sides – and it put us into the hat for a game which sparked huge interest when Reading's name was pulled out.

No one at Sunderland was that fussed about Reading of course. But they were fussed about the Royals' manager – one of Sunderland's all-time legends, Charlie Hurley. It was billed as 'The Return of the King'.

The build-up to the game was fantastic and I had to go to it. I wanted to see Sunderland get through and I also wanted to see the 'King'. Charlie was a legendary player and captain at Sunderland in the 1960s and was adored by the fans. On the pitch he had been a colossus for the club and off it he was charming and charismatic: a real *Boy's Own* hero. His return to Roker Park lived up to expectations.

Before the game, Sunderland fans still in love with him in the 34,000-strong crowd were chanting: 'Charlie, Charlie,' rather than 'Sunderland, Sunderland.' I can remember him coming out and lapping up the adulation like he was born to it. We drew that game and won the replay 3-1 but I couldn't make the trip to Elm Park because I was involved in a youth game.

The important thing was that Sunderland were through to the last 16 and had drawn one of the biggest, sexiest names in the game with Malcolm Allison's Manchester City. It was only now that cup fever really started to kick-in.

The team had been doing well in the league so the pressure was off there and, of course, Manchester City were this colourful, exciting side with Allison leading the way with a glass of champagne and a cigar.

No one gave Sunderland a chance of beating them at Maine Road but in the end City were lucky to get away with a 2-2 draw and I remember before the replay there was tremendous optimism both inside the football club and outside on the terraces and in the town itself.

I missed the game at Man City because it was played on a Saturday and I was involved in a youth game. But I was there for the replay, by which time the mood in Sunderland had been completely transformed.

After the first match and before the replay was where it all took off, where cup fever really began to sweep the place. You could sense it in the streets and in the homes – no doubt in the pubs and clubs too – but as someone who was going into training every day and watching them, I could see it never really affected the lads themselves.

That is something that has always struck me about the cup run: as all this excitement was building to fever pitch around them, the first team themselves were not affected by it.

Don't get me wrong, there would be a buzz and a good atmosphere around the place after a good win. But there was no sense of nerves among the players, of over-excitement, of a player suddenly becoming 'Billy Big Time' or getting carried away. They just never changed. The players remained very laid-back, the camaraderie just the same.

Although the Sunderland players were taking it all in their stride, the town was buzzing after that draw at Maine Road and that excitement truly burst the banks in the replay. There was a poll not long back about the greatest games ever played at Roker Park and it was the replay against Manchester City on February 27, 1973 which topped it.

I wouldn't argue with that. I was in the crowd of 51,872 –

though, like everyone else who was there, I believe it was a heck of a lot more – and it was the most intense, charged and excited atmosphere I have ever experienced in a football ground.

It was a night match, of course, which I think really helps: the dark and the floodlights enhancing the atmosphere. And there's no doubt that many supporters had taken advantage of the evening kick-off to enjoy a proper bit of 'refuelling' in the pubs and clubs in the hours beforehand.

That can only have cranked up the decibel levels. What I remember of the game is the goals – especially two absolutely brilliant ones from Vic Halom and Billy Hughes in the 3-1 win – and the noise and power of the crowd. I was on the Fulwell End that night and it was the best experience you can imagine having at a game.

I don't think you can get that atmosphere in modern stadiums because they are all-seater. Standing up in a massive crowd of people – all standing along with you – just seemed to add that extra charge of aggression and passion.

We were absolutely packed into the Fulwell that night and when the crowd moved, you moved. There was no control over where you were going when there was a surge, although because people were packed so tightly, you didn't fall over and the weird thing was that although you had no control of your movement, when the surge was over, you always ended up back in exactly the same spot!

The noise, the atmosphere and the team were brilliant that night and it was the best match day experience I have ever had. It was magical.

There was talk – probably apocryphal – of television technicians asking where the amplifiers were kept because they couldn't believe the noise. I don't know if that is true.

But I know that the very next day, we were in Roker Park as the young apprentices pointed out to each other where they had been on the terraces and told their stories of that night.

And there – in a nutshell – was my own unusual experience of that cup run: being a part of it both as a fan and as a member of the football club.

The day of the replay, I had been into training before leaving, getting ready and joining the rest of the fans on the terraces. I must have left Roker Park that night about 10.30pm and less than 12 hours later I was back there to do apprentice chores and clean the first team's boots.

I remember that day in particular everything seemed a bit surreal. Just a dozen hours earlier it had been dark, intense, explosive, a cauldron of noise. And here I was now, sitting in the deserted, silent stadium with nothing but the sound of the seagulls and me and my mates, cleaning the boots of the heroes.

The boots arrived in the skip and I remember they all got an extra shine on the back of the previous night. Billy Hughes' boots though were passed around reverentially and got twice the shine of everybody else's because he had scored two goals! Helping to keep the first team's boots right felt like a privilege.

That Man City game was a landmark win in the cup run because after that, people started to believe that our name was on the cup. It also pretty much did for Malcolm Allison. His star-studded team had missed out on the league title after blowing up in the home straight in the previous season and after that he had been under pressure. Indifferent league form in the 1972-73 campaign eventually saw them slump to mid-table and having been dumped out of the FA Cup by Sunderland – when he had been predicting that City would win it – the writing was on the wall for him.

Sunderland fans had a love-hate relationship with Big Mal and years later I had the chance to discuss it with him when I bumped into him in a pub in Yarm. It was after my playing career was over when a landlord of an upmarket bar pointed out Mal and introduced me. Growing up, he had been one of the sport's genuinely flamboyant and colourful characters in an era when football was not overburdened with them. He was great company and I had an hour with him in which we discussed the Sunderland and Manchester City replay and he actually said it was a great memory for him, even though his side had lost. He said he loved the sheer sense of occasion of that night and the banter that went with it.

That last part didn't really surprise me too much because he enjoyed his rapport with rival supporters. A few years after the tie, he was back at Roker Park as manager of Crystal Palace getting stick from Sunderland fans. These days it would just be ignored but Mal relished being noticed and strolled over to the Fulwell End waving his fedora and cigar to the crowd. I remember being there and watching it and thinking: 'Good for you!'

After City had been vanquished, the excitement levels went through the roofs of Wearside. We had known since before the replay that if we could somehow get past City, the reward would be a quarter-final tie against Luton Town – the only other Second Division side left in the competition.

It said a lot about Sunderland that we drew the biggest attendance of the four FA Cup ties played in the quarter-finals – 53,151 – especially when you consider this was two Second Division sides up against each other and the others were all-First Division affairs.

Actually, the crowd figure was even a little higher than the official attendance because late in the game, a bunch of Sunderland youth players swelled the crowd ever so slightly.

We had been playing a youth game at Washington which kicked off an hour earlier so as a result we missed all the excitement and build-up of the match but we were determined not to miss out on it completely.

As soon as our game was over, we high-tailed it down to Roker Park and were lucky enough to catch the last 20 minutes. We went through the front doors, detoured through the laundry room and ended up in the paddocks!

It was actually a feature of my first year that I played very little competitive football. I was there to learn and I learned more in training than the games, especially if everyone was in together; youth players, reserves and first team players.

It was an eye-opener for a kid to be in that environment. Even the general warm-up runs with the senior players seemed to rub off on you. You got to know your heroes and you learned you had to be dedicated to achieve your goals.

The Luton tie is probably the least-remembered match of the whole FA Cup run and it was the first one not to go to a replay – we won comfortably on the day.

I described the Notts County game at Roker Park as a routine win but the one against Luton was even more so by all accounts. Luton did the league double over us that season – their second win coming just a week before the cup tie – but everyone knew this was going to be a different prospect altogether, especially with the influence of the Roker Roar.

Within a few minutes of setting eyes on the game I could tell Sunderland were in complete control and I heard that they had been all game. We had taken the lead early in the second half through a Dave Watson header and so on top had we been that Luton hadn't had a single shot on target. They didn't muster one in the 20 minutes I saw either. Although I was lucky enough to see Sunderland score their clincher – Ron Guthrie swivelling on a shot to make it 2-0 in the dying stages.

It was a collector's item for Ron, who rarely scored, and the fact the two goals came from defenders only seemed to underline that everyone in the team was pulling together for each other.

Luton had been the draw we wanted for the quarter-finals but there was no easy tie when it came to the semi-finals – Arsenal and Leeds United were cream of the crop, while Wolves also had a very good top flight team.

We drew Arsenal, which was to be played at Sheffield Wednesday's Hillsborough ground, and looking back I am struck by the confidence in the camp at that stage.

It was crazy really because Sunderland were still not too far outside the Second Division relegation zone while Arsenal were a possibility for a second league and cup double in three years. But I remember Bob and the players fancying the game because they thought they could get at their defence.

Despite that, it was business as normal on the training ground. Meanwhile, the profile of the club was now massive with Sunderland in the semi-finals.

The FA Cup final was a much, much bigger thing in football in those days and Sunderland were suddenly big news. I was picking up national newspapers which had big features on the club, the ties were being mentioned in television interviews and the games were being televised. Sunderland AFC were the biggest thing in the world to me as an apprentice at Roker Park but I felt fantastic pride in the fact that we were now getting noticed beyond Wearside.

And yet in training itself, nothing much seemed to change, the players had a great togetherness and team spirit and just got on with it. I suppose there was also the art of good management involved too because Bob Stokoe and the rest of the coaching staff just kept things level. It never became a circus and no one was allowed to get carried away.

That was a good thing because the semi-final against Arsenal was as big a game as Sunderland had seen in a generation – at least since the 1963-64 promotion season and, beyond that, maybe bigger than the last FA Cup semi-final in the 1950s, in an era when the Rokerites pitching up in the last four was much less of a surprise.

Arsenal, like Man City, were a 'Champions League' outfit decades before the Champions League was launched. They were simply a big, big club with a lot of famous players, used to success, and they were gunning for their third FA Cup final in a row.

When you stopped to think about that, it was intimidating. But no Sunderland fans were thinking fearfully when the two teams ran out at Hillsborough to a fantastic roar.

It was wall-to-wall red and white but it was clear from the start that as well as the 23,000 Sunderland supporters on the giant, open kop, our fans also dominated the neutral sides too.

I was lucky enough to be among the fans on the kop and it was a great feeling to be part of such a giant sea of Sunderland fans. That massive bank of support must have given a huge lift to our players but I recall it was still a tough, tough game for us.

Arsenal had a few injury problems, in particular the loss of their captain, Frank McLintock, who was an important player for them, but I still remember them oozing ability and pushing us all the way.

From the terraces though what you could see was the confidence in our players. They believed in each other and their focus was on not allowing Arsenal to settle or play.

We went one up, two up, and the roars were deafening. It was unreal – the noise and the scoreline – but Arsenal were comeback kings and I never felt they were completely out of it. The Gunners got one goal back late on and I remember then feeling anxious but we got over the line and the celebrations were awesome.

My two abiding memories of that game as a youngster watching in wonder was that feeling at the final whistle – the thrill, the buzz, the exhilaration in knowing we had done it and we were going to Wembley. The other is being part of that crowd chanting for Bob Stokoe to come out afterwards.

Sunderland supporters would not leave until Bob came out and once people realised that was the mentality of the kop, they started joining in as well.

It felt like ten or 15 minutes afterwards because the ground had emptied apart from our fans but eventually Bob came out and I can still see him now if I close my eyes, standing there with his arms raised aloft.

It was not unlike Dick Advocaat in the recent Arsenal v Sunderland game when the manager had tears in his eyes. For Dick, it was the emotional realisation that he had completed his mission and kept Sunderland – a club he had become drawn to – and their fans in the Premier League.

The emotion got to Bob too and he wiped tears from his cheeks because he knew that he had delivered those fans who were worshipping him a Wembley cup final.

People talk about Bob being a very emotional man and I would agree with that view. But I would also point out that you would have had to have a heart of stone not to be moved by the outpouring of joy and affection towards him from the kop end of Hillsborough.

There were 10,000 or more fans on the kop that day than had been at Roker Park for Bob's first game in charge just a few short months previously! It was a lifetime highlight for Bob, the team and the fans.

When we got back to Sunderland, we were exhausted. But the town was alive and we got a fresh breath of life. The atmosphere was intense and it is no surprise to me that apparently John Peel later said the best gig of his life was supporting Rod Stewart and The Faces at the Bay Hotel in Sunderland that night.

Back at the Washington training complex in the days after

the game, it was business as usual and once again it was part of the feature of that cup run how much the players took the whole thing in their stride.

Training was serious, especially when Bob was around, but they were still so relaxed. As a youth team player, I had no problem getting a ticket to the final.

But I wanted to travel down with the fans rather than with the transport the club was laying on for staff. So, as a result, I journeyed to Wembley in a supporters bus with my old schoolmates Glenn and Gordon, two lads who had been with me at that first game at Notts County.

Before that, the whole media world was knocking on Wearside's door. In the month between the semi-final and the final there were loads more press at the ground. It was a great story, a fairytale and the time between April and May 1973 was magical for everyone at the training ground because you have to remember how miserable and down and shrunken the club had been just before Alan Brown left at the end of 1972 and how suddenly it had all come alive. It was as though the real Sunderland had been hibernating and now the great club that everyone had told us it had once been had come back.

It was Dennis Tueart, Vic Halom and Billy Hughes who were the focus of most of the media attention and I think Bob Stokoe and the coaching staff finally relaxed enough to let the media really do their thing. In a way, they would have had little choice because the FA Cup final was *such* a big thing and Sunderland were *such* a big story.

But I also think they had realised that the players themselves were not going to have their heads turned by the attention, and also that talking us up would not be doing our Wembley rivals Leeds United any favours.

If there was one team that was going to provide a tougher challenge for us than Manchester City or Arsenal, it was Leeds.

This was a team still in Europe and going for the treble that season of First Division, FA Cup and European Cup Winners' Cup.

Don Revie's side were a machine, a steam-roller and utterly formidable and it is always worth remembering that no one outside of Sunderland supporters really gave us a prayer on FA Cup final day.

The rest is history and you don't need me to go over all the details again: Ian Porterfield's goal, Monty's saves, Bob Stokoe's sprint, Bobby Kerr's FA Cup lift. All were unforgettable parts of what, as I said at the start of this chapter, is surely the greatest FA Cup final of all time.

For Sunderland's success-starved fans, the day was one big highlight from beginning to end. And for a young lad in his first full season of apprenticeship at Roker Park, it was fantasy football stuff.

My friends and I were low down in the Wembley terraces and right behind the goal for the two great moments of the day – Ian Porterfield's goal and Monty's saves.

The story was immense and I came back on the bus the same night grinning all the way: Sunderland AFC – FA Cup winners. Talk about living the dream!

It was the perfect end to the cup run, although not quite the perfect end to the season. Sunderland's last game followed a few days later at Roker Park against Queens Park Rangers. Perhaps predictably in the aftermath of the cup victory, a sapped Sunderland lost 3-0 but that didn't matter to a crowd of more than 40,000 who had come to see their heroes and the FA Cup on display.

The game is remembered for QPR's flair player Stan Bowles taking a pot-shot at the cup and sending it flying into the air. The crowd was absolutely incensed by that and didn't see the funny side of it. The mood turned really dark and for a second it looked like there would be a mass invasion, for a second I thought I would be on with them too.

Thankfully the crowd didn't swamp the pitch *en masse* and luckily for me I didn't either – I had a half-decent first season as an apprentice at Sunderland and it would have been a black mark to end it had I been arrested and banned from my place of work!

The following season was so different in so many ways from the one that had gone before – for me, for the team, and for Sunderland AFC generally.

Bob Stokoe outlined the difference at the club in one of the very first squad meetings back. He told us we were the FA Cup holders now and that came with certain standards. Being the FA Cup holders was a big deal. It meant that we needed to be more professional as individuals and as a club than we had been previously. And he was right. We were a big deal nationally. We were media darlings.

Wherever we went that season we were a big draw and the clubs we played tended to attract their biggest crowds of the season. We had always travelled to games with a big away support, the difference now was that we were putting thousands on the gates of our opposition with *their* fans turning up to see the famous FA Cup winners. We were box office.

But along with the extra scrutiny and the pressures that came with the fame, was the issue of sides raising their game against us. As a result, the team struggled to maintain momentum and although there were no relegation worries in the 1973-74 season, we didn't manage to finish higher than sixth.

If the club was different though, then so was I. The summer had been good for me and it was great being part of the club, even though I was down the pecking order. Physically, I had filled out and was stronger and fitter. It was simply the natural consequence of the transition from 16 to 17 for me – less of a boy, more of a man – but I had developed and it made a big difference to me in terms of how I was able to play the game.

Suddenly you cope with the physical side of things. Because of that, I started to be a regular in the youth team and because of that I started to get reserve team games playing with the likes of Ian Porterfield and Billy Hughes, if they were coming back to fitness from injury.

I was still working under youth team coach Ray Yeoman but as a 17-year-old, I now had my eyes on progress. At Washington, we had a first team dressing room which was also used by squad players; the other one was used for the under-21s and you looked to graduate from one to the other. The FA Cup win had changed everything and it had changed me too. The previous season I had been as much of a fan as I had been an apprentice. Now, the priority of progressing up the ranks within the club was uppermost in my mind.

The FA Cup run had inspired me and I felt like I too had a responsibility to aim for higher standards. I knew when I came back I had to be more than just a fan or a cheerleader, I had to try to become a professional. Suddenly we were a serious club and I had to be serious about getting on, rather than just enjoying myself with the lads and looking to learn as I went on.

It was the inspiration of the FA Cup success which made all the difference to me in terms of making me absolutely certain that being a Sunderland footballer was not just the thing that I wanted but the thing that I was going to make happen.

I still looked up to the players I had looked up to the previous season – I look up to them still – but now I started to see them as prospective work colleagues in the making rather than as heroes beyond the reach of a teenager.

I worked hard, used my strength, worked on my game, always tried to learn and I improved as a player over the course of the next couple of years. The 1973-74 and the 1974-75 seasons were too soon for me and there were plenty of senior players ahead of me at the time. But the management started to involve me gradually and then more and more in the first-team squad and by the 1975-76 season, I felt I was almost ready and it seemed, so did Bob Stokoe.

I remember me and another young lad, Mickey Henderson, being taken to an away game with the first team squad for the first time. We were two unused reserves and I remember being on tenterhooks having my first pre-match meal with the first team. It sounds nothing but you have to adapt to a lot of new things as you get closer to the first team and looking back now, I can see what Bob Stokoe was doing.

It is not just the 90 minutes on the pitch, it is the training, travelling and the growing comfortable with what is expected of you on these occasions. You learn things through watching closely as well as by practising hard.

I didn't model myself on anyone at the time but a player I came to admire was our FA Cup-winning captain Bobby Kerr. He typified everything I loved about Sunderland. He had led the team in the cup final, he was lively in the dressing room, he would help in his occasional serious moments and he was a mainstay of the side. He also played in midfield which – a lot of people forget – is where I started my career and played a substantial amount of it.

Later, when Tony Towers joined, I learned a lot from him too. I even learned from seeing the way he warmed up. He was a central midfielder – my original position – and he was a fabulous player; someone who perhaps deserves to be better remembered by Sunderland fans than he is today.

You learn from your team-mates and from the opposition – you learn all the time at every stage you go up in football. I had learned from occasional games with first team players in the reserves. Now, in training, I benefited from working with the likes of Billy Hughes, Vic Halom and Ian Porterfield. I learned from opponents too. I remember Trevor Brooking and Billy Bonds playing in one of my early games against West Ham United – so you get done a few times and you pick things up.

It took the arrival of Jimmy Adamson as manager to switch me from central midfield to left midfield and encourage me to get in the box. He said I should aim for ten times in a half. I got chances and that is when they started to move me forward more and more.

Before any of that though, I was simply trying to knock on the first team door.

It sounds as though I was putting myself under a lot of pressure but if I was, I didn't feel burdened by it. There was fun and excitement in making sure you progressed.

Bob Stokoe never told me how he felt about my developmnent. I had to rely on what he said to others. And one interview he gave to the press in the summer of 1975 made me realise I was really closing in on a first team appearance.

I have never been one to keep press cuttings particularly but I still have the clippings from that interview he gave because it made such a big impact on me.

Bob said: 'I don't want to weigh this lad down with a fancy tag. That's happened to so many in the past and they haven't been able to live up to reputations they hadn't even earned. But I can't help admitting there's something about Gary that excites me. I've handled young players in the past who have gone on to become top players – players like Colin Bell when he was at Bury. You know quite early with the good ones that they have really got it and that's the feeling I have now. The things that stand out most are his natural skill, the way he uses a ball so well, his competitive spirit and temperament.'

This was so much more than he had ever said to me personally and it focused me more than ever into showing I was worthy of his faith. It was more difficult to get into the team in those days because there was only one substitute. They did rotate the player on the bench from time to time but with there being only one, the manager had to be really sure about you.

On December 13, 1975, in a home game against Oxford United, that substitute's role fell to me. I went into the dressing room at 2pm, saw all the shirts and for the first time, one of them was mine. It felt fantastic.

I will accept it was hardly an auspicious occasion for everyone else – Sunderland's lowest crowd of the season, 22,501 – saw it. The Wembley hordes had been eroded by a couple of seasons of disappointment.

It was freezing on the bench but that didn't particularly affect me – I was too focused on the game itself. After waiting so long for this opportunity, you might wonder if I was nervous? Not a bit of it – I was actually just really anxious to get on. The reason for that was that I knew I was so close to fulfilling my dream I could almost reach out and touch it.

Getting on the team sheet was an achievement in itself but getting on the pitch, running out in red and white in front of the fans… that was what it was all about.

What happened if I didn't get on and didn't get anywhere near the substitute's bench again? Well, midway through the second half came my moment – I got on.

I didn't get the chance to do much in the game but I didn't let myself down and when I walked off, I knew I was part of the club's history – no one could take that first-team appearance away from me.

The *Sunderland Echo's Argus* noted in his match report: 'There was little chance for Rowell to make a great deal of impact but he certainly did not look out of place and showed neat touches on the ball.'

Afterwards in the dressing room I was in seventh heaven,

sitting alongside five of the 1973 FA Cup heroes – Ian Porterfield, Jimmy Montgomery, Bobby Kerr, Vic Halom and Dick Malone. At that point, I knew I had achieved my goal as an apprentice.

More than that, those players who had inspired me so much were now sitting alongside me as team-mates. I could die happy.

The final piece of icing on the cake that day? We won 1-0 and Ian Porterfield scored the winner! Déja vu!

On the day of my debut, I could have had no idea that I would go on to make so many more appearances for the club that I loved and would rack up so many goals. If you had told me then that I would go on to score over 100 Sunderland goals and beat Len Shackleton's post-war record I would have thought you were mad. I had only just made it into the first team, I had no idea whether I would get back in again, let alone become a regular.

I only made a handful of substitute appearances and first team starts that promotion season. It was to be midway through the following season, when Sunderland were back in the top flight, that I finally got a run of starts.

My first goal came in a 4-1 win, away at Hull City in mid-April, in my debut season. By that stage, we knew we were finally going to get back into the First Division – something which must have given an enormous sense of vindication to the remaining members of the Wembley squad.

There were to be so many more good times ahead for me in Sunderland's famous red and white stripes: I was to score the winner at Anfield and notch goals against Manchester United and Arsenal. Goals also came for me on visits to Manchester City, Nottingham Forest and Spurs.

I eventually beat Shackleton's 100-goal record and, of course, there was the hat-trick against Newcastle United in the 4-1 win at St James' Park.

But all of that joy and success stemmed from strong roots and from what I learned in an apprenticeship served in arguably the most inspirational spell in the club's history.

Fans first saw me play for the club at Roker Park in 1975. But my career in football began with Stokoe, Sunderland and '73.

Gary Rowell is one of only three Sunderland players to have scored more than 100 goals for the club since the Second World War. In total, he netted 103 times for the Red and Whites. Today, he writes a column for the *Sunderland Echo* and enjoys legendary status among Sunderland fans, largely due to his hat-trick at Newcastle United in 1979.

12

Sunderland were not among the 12 founder members of the Football League in 1888, although they had a team that probably deserved inclusion.

But, once they were admitted, they wasted little time making their mark.

They won three championship titles and were runners-up once in their first five seasons in the league.

Let **Rob Mason** introduce you to the Team of All The Talents.

THE TEAM OF ALL THE TALENTS

BY ROB MASON

Preston North End are still known as 'The Invincibles' after being unbeaten when they became the inaugural champions of the Football League in 1888-89 although they did lose 4-1 at Sunderland on April 29, 1889.

Sunderland hadn't been able to become one of the 12 founder members of the Football League. Out on a limb geographically, they had to be content with friendlies against Football League outfits, all of whom were based in the Midlands or north west. Wolverhampton Wanderers came to Wearside twice and drew both times but Preston were one of five other Football League visitors, all of whom lost, each conceding four goals.

Nottingham Forest, The Wednesday of Sheffield and a team called Halliwell were the three clubs who applied for membership of the original Football League without success. Sunderland, though, would become the first to be admitted to the Football League, replacing Stoke in 1890, in time for the third season.

Two years later they were champions. They would retain the title, finish runners-up a year later and be crowned champions for a third time in four seasons in 1895. That year, Sunderland travelled to Edinburgh to face Scottish champions Heart of Midlothian in a match billed as the 'World Championship'. Football had barely begun to spread across the globe as The Lads laid claim to being the best team on the planet.

By this time, Sunderland had become the first side to score 100 goals in a season. They had also set a record that has never been equalled – that of maintaining a 100 per cent home record in the top flight.

Moreover, Sunderland had been the last ever winners of the single-division Football League and, after the Second Division was formed at a meeting in The Queen's Hotel, in Fawcett Street, Sunderland, The Lads duly became the first ever winners of the First Division. As Sunderland retained their crown as champions in 1892, local rivals Newcastle United came into being. At no time have Newcastle ever held as many league titles as Sunderland and currently remain two championships behind the Red and Whites – the Black Cats having always been top dogs in the hotbed of soccer that is the north east.

So who were those men who made Sunderland one of the traditional powerhouses of English football? Sunderland are the last team to win the title winning stripes – in 1935-36 – and in the eight decades since have seen their tally bettered by only five clubs: Manchester United, Liverpool, Arsenal, Aston Villa and Everton.

Sunderland had been founded in 1879 by a Scot, James Allan. The Scottish influence was to be key to a side that was dubbed 'The Team of All The Talents.' Led by Tom Watson they gained their place in the Football League at a meeting at The Douglas Hotel, in Manchester, where, represented by James Marr and the Reverend Robinson Hindle, their prowess on the pitch was enhanced in the corridors of power by an offer to pay the travelling expenses of every team's long trek on Victorian roads or rails to the far flung north east.

That prowess on the pitch was illustrated in a 6-1 away win over Aston Villa in September 1892. Watching Villa chairman and founder of the Football League, William McGregor, stated: 'Sunderland have a talented man in every position.' Indeed they did and The Team of All The Talents indelibly imprinted Sunderland's name on the game as one of football's giants. The Lads might well have been a sleeping giant for more post-war years than supporters would like, but sleeping or otherwise no one has ever doubted the giant label – and that is due to this side.

Ted Doig, Jamie Millar, Johnny Campbell, John Auld and Hugh Wilson. These names might not be as famous as Costel Pantilimon, Steven Fletcher, Jermain Defoe, Lee Cattermole or John O'Shea nowadays but in their day they were the equal of Thibaut Courtois, Sergio Aguero, Wayne Rooney, Steven Gerrard or John Terry.

Goalkeeper Doig and forward Millar would win four league championships with Sunderland (also featuring in the 1901-02 title-winning team). Millar, who had become the first man to score five goals in a game for Sunderland (only three have done it since) in a record 11-1 FA Cup win against Fairfield in 1895 had won Scottish title medals with Rangers between two spells on Wearside. Campbell remains Sunderland's fifth top scorer while Auld, the Talents' first captain, helped keep the club afloat financially during the First World War (by which time he was a director of Newcastle) and even paid for Campbell's funeral. Wilson, meanwhile, was a man of firsts. Also a captain of the Talents, he was the first Sunderland player to score a penalty and also the first to be sent off.

Sunderland enjoyed an impressive home record in challenge matches against Football League sides in the two years that the league was played prior to their admittance. Of 17 games played, 11 were won with only two defeats at the hands of Bolton Wanderers and West Bromwich Albion.

The Lads found it tougher when they started the real stuff; losing their first two league games. Long-serving goalkeeper Bill Kirkley paid the price, being dropped to make way for a man who played more games than anyone in the club's history other than Jim Montgomery and Len Ashurst.

That man was Ted Doig. Indeed, Doig can lay claim to have played more games for Sunderland than anyone. His official tally of 457 applies just to competitive league and cup matches but back in his day there were also many lucrative friendlies and these weren't tame kick-abouts but keenly contested challenge matches. In total, he played around 1,000 times.

The record score in the history of British football is the 36-0 Arbroath wracked up against Bon Accord in 1885. Doig was on Arbroath's books at the time. He didn't play in the game and it is not known if he was at the historical occasion or perhaps playing a reserve game elsewhere that day but he did go on to be capped twice by Scotland while with the Red Lichties and to this day he is the only player to win a full cap while on Arbroath's books. In November 1899, he played for Blackburn Rovers in a 9-1 thrashing of Notts County but then went back to Scotland.

It was almost a year later that Doig returned to England to make his club debut in Sunderland's third game in the Football League. The opening two games had both been lost at their old Newcastle Road ground when seven goals were conceded to Burnley and Wolves. The Lancastrians triumphed 3-2 in the club's inaugural league fixture on September 13, 1890. Two days later, Sunderland led 3-0 at half-time against Wolves, only to succumb 4-3. The match marked the first occasion a Sunderland player could be recorded as making a final league appearance. Blamed for the defeat, Bill Kirkley, who had been at the club for eight years and had played in their first FA Cup tie in 1884, made a swift departure to locals rivals Sunderland Albion, a short-lived outfit formed by Sunderland's founder James Allan, who had fallen out with the original club. (Sunderland Albion had ambitions but these fell away with Sunderland's success and they became defunct in 1892). Kirkley was still part of the furniture at Sunderland half a century later when he could be found looking after the billiards room at Roker Park.

Kirkley was yesterday's man but Doig made a definite difference. His debut at West Brom brought Sunderland's first clean sheet and first victory, handsomely 4-0 – but no points for he hadn't been properly registered as his previous appearance in English football for Blackburn had been overlooked and Sunderland were fined and docked the two points they had won. Sunderland would finish seventh out of 12 clubs in their first Football League season. Without the points deduction, they would have been fifth.

A 3-3 draw at Burnley would produce Sunderland's first point that was allowed to stand but it was at home that The Team of All The Talents began to really shine. From Doig's home debut on October 18 – almost 11 years to the day since the club was formed – until the end of the 1895-96 season only one match was lost at home, spread over six seasons. It was a fabulous record of 67 wins, 14 draws and a solitary defeat. It was the backbone of three league titles and a runners-up berth in four seasons. By now you should be realising that for all the triumphs of later teams, this was the greatest team in Sunderland's history. They weren't called The Team of All The Talents for nothing.

By Christmas 1890, Sunderland had got used to league football and were ready to dominate it. They were bottom of the league going into the game before Christmas and Everton were en route to their first league championship. They had won their previous three games, scoring six last time out and they would go on to win their next four, scoring 19 times – but they were to lose 1-0 on Wearside. Within a month, another Doig clean sheet, this time at Anfield (then Everton's home), combined with a Johnny Campbell goal, gave Sunderland victory in their first FA Cup tie as a league club By the time of this cup win, Sunderland were flying. From the December meeting with The Toffees, seven of the next ten league games were won with just one lost. About to become kings, Sunderland played the role of kingmakers in their first season. Preston had won the first two league titles but would finish runners-up, two points behind Everton after taking just one point from two games with Sunderland.

Between the two PNE games, Sunderland had played an FA Cup semi-final and replay with Notts County, both at Bramall Lane, in Sheffield, going down 2-0 in the second game. The Talents would be no strangers to FA Cup semi-finals, reaching that stage in 1891, 1892 and 1895 but they could never get to the final – some believing there was a curse preventing it.

There were no goal nets in 1891 and just a piece of rope for the crossbar. The initial 1891 semi-final, which ended 3-3, included a Johnny Campbell goal that was disputed as to whether the ball had gone under or over the bar. Perhaps Sunderland should have gone on to meet Blackburn at Kennington Oval in the final in their first season in the league? On the other hand, Tom Porteous handled the ball near his own goal but as penalty kicks hadn't been invented either, Sunderland got away with that one.

As a first season it was satisfactory. Sunderland had shown they were a fine side who could beat the best, albeit away form could improve. There were three wins, five draws and five defeats on the road. It is worth considering that on the roads and rails of the early 1890s, every other team had one long journey – to Sunderland – whereas every trip was an adventure for The Lads.

Although the final competitive fixture was completed on March 21 the 'season' continued with Sunderland playing 13 friendlies, winning 12 and drawing one. Friendlies throughout the season were a common occurrence and, in total, Sunderland played 56 games, winning 25 of the last 31.

1891-92 would be the Football League's fourth season, Sunderland's second and the last year of a stand-alone league. Sunderland were to be the last ever winners of the single strata Football League and the first-ever winners of the First Division. In 1891-2 they also became the first and only team to win every home game while in 1892-3 they became the first team to score 100 league goals in a season – which was some going in a programme of 30 games.

Sunderland warmed up for what would be their first title-winning campaign by beating a touring Canadian travelling side and then hammering Newcastle West End 8-1 away a day later. When the real stuff got started, Wolves were the opening day visitors to Newcastle Road. A year earlier their four second half goals had brought about Bill Kirkley's demise but this time Sunderland bagged three after the break to win 5-2; with Jamie Millar grabbing a hat-trick. Worryingly, the away form that so needed improving showed no signs of doing so and three away games were lost. Seven goals were scored in those games but with a dozen conceded, Sunderland were bottom of a 14-team league, extended with the admission of Stoke and Darwen, who would end up as the bottom two.

Defending champions Everton brought the best out of the Talents. They were duly defeated to spark a run of four wins. Sunderland were just warming up and a 3-1 reverse at Blackburn was followed by a run of 13 successive league wins that still stands as a club record.

The sequence began in style with five first-half goals racked up in what became a 7-1 win over Derby; Johnny Campbell bagging four. Having been bottom after four games, giving the rest of the league a head start, it took The Lads until the penultimate match of those 13 consecutive wins to hit the top of the table – but once there, there was no relinquishing the position.

So March 26, 1892 was the day Sunderland reached the pinnacle of English football for the first time. Goals from Hugh Wilson and James Hannah overcame Aston Villa in a 2-1 win and the highest home league gate so far of 17,000 crammed into Newcastle Road to see it. Villa had scored 12 in their previous league game against Accrington and had summarily ended Sunderland's hopes of a 'double' by beating them 4-1 in the FA Cup semi-final at Bramall Lane a month earlier.

Sunderland's top scorer in the first three seasons was Johnny Campbell. In 1892 and 1893 he scored more goals than he played games as he spearheaded Sunderland to their first two titles. On the day Sunderland mathematically sealed their first league title, he scored four in a 6-1 home win over Blackburn. Rovers were the glamour side of the time. They had won the FA Cup in both of the previous two seasons, and five times in the last eight years, so could evidently rise to the big occasion. Coomb Hall did just that, heading an equaliser to cancel out an eighth minute lead Campbell had provided. Sunderland's response was instant: Jamie Millar heading home a cross from Hugh Wilson. Seeking to take the game away from the potential of another equaliser, Sunderland pressed hard and were denied by the woodwork three times before Campbell made it 3-1 before the interval (some reports credit this goal to David Hannah). There was no way determined Sunderland were going to slip up. Campbell headed home two corners with Jimmy 'Blood' Hannah (no relation to David) complete the scoring.

If you think a win over Newcastle is a big deal in modern day football, the rivalry with Sunderland Albion was even fiercer and 48 hours after becoming league champions, Sunderland met Albion in a friendly, beating them by the same 6-1 scoreline they had dished out to Blackburn. Albion just couldn't compete and they were defunct by 1892. Unlike Birmingham, Bristol, Liverpool, Manchester, Nottingham, Sheffield, Stoke and London, Sunderland has long been a one-team city. Perhaps that is part of the legacy of The Team of All The Talents? Sunderland's modern day support would be diluted if there was another team in town.

The two friendlies against Sunderland Albion were accompanied by three others before Sunderland completed their league fixtures with two further league victories leaving them five points ahead of Preston.

Many a modern day manager has grumbled about the expectations of Sunderland fans. Maybe The Team of All The Talents have to ultimately take the blame (or credit) for this. After all, it was The Talents who impressed upon the people of the north east and beyond that Sunderland were a huge club.

If being league champions brought any pressure to the side they singularly failed to show it. Starting with a 6-0 away win at Accrington, only one point was dropped from the first eight games. The last of these brought an 8-1 win over West Brom which took the goals tally to 38 for with eight conceded. Amazingly they weren't top! Preston had also got off to a scintillating start and at this point were a point ahead of Sunderland, having played a game more.

In the final analysis though, Preston had to settle for the bridesmaid's position of runners-up once more. They would finish 11 points behind Sunderland; The Lads equalling the record winning margin over the nearest challengers set by PNE in the inaugural season. Moreover, Sunderland beat Preston home and away, rubbing in their superiority.

The third game of the campaign was particularly significant. It was played away to Aston Villa at Perry Barr. Villa were more than a decent team. They had finished fourth the previous season and had won all three of the games they had played prior to Sunderland's visit, conceding only one goal in the process.

Sunderland had many great days in this era and this was one of the finest. Inflicting Villa's record home defeat of 6-1, they were 2-0 up within five minutes with Hugh Wilson opening the tally with a cracking volley before goal machine Johnny Campbell notched a second. Campbell scored again to extend the lead before the break and while the visitors continued to dominate, Villa mounted a few attacks and pulled a goal back through England international Dennis Hodgetts. The goal only served to sting Sunderland who restored the three-goal advantage straight from the re-start with a Jimmy Hannah shot. It was soon 5-1 as John Harvie celebrated his first league appearance in 18 months. It was his 'second debut' for the club, having spent a year back in Scotland with Renton in the meantime. Sunderland weren't finished and in the closing stages toyed with the home team, adding a sixth goal ten minutes from time with 'Blood' Hannah notching his second of the match.

Watching Villa director William McGregor was a giant figure in the history of football. His statue stands outside Villa Park and he was one of the founders of the Football League. Following this performance he bestowed 'The Team of All The Talents' nickname stating: 'Sunderland have a talented man in every position.' Goodness knows what he would have thought if Jamie Millar had been playing. Millar was one of Sunderland's chief attacking threats.

While the moniker 'The Team of All The Talents' was coined on this day, the era marked by The Talents had already been in existence for a year or more. Perhaps the beating of reigning champions Everton almost a year earlier that sparked a run of 17 wins out of 18 as they strode to their first title had signalled that something special was happening at Sunderland.

In 1892-93, The Talents had to wait until Christmas to go top. A week after pacemakers Preston were beaten 2-0 at Newcastle Road a return to the Black Country saw a 3-1 win at

West Brom to take Sunderland top. Perhaps the celebrations were less than professional as two days later on Boxing Day they lost 2-0 at Wolves to a side that had won just three of the previous 11 games. The game at Molineux was watched by a crowd of 14,000, some 6,000 higher than their second highest league attendance of the season and their biggest since Sunderland's previous visit, which set what was then a record gate for the ground. The Talents, evidently, were a considerable draw.

A week later 'Blood' Hannah scored four as Wolves lost the return 5-2. The Midlanders would go on to win the FA Cup but beating them on Wearside took Sunderland top and as the first of a run of eight wins and a draw from nine league games, The Lads simply left the rest in their wake.

The FA Cup continued to be a problem though. For the first time as a league club, Sunderland failed to reach the semi-final, bowing out at Blackburn after knocking out Royal Arsenal and Sheffield United.

Securing the retention of the title – the only time any team from the north east has done this – was a considerable achievement but Sunderland had an extra challenge they wanted to meet. The most goals any team had ever scored in a season were the 93 Sunderland had recorded in winning the league the previous year. In a season that had 30 games, four more than the year before, the second highest scorers would be third-placed Everton with 74. The Team of All The Talents decided they wanted 100.

They smashed their own record when putting six past Newton Heath (forerunners of Manchester United) and went into the last match at Burnley needing three to hit the century.

Johnny Campbell, Jamie Millar, Jimmy Hannah and James Gillespie all went into the match already in double figures. Top scorer Campbell had become the first player to score 30 in a season, something that wouldn't be matched for 20 years. None of the leading quartet would score in the game (although some contemporary reports attribute one of the goals to Campbell). Nonetheless, Sunderland had reached their 100 goals target before half-time. John Harvie got the first with a 20th minute free kick, soon added to by Hugh Wilson before Harvie hit the magical 100th goal. While modern day goal celebrations can include rehearsed routines involving a daft dance, a rocking motion if a baby is due or pointing to the heavens if someone has passed away, back in Victorian times it was considered the norm to greet a goal with a slap on the back, a manly handshake and a Mart Poom-like determination to get back into position for the re-start. Not a bit of it when Harvie scored the landmark goal, apparently some of the players performed cartwheels in celebration. The wheels nearly came off in the second half as Burnley came back to 3-2 but remember Sunderland didn't just have the best attack, they had the tightest defence too and despite finishing with ten men, full-back William Gibson having gone off injured, they made sure they won the game.

Sunderland's achievement in scoring 100 goals was phenomenal. No other side scored 100 top flight goals in a season until after the First World War – when there were 12 more games in which to reach the century. You should be impressed – and doubly so by the fact that including friendlies and FA Cup ties that season, in total The Lads scored 199 goals.

Sunderland would be champions again in fine style two years later but taking everything into account it can be argued that 1892-93 saw The Team of All The Talents at their best.

Looking for a third successive title, Sunderland started the 1893-94 campaign modestly with a win and three draws. Seventh at an early stage was no reason to worry as the league had been won two years earlier when three of the first four were lost but alarms were rung after the next two games ended in defeat, the first of them 7-1 at Everton which doubled the record losing margin in a league game. Edgar Chadwick scored a hat-trick in a match that marked the final appearance of Tom Porteous, the first man capped while with The Lads. The full back had represented England in a 4-1 win over Wales in March 1891, in a game played at Sunderland.

By now Sunderland were a prized scalp other teams raised their game against. It took until Christmas to begin to put together a consistent run of form but ultimately The Lads would have to settle for being runners-up to Villa, who won the title by a handsome six-point margin. A run of 11 wins from 13 games falling short of closing the gap. Villa undoubtedly had the upper hand, knocking Sunderland out of the FA Cup in the Midlands after holding them at Newcastle Road.

With James Potts Henderson having succeeded Robert Thompson as president at the club's annual general meeting a month before the season started, Sunderland began the 1894-95 season determined to regain the championship. Indeed they literally couldn't wait to get started and kicked off against Derby even though the delayed referee Mr Kirkham hadn't arrived. Sunderland led 3-0 at half-time with an alternative official but Mr Kirkham turned up and insisted on re-starting the game at 0-0. Undaunted, The Lads romped to a record 8-0 win against a team that included perhaps the most famous figure in this early era of league football, Steve Bloomer, whose bust is now adjacent to the dugouts at Derby's home ground.

A Tom Hyslop hat-trick saw Burnley beaten 3-0 before a first away fixture at Aston Villa, who had likewise taken maximum points from their opening two games. Stephen Smith maintained his record of scoring in every game so far for the defending champions but The Team of All The Talents laid down a marker by winning 2-1 with goals from stalwarts Johnny Campbell and Jimmy Hannah.

Despite maintaining their 100 per cent record by beating

WBA a week later, The Lads couldn't claim top spot with Everton also having maximum points from a game more; The Talents having fitted in a friendly victory at Leicester Fosse a couple of days after seeing off Villa.

Sunderland and Everton would meet on Merseyside in late October when two first-half Jamie Millar goals looked like avenging the previous season's record defeat but the home side showed their mettle by fighting back to take a point, the result dropping Sunderland to fourth place – their lowest position of the season.

The Talents had played a trio of friendlies – taking them from London to Glasgow – between their previous league game and the trip to Everton but there would only be two more such challenge matches in the next five months (one of them being a 1-1 draw with the Rest of the League) as they got on with the job of regaining the title.

Only one point would be dropped from the next seven games before back-to-back defeats between Christmas and New Year. Having won a Christmas Day friendly away to Newton Heath and a Boxing Day league fixture at West Brom, there was a third game in as many days at Forest followed by another two days later at Preston which brought single-goal defeats.

The New Year began with a 2-0 win over Preston and just 24 hours later Aston Villa took to the Newcastle Road pitch for a game whose image is seen by every visiting team to the Stadium of Light today. The match was the subject of what is believed to be the world's oldest and biggest oil painting of a football match. Entitled 'A Corner Kick' the painting shows Sunderland defending a corner with only Villa goalkeeper Bill Dunning missing out as the only one of the 22 players not pictured.

Artist Thomas Marie Madawaska Hemy was mainly known

for painting boxing matches. The clue to this is that every player – bar one who has a hand splayed out on the ground – has his hands in a fist. Hemy couldn't draw hands – though perhaps it indicates the fighting spirit of The Talents? Hemy was also known for his seascapes. The name Madawaska is the name of the ship he was born on as his Tyneside family travelled to Australia.

Sunderland had gone top of the table with the previous day's win and would not be knocked off their perch for the rest of the season. Defending champions Villa had found their form. They had won their last six games, scoring 23 goals in the process and had kept three successive clean sheets. No wonder the occasion had a painting commissioned. It was a humdinger of an encounter, finishing 4-4 after Villa led 3-2 at half-time. This was a record scoring draw for Sunderland and equalled the Villa record.

The Team of All The Talents had what passed for a blip in 1893-94, merely managing a runners-up spot, but now things were back on track. The side weren't as free-scoring as two seasons earlier but the title would be regained in style – with a couple of magnificent bonuses in a record victory and the accolade of becoming world champions.

A home draw with Forest followed the Villa match before the goals rained in with big wins at Wolves and Stoke. In between Sunderland played a friendly at Newcastle and thrashed the Second Division side 4-1. The Magpies had yet to reach the top flight as Sunderland were en route to becoming Football League champions for a third time.

For all their superiority in the league, Sunderland couldn't win the cup. This season would see The Talents reach their third semi-final in five seasons but also for the third time in that spell dreams would be quashed by Villa. Sunderland's cup run began at the beginning of February with that record 11-1 win over non-league Fairfield. The Manchester-based team were Lancashire League champions in 1895 and this was the only time they reached the first round of the FA Cup.

A week after the Fairfield tie, a draw at Small Heath (later to become Birmingham City) marked the final appearance of the original captain of The Team of All The Talents, John Auld. He had lost his place to fellow Scottish international Andrew McCreadie while Hugh Wilson had become captain. Auld had debuted in Sunderland's first-ever league game and became the first player to move from Sunderland to Newcastle once both were members of the league. Auld went on to become a Newcastle director but never lost his affinity with Sunderland, acting as a financial guarantor for the club during the financially strapped times of World War One.

Following the Small Heath draw, six of the last seven league games were won as Sunderland marched to another title but the destination of the trophy came down to the final fixture. The gates opened two hours ahead of the scheduled 4pm kick-off against second-placed Everton. The 20,000 attendance was 8,000 higher than the second biggest league gate of the season and only the third time the Newcastle Road ground had squeezed in 20,000.

Eight of Everton's 18 wins had come in their first eight games but they had a chance of taking their second title if they won as they still had another fixture, at Villa, who were otherwise occupied as Sunderland met Everton, beating their local rivals West Brom in the FA Cup final.

Sunderland went into the match minus skipper Hugh Wilson but had too much for a spirited Everton, who were stern opponents. Andrew McCreadie gave The Lads the lead, converting a Millar free-kick ten minutes before half-time only for Chadwick to level ten minutes after the restart. Having scored a hat-trick in Sunderland's record defeat the previous season, he was a real danger in an Everton side for whom a win was essential. The visitors pressed so strongly that Sunderland's 75th-minute winner was against the run of play. Created by a clearance from full-back Donald Gow, who had missed most of the season through injury, the winner came from 'Blood' Hannah who, in scoring against the side he had debuted against in 1891, beat goalkeeper Jack Hillman, who had been in goal for Burnley when Sunderland lifted the title two years earlier.

Sunderland were champions again but there was more to come. Seven days after the Everton game, The Lads travelled to Edinburgh to meet Scottish champions Heart of Midlothian. Hearts had won their first Scottish championship, the five-point winning margin from Celtic being a record north of the border.

Since eight years earlier when Hearts' Edinburgh rivals Hibernian met Preston such a fixture had been staged between leading clubs of what were then the two strongest football nations in a world mostly yet to enjoy the spread of the people's game from the British Isles.

Johnny Campbell would score twice for Sunderland, having been part of the Renton side who beat FA Cup winners West Bromwich Albion in 1888. The 1895 meeting featuring Sunderland was the first such fixture where the respective league champions of England and Scotland met head to head for the foot high pewter trophy and therefore Sunderland could lay claim to being the first 'World Champions'.

Having travelled to Edinburgh on the morning of the match, Sunderland lunched at The Douglas Hotel, an establishment of the same name as the Manchester hostelry that held the meeting that had admitted the club to the league they were now dominating. Over 90 minutes on a drizzly day, Sunderland would extend their superiority, scoring five times.

Harry Johnston and Johnny Campbell gave a side

consisting of 11 Scots, a 2-0 half-time lead but Willie Taylor and two goals from Robert McLaren turned things to Hearts' advantage (some reports claim George Scott scored one of the goals attributed to McLaren). However, the most successful team to ever represent Sunderland, the team whom bestowed that word 'giant' on the club from the game's earliest days, raised their game and hit Hearts with three more goals to win 5-3. Jamie Millar struck the equaliser, Campbell regained the lead with his second of the match and with two minutes left, John Harvie confirmed Sunderland were not just champions of England but of the world. It was a title they could claim for the rest of the century as the fixture was not staged again until 1901.

Two days later, Sunderland completed their campaign with a 51st fixture of a season in which they became world champions, the first club to be crowned English champions for a third time, FA Cup semi-finalists and also established their record victory.

In contrast, 1896-97 was a quiet affair. The season started brightly with the champions top after three games but after losing at Villa they dropped to ninth after seven fixtures following a run of five without a victory. Villa would go on to replace Sunderland as champions but were beaten in the reverse meeting at Newcastle Road.

Not until the run-in when six of the last seven games were won did the team put more than two successive victories together. Consequently, for the first time since their inaugural season, Sunderland weren't part of the title race and there was equally little joy in the cup where elimination came in the second round at the hands of eventual winners The Wednesday. In the league, Sunderland finished fifth, level on points with fourth-placed Bolton but eight points off the pace.

It was the end of an era because legendary 'manager' Tom Watson left at the end of the season, going on to lead Liverpool to their first-ever league title in 1900-01. He would later sign Ted Doig, the pair of them in due course being buried within 20 yards of each other in Anfield cemetery.

In one respect, the departure of Watson signalled the end of The Team of All The Talents but the team themselves had one more season, managing one last hurrah with arguably their greatest victory.

Watson was succeeded by the step or half brother of Johnny Campbell. Robert Campbell's father had adopted Johnny, who was possibly his illegitimate son, though this is unproven. Four years Johnny's senior, Robert had followed him to Wearside on Christmas Eve 1899. The pair lodged with Watson, Robert working in the shipyards as a storekeeper and becoming secretary of Sunderland's 'A' team, or reserves.

When Watson left for a better financial offer at Liverpool, Robert Campbell succeeded him. But it was a time of change. A month prior to his appointment, the club had become a Limited Company under chairman James Potts Henderson, who had been the club figurehead for a year, and within another two years would open a new ground at Roker Park, after the club had outgrown Newcastle Road.

Watson quite possibly foresaw that it was time to go. The Talents had waned as legs aged. Campbell began his tenure with the worst run in the club's history. There were no wins in the opening eight games. Five defeats in that run being more than were lost in the whole season when the title had been retained just over two years earlier. Sensationally, Sunderland found themselves bottom of the league; Campbell no doubt hoping for more from his formerly prolific step brother who was yet to score.

The return of Watson with his new Liverpool side inspired his old charges with The Lads racing into a 3-0 half-time lead and hanging on to win 4-3. While the next game was won, a third victory wouldn't arrive until Christmas Day. With five conceded in defeat 24 hours later, wins remained rarities throughout what was the first dismal season in what had previously been a road paved with glory. However, there was still to be a spiritedly glorious encore from this greatest of Sunderland sides.

The Team of All The Talents had run out of steam. But while fitness withers, talent doesn't and they could still raise their game. One of the four league matches they won after Christmas saw them put four goals against eventual champions Aston Villa.

Nonetheless, the league campaign ended with Sunderland second-bottom despite finishing with a five-game unbeaten run. Six decades later, Sunderland were still able to boast that they were the only club never to have been relegated thanks to what was The Talents' last stand. Instead of automatic relegation in 1896-97, second-bottom Sunderland were obliged to take part in the Victorian version of play offs, known as 'Test Matches'.

Sunderland faced a quartet of games against the Second Division's top two, Notts County and Newton Heath. With none of the first three of these games won, all hinged on the final match with Newton Heath at Newcastle Road. A win for Newton Heath would see them promoted while a draw would suffice for the visitors should Notts County beat Burnley in the other fixture. For Sunderland only victory would do.

The Test Match would be the final appearance for five of The Talents but they went out with a victory as important as any in the days when they had been able to dominate seasons and not just individual games. Captain Hugh Wilson (who was finally capped by Scotland after his penultimate league outing for Sunderland in a win over England at Crystal Palace), Johnny Campbell, Donald Gow, Jimmy Hannah and James Gillespie bade farewell in style – particularly Gillespie, who scored in each half as Sunderland triumphed 2-0, (some reports credit Hugh Morgan with the opening goal).

Had it not been for this fitting finale the legend of The Team of All The Talents would not have had the same lustre. Their achievements anchored Sunderland in the game's history with so many records and achievements but relegation was not in the DNA of the players who made this one of football's greatest clubs. Ted Doig would win a fourth title with Sunderland in 1901-02 – as would Jamie Millar – but 1896-97 marked the end of The Talents as a team. There would be three end-of-season friendlies, the very last a 3-1 win at Stockton on the last day of April.

The rest of this book looks at other eras in Sunderland's rich history. There have been other truly great players and great teams but in a four-year period The Team of All The Talents won as many league titles as the rest of Sunderland's teams have managed in well over 100 seasons. If medals are being put on the table, The Team of All The Talents are more than a match for even the best of teams that have come since. When you think of the club's trophy-winning greats: Charlie Buchan, Raich Carter, Bobby Gurney and Jim Montgomery for instance, remember that – given Doig and Millar's later success – The Team of All The Talents won more top flight title medals than everyone else in the club's history put together.

Rob Mason is Sunderland AFC club historian and publications editor.

TALES FROM THE RED & WHITES

VOLUME TWO
WILL BE PUBLISHED IN 2016